CHOOSE
to do
RIGHT

A Proven Path to Criminal Rehabilitation

Andrew E. Matson

Outskirts Press, Inc.
Denver, Colorado

Choose to do Right
A Proven Path to Criminal Rehabilitation
All Rights Reserved.
Copyright © 2009 Andrew E. Matson
V2.0

Outskirts Press, Inc.
http://www.outskirtspress.com

ISBN: 978-1-4327-2862-5

Library of Congress Control Number: 2008931572

Outskirts Press and the "OP" logo are trademarks belonging to Outskirts Press, Inc.

PRINTED IN THE UNITED STATES OF AMERICA

Thank you to all those who have played a part in my life, and helped inspire this book. Especially my family - thank you for all of your love and support.

Mom - thank you for loving me, for believing in me, and for always being there for me. You are my hero.

Trish – thank you for your love, and for taking a chance on me. You have taught me so much.

Christy - thank you for your friendship, your insight, and your guidance.

I love you all so much.

TABLE OF CONTENTS

SECTION I
WHAT IS WRONG WITH ME?

CHAPTER 1

The Decision to Change

The Path to Prison

As a boy, I never dreamed I would end up in prison. I grew up in a loving home where I was taught good morals and values. I did well in school, participated in church activities, did my chores, and usually obeyed my parents. When I was 16, I even earned the highest rank in Boy Scouts – the Eagle Scout Award - and received a letter of commendation from then Governor Dick Lamm congratulating me on my accomplishment. I wasn't perfect, but I definitely wasn't a "criminal".

At age 19, I was sent to prison for theft and forgery.

So what happened? Did my change happen all at once? Why did I turn to crime? How could I have done the things I did? And, how did I get to the point where I am at now?

Simply put, I started making one bad choice after another. At first it was just "little things" – skipping school, smoking a cigarette, sneaking out at night, lying, cheating, and so on. These choices, combined with many errors in thinking and perception that I had developed over the years, led me down a long road of sorrow and regret.

I was an imaginative, adventurous child. By the time I was four, I had wandered off so much that my mother drew a line across the entry to our cul-de-sac and told me never to cross it. An hour later, she was astonished to discover that I was gone again – this time pushing my two-year-old brother in his stroller. I was found an hour later, with my brother, at a local grocery store a few miles away. I can't remember exactly what happened, but I am sure that I didn't cross that line – I just found another way around it.

3

I was also a perfectionist. I always "colored in the lines" and strove to be the best at everything I did. If I wasn't the best, I felt like I was a "loser" – even if I came in second place.

I wanted everyone to like me. "Friends" became very important at an early age. I wanted to please everyone. This meant that I would often act differently and pretend to like different things, depending on whom I was playing with. What others thought about me was more important than what I thought of myself. If I was with one of my church friends, I would play sports and do, and say, positive things. If I was with one of my "bad friends", I would shoplift, smoke cigarettes, or skip school.

I would often daydream that I was "special" and had magical superpowers. I wanted to be in charge. I wanted to be the quarterback, the pitcher, and the leader. I wanted to be liked by everyone and be the best at everything I did.

In reality, however, I was a shy, fat, "nerdy kid" who did well in school, but had a hard time making friends. I never felt like I fit in and often did stupid things in an effort to be accepted. I spent most of my time trying to prove myself – and not enough time in an effort to **im**prove myself. Since it was very difficult to always be the best at everything I did, I didn't like myself and often wished that I was someone else. And, because I didn't like myself, it was hard for me to accept that anyone really liked me.

As I entered high school, I started hanging out with other kids who had similar problems. Shortly thereafter I was introduced to drugs and alcohol. Even though I was raised in a family with strong values against drugs and alcohol, I was able to overcome my fears and doubts enough to "just try it one time". I was hooked after the first time. I liked using drugs and alcohol because they numbed me. When I was "high", nothing really mattered. The best part was that when I had drugs, everybody wanted to be my friend. I was the coolest kid in town.

As my drug problem escalated, so did my need for money to pay for the drugs. I couldn't ask my parents for money to buy drugs, and if I got a job it would have meant working weekends and missing all of the parties. So, I started stealing. At first it was shoplifting and stealing from my family, but soon I was breaking into lockers at school, breaking into cars, and finally breaking into houses. In the beginning, it was hard for me to steal because I knew it was wrong and I was scared I would get caught. But stealing soon became as habitual for me as combing my hair. The drugs helped to eliminate any fears or pangs of conscience that I felt.

Between the ages of 16 and 18 I was in and out of trouble many times. I was arrested for such things as shoplifting, possession of marijuana, and using a fake ID. However, once I turned 18 everything changed. There was no more being released to my parents who would ground me for a week and then want to forget about it. Within a year I spent time in jail on three separate occasions for theft, selling drugs, and burglary. The judges in these cases decided to give me a chance and instead of prison I was sent to a halfway house, and then to a drug rehab program. However, neither of these worked. I was an out of control teenager wandering aimlessly through life without goals or values, and with little regard for others – like a ship without a ruder.

On my 19th birthday, I was arrested for theft and forgery. This time I was finally sent to prison where I continued to live irresponsibly. I did drugs, lied, cheated, and stole – nothing changed. Prison was more like a vacation than a punishment. And, even though I promised myself that when I got out I would never return, it was an empty promise. I simply didn't do anything to change.

When I was released, I sought the best of both worlds. I wanted to be successful, but I also craved the high-octane excitement that came with living life on the edge. I wanted to reap the benefits of living responsibly, but I didn't actually want to live responsibly.

At first I did fine, because I had the structure of being in a halfway house. My time and money were accounted for, and I was being given a frequent urine-analysis to make sure that I wasn't using drugs or alcohol. I had to maintain full time employment. And, I even enrolled in college and did very well for a few semesters. However, everything went downhill once I was released from the halfway house. I simply wasn't prepared for the increased freedom and lack of structure.

Soon, I was going to late night parties and nightclubs on weekends with my old friends. At first I told myself that I would only drink alcohol, but it wasn't long before I was using other drugs again. I convinced myself that I was being responsible if I only used drugs and alcohol on the weekend. I fooled myself into believing that it was alright to lie and cheat every once in a while. And, even though I had promised myself that I would never steal again, I started taking food and other things from the supermarket I worked at without paying for them.

Soon, however, I was using drugs and alcohol every day. I started calling in sick to work and skipping school. And, I was stealing a lot more than the occasional sandwich. Even at this point I couldn't see myself ever going back to prison. I was living a life of lies.

To be honest, I went through phases where I would clean everything up and live responsibly for a few days and even weeks at a time. But, I always ended up falling back into my old ways. I didn't have the consistent focus or moral foundation necessary to overcome the temptations that confronted me.

It wasn't long before I got myself into trouble again. I am surprised that I made it as long as I did. Less than two years after being released, I was arrested again for burglary and theft - and sentenced to 30 years as a habitual criminal.

Back Inside

Naturally, I was devastated. And confused. I couldn't understand why I was again caught up in a way of life that inevitably led to pain, sorrow and regret. And, I was scared that I was destined to repeat this pattern throughout the rest of my life.

For the first few years after I returned to prison, I felt like just giving up. Although I still had the love and support of my family, I had lost faith in myself, not to mention that prison was much harder this time. I was in a real prison this time, not a camp. I had a much longer sentence and I felt like I was destined to spend my whole life in prison. My family pleaded with me to "figure it out" and do whatever I needed to do in order to make sure that I never again returned to prison once I was released. However, with a 30-year sentence it was hard for me to imagine ever being released. So, I spent the first few years back simply "doing time" – writing letters, watching TV, playing cards, smoking cigarettes, and just hanging out with the guys.

Initially, the shock of being back behind bars led to some shallow promises to my family, my friends, and myself about turning my life around. I told my family that this time would be different; somehow I was really going to change. But it wasn't long before I was once again lying, cheating, stealing, doing drugs, bragging about my criminal exploits, and discussing future ones. I was back to my life-long patterns of criminal thought and behavior, which became more pronounced as my resolve to change and lead a responsible life faded.

I believe that at this point in my life I was unable to understand what it meant to live an "honest" and "responsible" life. To me, living responsibly simply meant staying out of trouble; and staying out of trouble basically meant not being caught doing anything that might get me into trouble. In essence, living responsibly meant maintaining the illusion that I was living responsibly. It had nothing to do with consistently living an honest and open life in which I did nothing that could get me into trouble; a life where I made choices that actually caused the consequence of staying out of trouble.

One day during a visit, my mom told me, "Listen, son, something is wrong and you have got to figure out what it is before you are released again or you will just go back to prison. I would rather you just stay here than get out and go back again." So, I started on my journey. I decided to write a book and try to come to grips with why and how my life had taken this turn. Initially, I wanted to change the "'system". I believed then, as I still do, that there is a big problem with the justice system in America. The "revolving door" style of the prison system traps too many lives. So, I wanted to identify the roadblocks and obstacles which "set-up" individuals to fail in society. Then, I was determined to try and develop a system of rehabilitation that could help break the cycle of irresponsible and criminal behavior.

While researching why the current criminal justice system neither reduced crime nor rehabilitated the criminals who committed crimes, I collected statistics and data on everything from recidivism rates to the daily cost of incarceration. I saw myself writing about the futility of warehousing criminals; the detrimental effects of long prison sentences on prisoners, their families and society; and the unfair and disparate sentencing system. As a non-violent criminal who had been sentenced to 30 years as a habitual criminal, I was also very intent on airing my opinion about the inhumane and unjust practice of threatening to use the habitual criminal statutes to extract guilty pleas from non-violent offenders.

I was looking to blame everyone and everything else for my past choices – choices that had led to my present situation. Instead of accepting responsibility for my actions and looking inside for the cause of all my problems, I was attempting to absolve myself of the responsibility by convincing myself that I had no control over my own life.

However, the more I read, analyzed myself, and reviewed the decisions I had made in my life, the more I realized that I was in a prison of my own making. "They" didn't put me in prison – I put myself in prison. I had no one to blame but myself.

With this realization, I enabled myself to grow. By accepting the fact that I had control over my past, I acknowledged that I had control over my present thoughts, choices and actions – and my future. Regardless of where I was at, regardless of what they did to me, I had control over "me".

I finally concluded that the only way to turn my life around was to work on changing the one thing that I had control over – myself.

Postponing Change

As I looked back over my life, I realized that I had made this resolution to change many times - usually the result of being caught and punished. However, in the past, this desire to change would always fade quickly and the vicious cycle would start over.

One tiny irresponsible act would lead to another. Each act would become a little more irresponsible until eventually I was back doing the same things as before – or even worse. It was as if I were challenging the fates to bring me down. When they didn't, I rejoiced in my shrewdness. However, this short-lived merriment always ended with the painful slap of reality once I got caught...and resolved to change again.

It is hardly surprising that every criminal I talked to was caught in a similar vicious cycle. We had vowed to change at some point in our lives, only to revert back to our criminal ways. We would tell ourselves that we would never again use drugs, steal or hurt others. But, we did. None of us ever wanted to be arrested or return to prison. But, we did. We all wanted to be successful, important, and in control. We wanted to make our friends and families proud. But all we ever seemed to do was cause them pain and suffering.

The irony of this past way of life, as well as its painful consequences, stared me in the face. Still, as was my past pattern in life, I delayed making the effort required to change. I didn't want to totally give up my past way of life and I allowed the daunting task of change to overwhelm me. I liked thinking that I was in control, hanging out with the other convicts, and occasionally "bending the rules". And, I knew that it was going to be hard to break the many bad habits that I had developed over the years.

As usual, I had plenty of excuses: "I've got so much time left to serve, there's no point in making the effort to change yet." "It's alright to let go every once in a while as long as I don't do anything too bad." "I understand myself better this time, so I'll be able to stay out of trouble once I get out." And when those excuses didn't ring true, I'd tell myself that I didn't really know what I wanted out of life - and convince myself I really didn't care.

The desire to postpone the effort required to change was an enormous barrier. It was difficult for me to let go of a lifestyle and way of thinking that had become ingrained over many years.

Eventually, however, as I learned more about myself and gained a vision of what I wanted out of life, I began to recognize these excuses for what they really were - errors in thinking and perception which distorted reality and held me back from a more productive, satisfying, and meaningful life.

With no more excuses to rely on, I finally resolved to change and made the commitment to do whatever it took to turn my life around. Even though I still had many years left to serve in prison, I vowed to be ready when I returned to society.

The Educated Criminal

During my first stint in prison, I took part in almost every educational and substance abuse program offered. At the time, I believed that all I needed to do to turn my life around was get an education, stay away from heavy drugs, and keep out of trouble.

When I was released, I joined Alcoholics Anonymous, got a job, and enrolled full-time at the University of Colorado. For three semesters, I went to CU, worked, and did very well. Yet, I still returned to my previous patterns of crime and became just another statistic in an outrageously high recidivism rate.

I now realize that although educational, vocational, and drug/alcohol abuse programs all play an important role, they are secondary to the development of personal character. No matter how skillful or brilliant we are, we cannot be successful if we lack integrity, self-control, self-esteem, and empathy for others. It is impossible for us to grow through deceit and insincerity. A fundamentally flawed character can only lead to distorted thoughts and perceptions. This then often leads to irresponsible behavior.

Current educational and vocational programs offered to criminals lack the basics required to help us lead a responsible life. Solely educating a criminal will only result in an educated criminal – not a changed criminal. These programs simply do not provide the knowledge or demand the intensity of focus or conviction necessary for the enormous amount of change required. We may gain skills and knowledge, but if we retain our errors in thinking and perception, we will remain fundamentally flawed.

Drug and alcohol programs are similarly ineffective because they simply focus on one aspect of our criminal nature. Certainly, drugs may lower inhibitions, but they do not put criminal thoughts into our minds. So, although drug and alcohol programs may help to eliminate some of the symptoms, they do nothing to cure the disease.

A Principle-Centered Life

In order to truly change, we must learn to live a "principle-centered life".[1] As its name suggests, it is a life that is centered on responsible values and qualities that include integrity, obedience, empathy and compassion for others.

A Principle-Centered Life	
Integrity	Effort
Humility	Thrift
Obedience	Fidelity
Courage	Empathy
Patience	Compassion
Industry	Helpfulness

These principles are deep fundamental truths that are self-evident, enduring, and universally applicable. They govern any human growth, happiness and effectiveness.

To achieve permanent change, we need to identify the habitual irresponsible and criminal thinking patterns that have distorted our perceptions and guided our behavior in the past. Next, we need to eliminate them and replace them with new thinking patterns based on these principles – principles that are often foreign to our past way of life.

It was when I finally accepted the importance of my own thoughts and perceptions that I abandoned my initial book outline. Rather than using this book as a forum to blame everything and everyone other than myself, it became a personal call to action. Its purpose was to help me stay consistently focused on recognizing

---

1   Covey, Stephen R., "THE 7 HABITS OF HIGHLY EFFECTIVE PEOPLE - POWERFUL LESSONS IN PERSONAL CHANGE" (New York: Simon & Schuster, 1989)

my own errors in thinking and perception so that I could correct them by implementing more responsible, "principle-centered" ways of thought, perception and behavior.

Throughout my life, my thoughts and perceptions had usually led me towards self-destructive behavior. The time had come to question and change this. The only alternative was to resign myself to a meaningless life, in and out of prison, with my only accomplishment being the pain and suffering I caused others and myself.

Defining our Purpose

As thinking beings, we're all capable of self-examination. I used this ability to "stand apart" from my present self and imagine that I was old and had already lived my life. By using this technique, I easily recognized that if I continued to follow my previous path it would only lead to further regret and sorrow. Then, I imagined that I had a chance to go back and change it; to live my life over again and repair the mistakes I made the first time around. This time I wanted to be happy and make those around me happy - something that is very difficult to achieve from a prison cell.

To be successful, I knew that it was important to formulate a clear purpose in my life. First, I needed to discover what was important to me. Then I needed to define what direction I wanted my life to go; what I really wanted out of life. Once defined, this purpose had to become the standard by which I evaluated my life, judged myself and guided my decisions. In time, this purpose became a valuable source of self-esteem, direction, wisdom, consistency and power.

After much thought and honest introspection, I formulated a purpose for my life. It was:

I want to lead a productive, satisfying and meaningful life in which I bring joy and happiness into my life and the lives of others.

Then I listed how I would achieve that purpose:

- I will follow the rules.
- I will stay sober.
- I will help others.
- I will be honest and open to myself and others.
- I will live a principle-centered life full of integrity and hard work.
- I will have love, empathy, and compassion for others.
- I will love and respect myself; otherwise it will be impossible for me to love and respect others.
- I will place my faith in God.

I knew that if I could only learn to live by this purpose, my life would be a success.

Next came the hard part. Once I had defined my purpose, I needed to apply it in my life. I knew what I wanted out of life, and what was necessary to be happy and successful. Now my challenge was to make the consistent effort necessary to live responsibly.

Creating a Solution

I have often heard that taking responsibility is the key to **finding** a solution. I would like to take this one step further: taking responsibility is also the key to **creating** a solution. Rather than simply accepting the consequences of our behavior, taking responsibility for our life means actively using our abilities of examination and imagination to create the consequences we want in our life. Living responsibly entails taking control of our life by choosing to respond to all of the challenges we face in a manner that is directed by our purpose, our goals, and the reality of our situation. With each choice we make, we create our own consequences and we create our own opportunities.

From the outset, it is important to understand that as criminals we all have the same errors in thinking and perception that serve to form our criminal point-of-view. We may think our life, our way of thinking, and our problems are unique - they are not. My research and experience demonstrates that every criminal, to some degree, has every error in thinking and perception that I will describe in this book. Whether we are white-collar criminals, thieves, rapists, or murderers, the errors in thinking and perception that lead to crime are basically the same. And, in order to achieve a true and lasting change, we need to develop more realistic and more responsible ways of thinking and viewing the world.

Simply changing our environment or our behavior by avoiding irresponsible friends or staying away from drugs isn't enough. We must totally change whom we are inside. True change can only happen from the inside out. And, for that change to be effective and lasting, we must begin by changing the most fundamental parts of ourselves - our thinking and perceptions. We must be reborn and become a new person with new habits, new thoughts, and a whole new perspective on life. We must learn to function at an impeccable moral level, endlessly seeking reality and living a principle-centered life. Anything less and we are doomed to eventual failure.

Complete and Total Change

The first time I was released, I didn't think there was a need for a complete and total change. I believed that dabbling with irresponsibility was acceptable as long as I didn't cross the line. I could drink and party as long as I didn't do any "heavy drugs". I could lie and cheat at work as long as I didn't do anything that I could get arrested for.

However, I now realize that whenever I allow myself to start acting irresponsibly, I always end up crossing that line. That is just the way I am. One irresponsible act always leads to another even more irresponsible act. Step-by-step my behavior snowballs and it becomes harder and harder to control myself. As time passes, I want to do something a little more exciting and a little more daring. I want more risk and more "fun". And, eventually I lose sight of reality.

In this regard, I am much like the alcoholic who only intends to have one drink, but ends up losing control and getting drunk. Certainly, some men and women can think and act irresponsibly at times and yet never cross the line. Or if they do, they can pull themselves back and regain control. However, some of us cannot. Just as an alcoholic can never take the first drink, we cannot allow ourselves the first irresponsible act.

One Choice at a Time

Although most criminals leave prison with the intention of never returning, the high recidivism rates prove them wrong. The fact is that no true change can ever happen without the proper focus, effort and endurance. No one is going to eliminate a lifetime of irresponsible thoughts and behaviors overnight. True change doesn't happen magically – it requires you to do something.

If our primary goal is to live a happy and productive life outside of prison then this goal must invade our thinking and captivate our lives. There can be no halfway point - it is all or nothing. We must learn to think and behave totally responsibly. We must be willing to say good-bye to who we are, in order to say hello to who we want to be. There can be no regrets - no nagging questions about our true desire to change. Without a total, unconditional severance from our old self and old way of life, we cannot grow and move forward.

The choice to live responsibly is only the first of an infinite series of choices. Realistically, the decision to live responsibly must be made again and again, each day, with each choice we make. This is not easy. However, most of us are very stubborn when it comes to getting what we want. There isn't much we can't do when we set our minds to it. Thus, if we can simply focus this passion and single-mindedness away from criminal activities and toward responsible living, we are bound to succeed.

Ultimately, we must ask ourselves:

- What am I willing to do to make my life more meaningful, productive and satisfying?
- What am I willing to do to stop this cycle of pain and suffering for me and the ones I profess to love?
- What is my freedom worth?

- What am I willing to do to be happy?

In the end, those of us who do not change are those who won't give ourselves completely to the process of changing. Change, like any activity, takes effort and sacrifice - good intentions are not enough.

<u>Acceptance</u>

➢ Step 1 – Acknowledge Weaknesses

Our first major step towards change involves reviewing our life's choices and their consequences. We must admit to ourselves that we are a criminal – we are guilty of committing a crime – and that we need to change. Certainly, there may have been times when we've acted responsibly and honestly. And even times when we have been very helpful and loving. However, these positive instances do not, and cannot, make up for the damage done by even one criminal or irresponsible act.

Few of us are willing to admit that there may be something wrong with us. We feel that it is a sign of weakness to do so. Even while sitting in a prison cell, I didn't view myself as a criminal or a threat to society. I saw others as the real criminals. Guys that were in prison for murder and rape – those were the real criminals. I convinced myself that my property crimes and drug offenses weren't violent, and that nobody really got hurt. I told myself that I was basically a good person who had just made a mistake.

The failure to accept that we are criminals and admit that we need to change can be one of the biggest obstacles to overcome. Almost every criminal has an excuse for his or her criminal and irresponsible behavior. Some claim that they are the victim of a racist or corrupt system. Others blame drugs, the people they hung around with, their childhood, or even the victims themselves. Many of us hearken back all the good things we have ever done and believe that this somehow atones for our mistakes. Or, we self-righteously list all the crimes that we would never commit, while overlooking the pain and suffering we have already caused. Yet, "until a person can say deeply and honestly 'I am what I am today because of the choices I made yesterday' that person cannot say, 'I choose otherwise'." [2]

Much of the time, we're not the only ones who downplay the impact of our actions. Often family and friends will unintentionally deny our need to change by maintaining that we just made a mistake. They blame our actions on our friends, on drugs, or on some other scapegoat. Although this may be comforting for everyone, it can be harmful if it prevents us from acknowledging our need to change.

Certainly, not everyone in prison is a criminal - and not all criminals are in prison. However, if you have committed a crime and making mistakes has become a pattern in your life, then you are a criminal and you need to figure out what is wrong.

➤ Step 2 – The Commitment to Change

Once we have accepted our weaknesses and acknowledged a need to change, the next step is to make the commitment to do anything, and everything, necessary to change. If we want to be successful, we can't go into this half-heartedly; we must be willing to do whatever it takes. This entails not only making the commitment to ourselves, but also to other people in our lives who can help us stay focused.

Making this commitment isn't easy, but neither is spending your life in and out of prison. This book can offer some insight and guidance for change if you use it properly, but it can't force you to change. The decision to change is totally up to you. No one is coming to save you, or live your life for you, or suffer your consequences. Not your family; not your friends; not anyone. Sure, these people will help as much as they can, but they can't do it for you.

It's the ultimate choice. We can decide to embrace change and put all our efforts into living a totally responsible way of life, or we

2 Covey, Stephen R., "THE 7 HABITS OF HIGHLY EFFECTIVE PEOPLE - POWERFUL LESSONS IN PERSONAL CHANGE" (New York: Simon & Schuster, 1989) pp. 72

can live life the way we always have and continue to suffer the same consequences. Looking back, it is hard for me to accept that I fought so hard to live my own life while consistently risking everything worth living for. The aim of much of my criminal behavior was to get me ahead in life. I somehow thought that I could take shortcuts to success by bending a few rules, and I selfishly didn't care who was hurt along the way. However, I now realize that criminality can never lead to happiness or success. My irresponsible actions didn't lead to shortcuts - they led to wasted time and delays.

I now believe in the utter hopelessness and futility of a criminal way of life - a lifestyle where I could never honestly accomplish anything or hope to realize my potential. A lifestyle doomed to failure from the very beginning.

> Step 3 - Preparing for Change

For our change to be effective we must first prepare our inner selves - much like a farmer prepares the soil before he plants his seeds - so that the seeds of change and responsibility can firmly take root and grow in our lives.

Recognition

To prepare for the change process, we should first:

- Formalize the acceptance of our problems and confirm our commitment to change. We can do this by declaring, not only to ourselves but also to another person, that we are a criminal and that we intend to do something to change that.
- Accept full responsibility for our past, present, and future choices.
- Stop blaming others for our problems and seeing ourselves as victims of life's circumstances when we suffer the harsh consequences of our actions.
- Recognize and accept that our success, or failure, in life is

fully dependent on the choices we make.

As human beings with intelligence, self-awareness and free will, we have the responsibility (response - ability) to be the cause of the consequences we want in our lives. We have the **ability** to **respond** to the circumstances in our life in a way that leads to success and happiness.

Taking Inventory

The next step in our preparation to change should be to take an inventory of our lives. In order to take a proper inventory we need to:

- Write down all the things we have done wrong in our lives and list the consequences – for ourselves and others. This step will take some time. It is not good enough to quickly scan our lives and say, "I've made a lot of mistakes and being in jail has been miserable for me," and then be finished.
- Be thorough. For our list to be effective, we must drop all our defenses and write down every crime, irresponsible behavior and lie that we can remember.
- Search out all the flaws and faults in ourselves which may have contributed to this criminal lifestyle. It is important to figure out why we have made the choices that we did.
- List our fears and resentments.
- Make amends and restitution whenever possible. There will be some wrongs which we can never right, but we must make an honest attempt to make things right.

Confession

Next, we must confess all of our past crimes and misdeeds to someone else – someone who is important to us. We must clear our conscience – our inner guide – before we can begin to heal.

For this confession to be of worth there has to be some risk involved, so it can't just be to a stranger or some other convict. It needs to be to someone who is important to us – someone we've probably hurt in the past. This is the only way we can forgive ourselves and move forward. Actually, the harder that it is to make this confession, the more beneficial it will be in the end. Fortunately, most people are very understanding and forgiving. However, we should accept that some won't be.

We need to be prepared to suffer some consequences from the honesty that this step requires. There may be family and friends who weren't aware of the full extent of our crimes. They may regard us quite differently when we tell them the complete truth about ourselves, and this may be difficult. However, we cannot change and learn to live responsibly if we are always worried about hiding skeletons in our closet. We need to clear all the irresponsible remnants of our past from our conscience. If we don't, we risk the chance of these deep, dark secrets festering and returning to distort our perceptions and diminish our resolve to change. It is much like a cancer that has not been totally removed can return and overwhelm the body.

This confession, however, does not clean the slate so to speak. We must accept responsibility for our actions and then do whatever is necessary to ensure we never commit a crime again. Without this, our confession is worthless. Rather than absolving us of responsibility, true confession and remorse should help us focus on the responsibility we have for the future.

Self-Forgiveness

It is also important that we work on forgiving ourselves as well as anyone who has wronged us in the past. We must acknowledge our own imperfections and those of others. We should not hold grudges, because they will harden our hearts and distort our vision of what is important in our lives.

However, we must realize that forgiving ourselves does not mean that we can excuse, condone, or diminish our past wrongdoings in any way. Self-forgiveness does not imply self-deception; it only means that we should have compassion for ourselves.

True self-forgiveness is not easy. It takes time, courage, and inner strength to be able to truly accept and forgive ourselves. Through self-examination, we need to understand all the thoughts, beliefs, and perceptions that contributed to each one of our crimes and irresponsible acts. It will take a lot of focus and effort. However, this is the only way that we can begin to understand ourselves and reduce the likelihood of these things ever happening again. In time, this newfound self-awareness can even help to fuel our desire to change.

A Higher Power

In order to provide the moral foundation and guidance necessary to turn our lives around, I believe that we must find and accept a power greater than ourselves. Accepting the existence of this higher power can help strengthen us and help us find the consistency, resolve, and courage we need to change.

Some people may find it difficult to believe in a higher power. For much of my life, I was the same way. But then I looked at the world around me and realized that it couldn't have happened by accident. Believing our world and universe was created by some sort of random explosion is like believing that we could detonate a pile of garbage and then, when the dust cleared, have a fully furnished house complete with cable television and a well-stocked refrigerator.

There is just too much purpose and harmony in this world for there to be no purpose in life. There is too much diversity. Our existence is too structured, too balanced, and too wonderfully beautiful for there to be no divine providence.

However, even though I truly believe in a loving God who wants the best for each of us, I am not trying to convert anyone to my religious beliefs. Your higher power or higher purpose may take any form you envision. It may be God. Or it may be honesty, truth, family, love, freedom, or even success.

Mental health requires that the human will submit itself to something higher than itself. To function decently in this world we must submit ourselves to some principle that takes precedence over what we might want at any given moment.[3]

Sadly, many believe that faith in a higher power or some form of spirituality is a sign of weakness. Realistically, however, spirituality is a sign of personal strength. Our faith in a higher power and higher purpose in life gives us the fundamental principles, moral foundation, and consistent strength, focus and desire we need to persevere and be successful in changing ourselves. Consequently, our physical well-being should always come second to our spiritual well-being. We must never sacrifice our morals, values, or spiritual focus in order to be liked or to get ahead in life.

As I looked back over my life, while doing my personal inventory, I realized that one of my problems was my need to be liked and accepted. I had low self-esteem and I started my life of crime by stealing cigarettes and smoking to impress some older friends from school. And then, little-by-little, I progressed to bigger crimes. Certainly, peer group pressure is an amazing force at that age. However, I wonder if I'd had a testimony of God when I was younger whether or not this need to impress a couple of 16-year-olds would have been quite so important for me – or so destructive.

A spiritual way of life must be much more than an idealistic dream or a passing fancy. In order to live responsibly, we must learn to humble ourselves and continuously focus on making spiritual progress. We must actively follow a life of meditation, sacrifice, and spiritual redemption. Each morning, before our day starts, we should spend a few minutes meditating. We should think about our short and long-term goals, our purpose, and our progress in life. We should reaffirm our commitment to changing our lives and living responsibly. And we should pray to our higher power for the strength and guidance to do so.

Then throughout each day, we should continually remind ourselves of our purpose and all the reasons why we wanted to change our lives in the first place. Our purpose and higher power should

---

3   Peck, M. Scott M.D., "PEOPLE OF THE LIE: THE HOPE FOR HEALING HUMAN EVIL" (New York: Simon & Schuster, 1983) pp 172

consistently guide our thoughts, choices, and actions. If we find ourselves behaving irresponsibly, we must immediately stop and confess our wrongdoing to whomever it affects, ask for forgiveness, and make amends. We cannot be perfect, but it is important for us to try and keep a clean slate. Attempting to hide even a small misdeed can quickly defile our conscience and cause us to revert to our old ways of thought and behavior. When the day finally ends, we should again meditate, evaluate our progress, and pray.

We should be like the professional body-builder who continually looks in a mirror to assess his physical development and identify any problem areas. For us, meditation and self-reflection is a moral mirror where we can evaluate our spiritual progress and identify what parts of our lives we need to focus on - work, relationships, communication, giving up control, etc.

As part of our daily inventory, we should ask ourselves:

- Did we reach our goals for the day?
- Are we happy with the way the day went?
- What thoughts did we have that weren't in line with our purpose and choice to change?
- What choices did we make today that were in harmony with our purpose to change?
- For each of the thoughts, choices and behaviors that were not in line with our purpose, what was the motivation behind them?
- Why were we motivated in that way?
- What were some responsible ways we could have responded to these circumstances?
- If the same thing were to happen tomorrow, what would we do?

Ultimately, we have the ability within ourselves to identify our faults and weaknesses, critique ourselves, and then find ways to overcome our weaknesses and move forward in our lives.

With the help of a spiritual focus, we stand a much greater chance of overcoming our lifelong patterns of irresponsibility and crime. However, we must remember that faith and prayer alone will not make us responsible. Spirituality can help provide us with:

- the principles and rules to live by
- the moral ability to judge between right and wrong
- strength to do what is right
- a conscience which can help guide us

However, we alone are responsible for using this spiritual direction or ignoring it. No one else can change the way we think and behave or what we believe - we must do that ourselves.

The Consequences of Change

We can further prepare and motivate ourselves to change by writing down our goals and all of the benefits of living responsibly, along with the consequences of continuing to live irresponsibly. This will give us a vivid image of the future rewards that our change can bring, and remind us of everything we lost because of our irresponsible actions.

It is important to understand that all thoughts, choices, and behaviors have consequences.

> While we are free to choose our actions, we are not free to choose the consequences of those actions. Consequences are governed by natural law.[4]

When we act irresponsibly, we may benefit somewhat in the short-term, but in the end, we will suffer a consequence because of the nature of cause and effect. If we call in sick to work because there is something else we want to do, we may benefit for the moment because we get to do that thing. But, we also risk losing our job and the things our salary provides. And, even if we are not caught, we may lose our pay for the day and also risk damaging

---

4   Covey, Stephen R., "THE 7 HABITS OF HIGHLY EFFECTIVE PEOPLE - POWERFUL
     LESSONS IN PERSONAL CHANGE" (New York: Simon & Schuster, 1989) pp. 90

our sense of self-esteem as a result of lying. Likewise, if we choose to watch television instead of studying for an important exam, it may be easier at the time, but we won't do as well on the exam and we may even fail. These consequences don't happen as a punishment, but simply because that is the way life is.

In my own life, I have found the same thing. My irresponsible choices usually had some short-term benefits, but they were far outweighed by the long-term consequences. Living irresponsibly is like buying on credit. By the time we pay it off, we've paid far more than it was worth. Conversely, while responsible choices may require sacrifices and take effort, they usually lead to increasingly positive rewards in the future. Struggling to live responsibly is like making an investment - an investment in our future – that will pay dividends. I've found that responsible behavior usually pays dividends. The total benefit of my responsible actions is often greater than my initial investment of time, energy, and effort.

Every little thing we do - every choice, every thought and every act - unquestionably plays a role in dictating the consequences of our lives. And although we can choose to pay now or pay later, eventually we will always pay.

Consequences of Responsible Living

In order to prepare ourselves to live responsibly, it is important to recognize and accept all of the consequences of our decision to change. Not only must we understand the rewarding consequences, but also the difficult ones. If we ever hope to change in a lasting way, we must start by understanding what change really means – and what it entails.

The consequences of our decision to live a responsible life can be as difficult as they are rewarding and enjoyable. Living responsibly requires more effort and sacrifice than simply doing what we want when we want to do it. Taking responsibility entails problem solving, fact finding, sacrifice, and self-motivation. We must learn to deal constructively with disappointment and adversity. And, we need to accept restraints and acknowledge that we cannot control everything.

We will also have to do things that, in the past, were difficult for us. We will need to swallow our pride and resist our desire to get even when we feel disrespected. And, we will be required to put the needs and feelings of others above our own.

To live responsibly, we will have to follow <u>all</u> the rules - even those we don't understand or agree with. We might not comprehend the necessity of a certain rule, however, that does not give us license to disregard it. Certainly, if we do not understand a rule or think it is unfair, we can attempt to have it changed. But, we cannot ever behave as if it doesn't exist just because it doesn't fall in line with our own idea of what is right.

As we begin to struggle with responsibility, it is inevitable that at times we will become bored and even somewhat depressed. We will miss the excitement of our past way of life. However, we can relieve the boredom by continuously focusing on all the little details of changing ourselves and learning to live responsibly. Details such as:

- recognizing and correcting our errors in thinking and perception as they happen
- implementing responsible patterns of thought and perception
- critiquing ourselves at every turn
- developing true self-awareness, self-esteem, and empathy for others
- being totally honest and realistic in all areas of our life
- responsibly working toward our goals
- following a strict routine

If we are properly focused on living responsibly, we will become so engrossed in the many details of our change that we won't have time to be bored.

Learning the moral lessons and responsible patterns in life can be a struggle because they are so foreign to our way of thinking. If we really desire to change, it is important that we transform our lives into ones of humility, integrity and honesty. We must give up trying to control everyone and everything around us, and instead focus on controlling ourselves. We should be meticulous in controlling our own thoughts, emotions, desires and behavior.

Initially, the journey down a responsible path can seem like an impossible mission. But like all worthwhile achievements, it begins with one step - one choice. Then it simply requires us to focus on one thought at a time, one choice at a time, and one day at a time.

For me, change didn't begin as a desire to live responsibly. It's impossible to desire something you know nothing about. Rather my change sprang from a desire to avoid more suffering - more jail time, more family members losing faith in me, more mental anguish. For me, living responsibly was a means to that end.

Ironically, the desire to live responsibly only comes after we have lived responsibly for some time and have made some responsible gains in our lives. These gains then reinforce the intrinsic worth and value of the responsible way of life. In the meantime, however, just as I took a leap of faith and committed to live a totally responsible way of life, day-by-day, choice-by-choice, so can you.

Rewards of Responsible Living

It is important to start our responsible journey with a positive perspective and attitude. We've all lived responsibly at various times in the past. To succeed now, we must simply put together a series of these responsible choices and begin to stabilize our lives. And we must believe in ourselves.

Responsible living has many rewards. A major one is the peace of mind that comes with a clean conscience. We will no longer need to constantly look over our shoulder, and worry about being caught and punished.

Living responsibly also brings with it true personal freedom.

- Freedom to realize our potential
- Freedom to use our talents

- Freedom from personal jeopardy
- Freedom to grow and develop
- Freedom from the misery of a guilty conscience
- Freedom to openly be ourselves.

The constant worry and anxiety that are part of living a life of lies will disappear. Instead, there will be a sense of pride, self-respect and integrity. Spiritual and intellectual suffocation will be replaced with the sense of accomplishment and self-esteem that comes from an honest day's work. Gradually, we will begin to trust ourselves and earn the trust and respect of others.

These rewards are non-existent in the criminal way of life. As criminals, we are never satisfied. The more we get, the more we want. The more we succeed, the more we crave success. The more we prove ourselves, the more often we feel the need to prove ourselves again. Nothing is ever good enough for us, not even ourselves.

Sure a criminal life can be exciting, but that's not to say that a responsible life is devoid of excitement or pleasure. It simply takes a different form. And over time, it becomes even more exciting, pleasurable, and fulfilling as we begin to build a life for ourselves and start earning the trust and respect of others. With this comes an inner peace that money can't buy.

Eventually, I lost my taste for the high-octane excitement of criminal behavior and became increasingly satisfied with the more fulfilling, purposeful, and less destructive excitements of a responsible life. Now I love to be with my family, play sports, and work. It is like someone who goes on a no-salt diet. Initially, everything tastes bland. But then, they lose their taste for salt and salted food actually becomes almost inedible. In the same way, I have lost my taste for irresponsibility and it has become easier to maintain a new, more responsible, productive, and purposeful way of life.

Moving Forward

Discontinuing Criminal Behaviors

Once we have cultivated the desire to change and have committed ourselves to the lifelong journey of responsibility, we must stop all irresponsible and criminal behavior. Although most of us know right from wrong, this can still be a very difficult task. We simply don't have the experience. So there will be times when we don't recognize we're being irresponsible until it's too late and someone points it out. There will also be times when we miss the opportunity to initiate and implement responsible thoughts, choices and behaviors. Our understanding will come too late. Much like a small child cannot be expected to feed himself or brush his teeth without being taught these skills, we cannot expect to live a consistently responsible way of life without first learning and developing the necessary patterns of thought and behavior.

And our intelligence has nothing to do with our lack of responsibility. We are handicapped from years of viewing ourselves and the world in an irresponsible way. But as we grow and develop, our understanding of the elements of responsible living will also grow - with practice we will become better. And, the more conscious effort we put into our struggle to grow, the greater our understanding will become. There is great truth in the biblical promise of Jesus Christ who says, "Ask, and it shall be given you: seek, and you shall find: knock, and it shall be opened to you". [5]

In the beginning, though, it is vital that we consistently struggle to follow all the rules – even the little ones. We can't allow ourselves to ever lie, cheat or to commit any crimes. We mustn't come up with any of our usual stupidly insane excuses. There can be no more stealing, gambling, drinking, drugging, speeding, littering or even associating with other irresponsible individuals.

If you're still in prison, you're probably thinking that this is impossible. Irresponsible people surround you! But it can be done. I did it. Not associating with... doesn't mean that you can't talk to

---

5   St. Luke 11:9

them, acknowledge them or show them the same courtesy and respect that you would like to be shown. We just can't hang out with them and become involved in their criminal discussions and deception. Otherwise, we will be exposed to their beliefs and misperceptions. We simply can't allow ourselves to become engaged in 'criminal talk', criminal power plays, criminal boasting, or other criminally exciting behaviors that often become the center of an incarcerated person's way of life.

The door must be totally closed to all irresponsible and criminal behaviors and thought. Like anything else, the only way to learn to live responsibly is by living responsibly, and only by living a consistently responsible way of life can we gain a realistic perspective of what responsible living entails.

The Best of Both Worlds

In the past, many of us have sought the "best of both worlds". We would pretend to be responsible so we could continue to enjoy the comfort and affection of family and friends. At the same time, we would secretly enjoy the excitement and "proof of power" that comes with irresponsible and criminal behavior. Naturally, a responsible way of life cannot work this way.

If your goal is to be responsible, mixing responsibility with irresponsibility is like taking strychnine with your morning vitamins - the goodness of one simply cannot remedy the bad effects of the other. Our good deeds can never make up for our bad ones, and eventually we will suffer the consequences of trying to lead a double life.

This reminds me of a story I read of a young man who was constantly getting into trouble. His father, at a loss for what to do, told him that every time he got in trouble he was going to put a nail in the railing at the side of the barn, and every time he did something good he would take a nail out. The first day, several nails were driven into the side of the barn. The next day a few were taken out, but even more were driven in. After a week there were so many nails that it seemed that no one could ever do enough good to get them taken out. At that point the boy, ashamed with himself, committed to do everything he could do to clear the barn of the nails. One good deed led to another and soon many of the nails were gone. Finally, a few weeks later, the last nail was pulled out. As the young man stood there, looking at where all the nails once were, he started to cry. His bewildered father said, "Son, you have worked very hard and have finally done enough good deeds to remove all of the nails that were once here. Why are you so sad?"

The son, through the tears in his eyes said, "The nails are all gone, but the scars they made in the wood are still there." Good deeds can never make up for irresponsible behavior. And even though the scars created by irresponsibility and crime can heal, it takes time.

The key to spiritual growth involves consistency in both thought and action. Therefore, we must always be consistent in the way we apply ourselves to each choice. And, as individuals with a tendency towards misperception, we must learn to consistently evaluate our every thought, choice, and action to make sure we don't deviate from our purpose. There can be no in-between for us - we must keep focused on our goals and struggle to stay on the right path.

Since success will depend on a constant self-evaluation and positive focus, there can be no reservations about the commitment involved. Deceiving ourselves into believing that we can learn to be responsible now, and then some day be able to let loose and re-vert back to some of our old, exciting ways won't work. Only a complete commitment to the continuous struggle for spiritual and moral progress will provide a lasting change.

Just as Alcoholics Anonymous teaches each member to iden-tify themselves as an alcoholic, regardless of how long they have been sober, we must accept that we are criminals and must struggle each and every day to live responsibly. We have a moral flaw which won't allow us to tread the line without eventually crossing over. We will never reach a point where we can become compla-cent and tell ourselves we are no longer criminals. We can never allow ourselves to act even a little bit irresponsibly. Other people may be able to do these things, but we can't. To do so means we run the risk of opening the door to our past patterns of irresponsibility and crime.

Naturally, we won't be perfect. We will make mistakes. What we cannot do is continue to make excuses for them, rationalize them, or condone them. Instead, we must acknowledge our mistakes and then struggle to correct them, learn from them, and make sure that they don't happen again.

Breaking Old Habits

In order to stay focused on our objective of changing our inner thoughts and perceptions, it helps if, for some time, we have some sort of restraint on our freedom and a monitoring process. We need this structure to help us stay properly focused.

When I was released the first time, I found it difficult to stay away from the irresponsible situations that I was so used to finding myself in. It was just too easy to revert back to my former friends, hangouts and behaviors. I have found that if you don't consciously think about each and every choice that you make before you act, your subconscious programming (your habits) will lead you to make the same type of choices you made in the past.

So during the preliminary period of change we need extra effort, consistency and conscious focus. Habits, much like gravity, can hold us in their grasp. Initially, it can be difficult to break away from their pull, but once we do we free ourselves to grow. And then it will become increasingly easy to live without them.

Finding Our Responsible Guide

Of course, simply breaking old bad habits isn't enough. We must replace these habits with more productive ones. Therefore, we will need some guides - someone or something to help us along the way. While only we can provide the desire and determination to change, a guide can help make us aware of what it is we need to change and what important habits we must develop.

This book, and others like it, can be such a guide or road map to living responsibly. However, it is up to each of us, individually, to make the effort and sacrifice necessary to implement what we learn about ourselves. It is worthless to simply read this, or any other self-improvement book, without doing all of the exercises that it prescribes. In order to be successful, we must actively use the lessons we learn and the knowledge we gain to move forward in our lives.

As we struggle to change our lives, we will need someone who can provide support, strength and knowledge. Someone who will take us under their wing, so to speak, and teach us what it means to live responsibly. Naturally, we will need to pick our guide carefully.

First, they should be **someone we trust and respect**. Someone whose advice we will listen to and not question. If we neither trust nor respect them, we are likely to question their views and end up distorting what they are trying to teach to us. They also need to be able to be open and honest with us about their view of us and the world.

Second, we need **someone we can be open and honest with**. We need to be able to tell our guide about everything that is going on in our lives - our actions, our motivations and our thoughts. Even though we want to change, we may still be tempted to withhold information. We may be afraid that if we tell everything, we could endanger ourselves or incur undesired consequences. We may fear that our responsible guide will no longer respect or like us. Whatever the reason, the result is the same. If we aren't totally open and honest, our guide cannot help us. They must know what we are feeling, what we are thinking, and what we are doing.

Third, we need **someone to keep us motivated and focused**. At times, we may be tempted to change our minds about what we really want out of life and try to start down a different, less difficult path. Our guide must constantly remind us why we wanted to change in the first place and not be afraid to point out what our future will be like if we don't live responsibly. There will inevitably be times when we just want to give up. For many of us, giving up has become a pattern throughout our lives, so we'll need someone to be there who is willing to kick butt to keep us focused. Like an Alcoholics Anonymous sponsor, our guide must be willing to help keep us from becoming complacent in our desire to change.

Fourth, we need **someone who will express their own opinion** of us, honestly and precisely. Our guide should:

- help us identify our errors in thinking and perception
- help point out what we are doing wrong
- remind us of the consequences of irresponsible behavior
- help us to identify all the responsible options that we have

There can be no fear of hurting our feelings, and no "beating around the bush" when it comes to helping us avoid our old patterns.

Our guide must always be honest with us. Certainly there will be times that our guide will want to praise our progress. However, we shouldn't be praised simply for behaving the way we should have been behaving our whole life. Unwarranted praise can be detrimental as it reinforces our criminal perspective of being unique and special.

Lastly, our guide must be **someone who knows our criminal thinking** patterns and is able to incorporate this into their analysis and criticism of our progress. We think and view the world differently than responsible people. Our guide must understand this, be familiar with our criminal characteristics, and be able to point them out when we display them. Our guide must also be able to offer corrective suggestions in order to help us think and live responsibly. For us, true change will require the continuous repetition of lessons that include examples of responsible thoughts, choices, and actions; corrective advice; and constructive criticism.

Our Daily Progress Report

To be successful, we must develop structure and open communication with our guide. To do this, I suggest daily progress reports that outline our progress and our failures. We can start by talking about the irresponsible behaviors and choices we made during the past 24 hours. We should:

- discuss why we made them
- identify how we were feeling at the time
- determine whether we thought about the consequences before we acted on our irresponsible thoughts
- identify whether or not we realized they were irresponsible choices

Next, we should report on any irresponsible or criminal thoughts, feelings and desires we have had – even if we haven't acted on them. Criminal thoughts are the seeds of crime. So, the eradication of our irresponsible and criminal thoughts is just as important as eliminating the behaviors which these thoughts invoke. Significant thoughts may include:

- incidents where we became angry and thought about getting even (even if we didn't act on these thoughts)
- times when we felt the need to prove ourselves for one reason or another
- any time we thought about taking something that wasn't ours
- periods of boredom
- any thoughts or desires to behave irresponsibly or criminally
- any thoughts, choices, and actions that we are uncertain of

Due to our errors in thought and perception, and lack of experience in responsible living, we cannot let ourselves decide what is important and what is not.

Finally, we should discuss some of the responsible thoughts, choices, and actions we made during the past 24 hours. This can help to promote a sense of inner satisfaction and joy over the progress we have made.

Sometimes it will be necessary for our guide to treat us like a child; to tell us things that a responsible five-year-old should know. However, they must realize that we <u>are</u> like children when it comes to living responsibly. We need to accept our guide's observations

35

and criticism graciously, consider their relevance, and make whatever changes are necessary to implement what we have learned.

But we also must remember that our guide is just that - a guide. Our guides aren't there to solve our problems for us or direct our decision-making by telling us what to do. Our guide should simply help us understand the value of responsible decision-making processes, such as fact finding, identifying our options, and weighing all of the possible consequences of our options. Realistically, the only way we can learn how to make responsible decisions is by actually making them ourselves.

Conclusion

Once we have made the commitment to change and prepared ourselves for the difficult road that lies ahead, it is necessary to gain a better understanding of ourselves and why we made the choices we did. It is difficult to change if we don't fully understand what needs to be changed in the first place.

In the next few chapters of this book, I discuss many of the errors in thinking and perception that form the basis for our criminal behavior. My aim is to help identify why we make the irresponsible and criminal choices that we do. Hopefully, this knowledge will provide the personal insight and awareness necessary to trigger change.

As we learn about ourselves and begin to recognize our errors in thinking and perception, it is important to make this knowledge operational in our lives. True change can only happen when we fortify our knowledge with action - when we "walk the talk" and do what is necessary to consistently live a responsible way of life.

With the right focus and effort, a miraculous thing will begin to happen. You will start to build a reputation with yourself as being an honest and responsible individual. You will trust yourself and believe in yourself. You will develop a true sense of pride and satisfaction in the things that you do. Ultimately, it is changing this inner concept of yourself, your self-esteem - the part of you that no one else can see - which is the most important.

CHAPTER 2

Choices

When I first went to prison, I didn't view myself as a "real" criminal. Even though I took things that weren't mine, I reasoned that it didn't really hurt anyone. I felt like a modern day Robin Hood. I convinced myself that my victims really didn't suffer much, because their insurance would replace the things that I took. I couldn't begin to compare myself with murderers or rapists who, in my mind, were the real threats to society.

I also thought that I was very unique and that nobody else could ever understand what I had been through, how I felt, or how I viewed the world. In my mind, there was nobody else like me. I believed that I was destined for greatness and that somehow I should be better than everyone else around me. And because of this perspective, other people's thoughts and feelings just didn't seem to matter as much as mine. Paradoxically, I also often felt worthless, because I was unable to live up to my own lofty expectations of myself. During these times, I believed that everyone else viewed me that way as well.

However, after several years of research, observing and talking to many of the other men I was in prison with, and taking an honest look at myself, I realized that I wasn't so unique after all. I learned that although the individual manifestations of crime vary from criminal to criminal, there are many characteristics and traits that we all have in common. The fact is that most criminals don't see themselves as criminals – or threats to society. We all think that we are unique and that somehow our crimes aren't quite as bad as the crimes committed by others. We all think that we are special and a little bit better than everyone else – until we fall short of our own expectations. We also:

- can be very controlling and manipulative
- tend to blame others for our predicament and constantly complain when things don't go our way
- have a high sensitivity to what we call "disrespect"
- have an intense lack of trust
- have a thirst for power and excitement
- have the capacity to disconnect ourselves from the thoughts, feelings and emotions that normally serve as deterrents to crime

Based on these characteristics, and many others I will describe throughout this book, our point-of-view is very different from that of a responsible person. We see the world through a tainted lens. And, it is this "criminal viewpoint" and the associated errors in thinking and perception that combine to perpetuate our irresponsible behavior. Criminal behavior, then, is simply a choice - a choice which is based on this criminal point-of-view.

Irresponsible Behavior

What makes someone capable of choosing to commit a crime? To understand this you must first understand that crime is simply an irresponsible behavior. In fact, the consequences of non-criminal irresponsibility can be just as damaging to the self and others as criminal behavior, and may even last much longer. For example, while unprotected teenage sex may not be considered a crime, the potential consequences to the individual – potential pregnancy, disease, and the life-long responsibility which comes with raising a child - are potentially greater than the consequences of many crimes. And what about gambling? It's not illegal, but can lead to huge problems for the individual and everyone around them. Even eating disorders, such as anorexia (the choice not to eat) and extreme overeating (the choice to eat too much) can have more serious and long-lasting consequences than many crimes. They may result in health problems and even death. Psychological abuse of a child or spouse is also extremely irresponsible, but not a crime. From the perspective of many in society, the same can be said for abortion, lying, cheating, and failing to keep obligations. Just take a look at today's foreclosure rates.

In fact, although all crimes are considered irresponsible behavior, many irresponsible acts are not considered crimes. For example, some people see nothing criminally wrong with adultery or abortion, yet the individual consequences of these irresponsible acts (broken homes and hearts, anger, fear, loss of life, and stolen dreams) are ultimately no less horrific than those which crime may have on society as a whole. And even though suicide, a sad but completely irresponsible act, is not considered a crime, it has an enormous consequence on the self (self extermination) and on all of those left behind.

My point is that many of us occasionally do things that are contrary to what we know is right and in our own best interests.

We are the one species that can formulate a vision of what values are worth pursuing - and then pursue the opposite. We can decide that a given course of action is rational, moral and wise - then suspend consciousness and proceed to do something else. We are able to monitor our behavior and ask if it is consistent with our knowledge, convictions and ideals - and we are also able to evade asking that question.[1]

Realistically, there is a wide spectrum of irresponsible behaviors. Watching TV when you have other obligations may be irresponsible, but cannot be compared to committing a burglary. And where do theft, adultery, lying, and laziness sit on the spectrum? However, even though all of these behaviors vary in degrees of irresponsibility, they all arise from the same psychological thought processes - thought processes that enable an individual to do something that they know is wrong and contrary to the realistic appraisal of a situation, no matter how potentially extreme the consequences may be.

---

1   Branden, Nathaniel, "THE SIX PILLARS OF SELF-ESTEEM" (New York: Bantam Books, 1994) pp. 31

I assert that irresponsible behavior and crime are the result of a series of psychological mechanisms and errors in thought and perception, which combine to distort reality to the point that a particular irresponsible or criminal act seems justifiable, acceptable, or even necessary.

For example, let's say that a young, teenage boy has met a pretty girl at a school dance and as the night goes on he is faced with the choice of having unprotected sex with her in the back of his car. First, he has to justify this choice and convince himself that it's okay. He can do this through a variety of misguided thoughts and perceptions such as:

- All my friends have tried sex and they will think I am different or uncool if I don't do it.
- I may never get this opportunity again – I had better go for it.
- I am old enough to make my own choices and if I want to try sex, I will.
- I don't need a condom. It is only once and I won't get her pregnant or catch any disease.
- It is my life and I will do what I want. I'm not hurting anyone.

Or, if he has previously made up his mind, then he may simply choose not to think at all – until after he has sex. Then he may start worrying about these things.

Making an irresponsible or criminal act seem acceptable is only part of the whole picture. You also have to ignore the possible consequences of your actions and suppress any inner beliefs, morals, or values that may deter the irresponsible or criminal behavior.

Going back to the example of the teenage boy, the stronger the teenager's moral set against unprotected sex, the more errors in thinking he must use to justify it. If he is religious or his family values are at odds with this choice, then he must also contend with them. And, if it is his first time, he must also deal the fears of the unknown.

Once the choice to have sex has been justified in his mind and deemed as okay, he must then somehow distort or ignore the reality of any potential consequences, such as:

- the girl could get pregnant
- he could contract AIDS or another STD
- he may get in trouble and even be arrested if the girl is much younger than him

These potential consequences of his choice can be side-stepped by a couple of different mechanisms:

- he can simply not think about them by setting them aside and avoiding conscious awareness of them
- he can convince himself that these consequences somehow don't apply to him (for example: "I won't get her pregnant or catch any diseases because that just wouldn't happen to me.") - again distorting reality.

Ultimately, every irresponsible or criminal choice, from the smallest lie to the greatest evil, is filtered through much the same psychological thought process before it manifests itself in behavior. If we tell a lie, we must first justify the lie to ourselves. Then, we need to circumvent any beliefs or values we may have against lying. Finally, we must distort or ignore the possibility of being caught and any potential consequences for us and others.

Criminal behavior follows the same process. For a person to commit any type of crime, they must first justify or excuse the criminal behavior, distort any values that they, or society, may have against the crime, and then somehow avoid the reality of the possible consequences of their actions. Contrary to popular belief, very few criminals think it is appropriate or acceptable to commit crimes, so they have to go through the same justification and avoidance process. However, the more often you make an irresponsible choice, the easier it is to make them again and again. Once you have behaved in a certain way in the past, it becomes easier to make that behavior seem acceptable in the future. The fact that you have already done something wrong can actually become an excuse for irresponsible behavior.

I am not trying to make excuses for irresponsible or criminal behavior. Our behavior is ultimately a result of the choices we make. However, in order to fully understand ourselves, we must understand the thought mechanisms and perceptions that enable us to choose this behavior. My objective is to help provide the insight and motivation necessary to change these errors in thinking and perception, and to increase awareness of the internal and external consequences of irresponsible behavior. The way we think and view the world provides the foundation for the choices we make - so it is these thoughts and perspectives that are a key in our struggle to live responsibly.

Criminal Thinking

The impact of a man's thinking on his behavior has been recognized since the beginning of time and should not be underestimated. In the Bible it states "...as a man thinketh so is he,"[2] and in a passage from *The Miracle of Forgiveness* the effect of our thinking on our lives circumstances is eloquently expressed by James Allen:

A man does not come to the almshouse or the jail by the tyranny of fate or circumstance, but by the pathway of groveling thoughts and desires. Nor does a pure-minded man fall suddenly into crime by stress or mere external force; the criminal thought had long been secretly fostered in the heart and the hour of opportunity revealed its gathered power. Circumstance does not make the man; it reveals him to himself. No such conditions can exist as descending into vice and its attendant sufferings apart from vicious inclinations or ascending into virtue and its pure happiness without the continued cultivation of virtuous aspirations and man, therefore, as the lord and master of

---

2   Proverbs 23:7

his thoughts, is the maker of himself, the shaper and author of environment...Let a man radically alter his thoughts and he will be astonished at the rapid transformation it will effect in the material conditions of his life. Men imagine that thought can be kept secret, but it cannot; it rapidly crystallizes into habit and habit solidifies into circumstance. [3]

Our thinking guides our choices and crime is always a choice. We are not forced to commit a crime; we alone have control over our actions. We all have knowledge of right and wrong. Most of us are also capable of feeling the full effects of a guilty conscience and the dissonance associated with irresponsible behavior. We know it is wrong to murder, steal, and hurt others. That's why we attempt to cover up our crimes. And even when we get caught, most of us try to hide the full knowledge of our crimes from others.

In prison, I saw a man convicted of multiple murders convince another prisoner not to kill someone because he regretted his crime and knew that it wasn't the right thing to do. I've seen men break down and cry at the realization of the pain and suffering they have caused others. While most criminals try to cope by hiding the memories of their wrongdoing from themselves, at times this fa-çade crumbles to reveal men who cannot understand why they acted that way. They ask themselves, "How could I have done what I did?" Most of us are able to deceive ourselves and hide the true answer to this question from ourselves in order to maintain our inner status quo. Ironically, we hide behind the same justifications, lies, and scapegoating that enabled us to commit the crimes in the first place.

Even the criminal who has grown up around parents who are drug users knows that it is dangerous and illegal to use drugs and understands the consequences. In fact, they often have a greater understanding of the dangers than someone who has been spared from that environment. Sure, early life experiences such as these invariably have an impact on future choices, and they may make

---

3   Kimball, Spencer W., "THE MIRACLE OF FORGIVENESS" (Salt Lake City: Bookcraft Inc., 1969) pp. 105

choosing a responsible path more difficult. However, these learned experiences do not fully undermine our ability to assess what is right and wrong, and to make the right choices. Nor do these experiences eliminate our awareness and understanding of the potential consequences. Thus, drug use, or any other irresponsible behavior that may be passed from parent to child, is still a matter of choice.

Perspective – Our Point of View

An individual's actions are simply a reflection of the action in his mind. However, many different things combine to form the action within one's mind. The way a man thinks is not only influenced by what he knows, but more importantly, by his perceptions of himself, others, and the world around him - his point-of-view. In turn, the way a man perceives reality is influenced by many things, including genetics, assumptions and expectations based on past experiences and his relationship with himself - or his self- esteem.

Reality is concrete. What is, is. What is not, is not. However, the perception of reality varies from individual to individual. What an individual thinks, sees, and chooses does not depend primarily on reality or even the physical images their eyes see. They do not react so much to the facts in front of them as to what they understand or want to understand the facts to be.

Thus, when one person sees the cup as half full, another can see it as half empty. For one man, the sight of a particular person will evoke thoughts and feelings of joy, happiness and love. For another, the sight of the same person might trigger only fear or anger.

Now, let's imagine you are walking with your friend on a sunny day at the park and see a young boy running from an older man. You may perceive it as a man playing tag with his son while your friend may see a child running from his potential abductor. Perhaps you may find out later that the child has just stolen the man's wallet and was trying to run away. How would your perspectives change?

Similarly, a person's own self-image can be distorted by unrealistic thoughts and perceptions. Take the case of the anorexic who perceives herself as being fat even though she is so emaciated that her ribs are sticking out. In fact, studies have shown that up to 95% of women unrealistically evaluate their appearance by overestimating the size, shape and weight of their bodies. Since our self-image is an external factor, it is based not only on how we perceive ourselves, but also on our assumed perceptions of how others see us. Thus, I believe one of the reasons why so many women have an unrealistic self-image is because it is based more on society's portrayal of the perfect size and weight for women. It is not so much a reflection of what a woman physically sees as how she believes others see her.

I believe that the human perception of reality is usually distorted to some extent or colored in one way or another. However, we do have a choice as to how we perceive reality and how realistic our perceptions become. We have the ability to re-evaluate our perceptions and change our inner point-of-view or reference, so that our glass always seems half-full instead of half-empty. We can discover why certain things make us feel a certain way and then change these things if we so desire. We can seek awareness or we can avoid it. It may not be easy to face reality, but it can be done. To do it - or not to do it - becomes another choice.

Human consciousness is volitional. We have the option of seeking reality or not. We are also capable of avoiding reality if we fear, dislike, or are unable to accept our perceptions of reality. However, we also have the capacity to be courageous and overcome our fears and dislikes. We can make the conscious effort to focus on our thoughts and perceptions if we so choose.

The human tendency is to focus our conscious awareness on things that already support our point-of-view. We readily remember instances that support our way of thinking while tending to discount experiences or memories that challenge it. Thus, not only do our perceptions influence the way we think, but they verify it. In turn, the way we think also influences our perceptions.

For example, if we believe that the world is evil, we will tend to focus our conscious awareness on all the world's evils and fail to seek the awareness of any good in the world. However, if we believe that the world is basically good, then we tend to focus on all the good in the world while downplaying all of the evil. In this way we verify our own point-of-view, which can then serve to further distort our perceptions.

The big problem with our ability to focus, or not focus, our conscious awareness is that we can also use this process to support and confirm our errors in thinking. And, it can also allow us to avoid the awareness of our own morals, values, lessons learned from experience, and emotions such as guilt and fear.

Self-Esteem

Throughout our lives we all make choices (beginning in early childhood) that inevitably have an impact on the type of individual we become.

Through the thousands of choices we make between thinking and non-thinking, being responsible toward reality or evading it, we establish a sense of the kind of person we are. Consciously, we rarely remember these choices. But deep in our psyche they are added up and the sum is that experience we call self-esteem - the reputation we acquire with ourselves.[4]

Our self-esteem has a tremendous impact on the way we think and act by creating a set of expectations about what is possible and appropriate for us. It can also have an affect on our self image, or the way we think others view us. This, in turn, can play a huge role in the decisions we make, especially throughout our teenage years.

Our self-esteem plays a vital role in our thoughts and choices. When we have a healthy self-esteem we feel confident about coping with life's challenges. We feel worthy of happiness and respect. We are reality-oriented. Facts have a higher priority than feelings or desires. The truth is more important than being right. We know who we are, so we maintain a stable moral base on which to predicate our decisions. Joy is our motivation. Happiness is the state we wish to experience. Our purpose is self-expression

---

4   Branden, Nathaniel, "THE SIX PILLARS OF SELF-ESTEEM" (New York: Bantam Books, 1994) pp. 69

and to live up to our potential.

People with low self-esteem feel unworthy and incompetent. They live more to avoid inner pain than to simply experience life. They are too busy trying to prove themselves to experience the joy of their own existence. And because they always feel like they must prove themselves, it's a task that can go on forever. Nothing ever seems to be good enough.

When someone lacks self-esteem, the need to make choices can be very frightening. Rather than being steadfast in their knowledge of right and wrong, choices can become an inner source of endless debate. Unfortunately, while the debate rages, choices are based more on feelings and an effort to prove themselves than on reality.

> ... (If) I lack respect for and enjoyment of who I am, I have very little to give - except my unfilled needs. In my emotional impoverishment, I tend to see other people essentially as sources of approval or disapproval. I do not appreciate them for who they are in their own right. I see only what they can or cannot do for me. I am not looking for people whom I can admire and with whom I can share the excitement and adventures of life. I am looking for people who will not condemn me - and perhaps will be impressed by my persona, the face I present to the world.[5]

Contrary to popular belief, you can never have too much self-esteem. Although many people confuse an over-healthy self-esteem with egotism, pride, arrogance and boasting, these traits don't reflect a healthy self-esteem. Rather, they are manifestations of an unhealthy one. When you have a healthy self-esteem, you are not driven to prove yourself by measuring your worth against some comparative standard. You don't need to feel superior to others. You believe that everyone is entitled to the same feelings of happiness and self-esteem that you have, so you enhance these traits in others. You realize that there is enough sunshine in the world for

---

5   Branden, Nathaniel, "THE SIX PILLARS OF SELF-ESTEEM" (New York: Bantam Books, 1994) pp. 8

everyone. When you love, respect, and trust yourself, you show love, respect, and trust towards others.

An example of true self-esteem can be seen in the dog that happily runs around the backyard playing by himself and taking in all of the sights and sounds of a summer day. He isn't thinking to himself, "Wow, this is great. I have it so much better than the dog next door." Nor is he pondering what the dog down the street is doing or wishing that he had a backyard like his. He is simply happy to be himself and enjoying the fullness of his creation.

Striving for popularity, material possessions, praise from others, and a feeling of power over others does not create a healthy self-esteem. These things may enhance an individual's self-image, which can make them feel better for a while. They can also help them feel more confident and in control - and even make them feel more comfortable in certain situations. But this comfort and proof of worth can only fleetingly serve to fill the void in one's relationship with themselves. In the end, these things are just as likely to make a person feel worse, not better. Just think of all the famous people who seem to have it all yet turn to drugs or commit suicide.

> Nothing is more common than to pursue self-esteem by means that will not and cannot work. Instead of seeking self-esteem through consciousness, responsibility and integrity, we may seek it through popularity, material acquisitions or sexual exploits. Instead of valuing personal authenticity, we may value belonging to the right clubs, church or political party. Instead of practicing appropriate self-assertion, we may practice uncritical compliance to our particular group. Instead of seeking self-respect through honesty, we may seek it through philanthropy - "I must be a good person, I do good works. Instead of striving for the power of competence (the ability to achieve genuine values), we must pursue the "power" of manipulating or controlling other people.[6]

---

6   Branden, Nathaniel, "THE SIX PILLARS OF SELF-ESTEEM" (New York: Bantam Books, 1994) pp.52

Problems with an unhealthy or low self-esteem are often manifested as shyness, fear of change, and lack of confidence. However, an unhealthy self-esteem can also cause detrimental thoughts and perceptions as a result of its own avoidance. In an attempt to cover for an unhealthy self-esteem, our thoughts and perceptions will reflect the desire for control, confidence, and the sense of personal worth which are lacking. If we haven't internalized a sense of personal worth, we will seek to prove it in external ways. If we have no internal sense of confidence, we will seek recognition and praise from others. And, if we have no internal sense of control, we will seek to control others. The primary source of our self-esteem then becomes external or based on others' reactions to our actions – which can be very dangerous.

Of course, we may also choose to simply avoid the conscious awareness of our unhealthy self-esteem and just not think about it. Yet, even though we may be able to conceal our deficient self-esteem through a variety of mechanisms, we cannot be indifferent to its effects. At some level, the self is ultimately aware of our inner thoughts and choices - and the basis for these thoughts and choices. And, the more we struggle to avoid the awareness of our reputation with ourselves, the more we lose touch with reality. This, in turn, lowers our self-esteem even more. And, the lower our self-esteem becomes, the more we will feel a need to prove ourselves and to conceal our self-esteem by living mechanically and unconsciously. If not remedied, this can become a never-ending downward spiral in which the self has the most to lose.

Choices Lead to…More Choices

Our self-esteem is not constant; it fluctuates on a continuum. Instead of being something we either have or don't have, self-esteem varies in degrees. The lower our self-esteem, the less confidence we have in ourselves and the less worthy we feel. The higher our self-esteem, the more confident, competent, and worthy we feel. Self-esteem is also not something that we can earn and store away for later - like a retirement account. It is something we must earn daily - like a paycheck. And, although not all primary sources

49

of self-esteem are under our control (such as early childhood experiences and genetic make-up) it is primarily our thoughts, choices and actions which determine our level of self-esteem. Behavior and self-esteem are reciprocal. They are both a cause and consequence of each other. The more right choices we make, the more habitual it becomes to make right choices. On the other hand, the more wrong choices we make, the easier it becomes to make the wrong choices. This tendency is beautifully described by Erich Fromm:

> Our capacity to choose changes constantly with our practice of life. The longer we continue to make the wrong decisions the more our heart hardens; the more often we make the right decision, the more our heart softens - or better, perhaps - comes alive ... Each step in life which increases my self-confidence, my integrity, my courage, my conviction also increases my capacity to choose the desirable alternative, until eventually, it becomes more difficult for me to choose the undesirable rather than the desirable action. On the other hand, each act of surrender and cowardice weakens me, opens the path for more acts of surrender and eventually freedom is lost. Between the extreme when I can no longer do a wrong act and the extreme when I have lost my freedom to right action there are innumerable degrees of freedom of choice.[7]

It is important to understand that our self-esteem becomes healthier the more we:

- live consciously
- respect ourselves (and inevitably, others)
- admit (and either correct or accept) our imperfections and mistakes
- and, live with integrity by acting in a way which is consistent with our morals, values and knowledge of right and wrong.

---

7   Peck, M. Scott M.D., "PEOPLE OF THE LIE: THE HOPE FOR HEALING HUMAN EVIL" (New York: Simon & Schuster, 1983) pp.81

As a result, the increased confidence and trust we have in ourselves can make it easier for us to make responsible choices based on reality.

Conversely, when we act in a way that is contrary to our personal goals and values, we promote a reputation of distrust and doubt within ourselves. We lose faith in ourselves. Consequently, this tends to distort our thoughts and perceptions of reality to the point where our knowledge of right and wrong becomes debatable. Our choices are then usually based more on a yearning to feel worthy than on the reality of the situation.

I believe that as our self-esteem becomes more and more unhealthy, different psychological defense mechanisms are employed in an attempt to defend the self against whatever it may perceive as a threat. If reality is perceived as the enemy of our self-esteem, then our conscious awareness can be undermined, distorting internal thoughts, feelings, emotions and external perceptions. And if a certain person, or activity, is perceived as a threat, then that person or activity will most likely be avoided – or eliminated.

In an attempt to repair the damage to our self-esteem by proving ourselves through external means, we may become a workaholic (or any type of "-aholic"). Internally, a workaholic avoids the conscious awareness of his feelings by continually focusing his awareness on the task at hand while externally pushing himself to his physical limit to prove his worth to himself. In the end, however, this does not work, so he is continually left trying to prove himself.

Some people may hide behind food or drugs and alcohol. And others may attempt to prove themselves by physically hurting others, seeking praise, or in some other way attempting to enhance their self-image - the way they believe others see them. In fact, according to Nathanial Branden:

Apart from disturbances whose roots are biological, I cannot think of a single psychological problem - from anxiety and depression to under achievement at school or at work, to fear of intimacy, happiness or success, to alcohol or drug abuse, to spouse battering or child molestation, to co-dependency and sexual disorders to passivity and chronic aimlessness, to suicide and crimes of violence - that is not traceable, at least in part, to the problem of a deficient self-esteem.[8]

As young children, we don't have a healthy self-esteem, but only because it has yet to develop. We are still creating our reputation with ourselves through the conscious and subconscious evaluation of our behavior and its consequences. Self-esteem in children is founded on others' reactions to their actions - it is external. And eventually, "if we develop properly, we transfer the source of approval from the world to ourselves; we shift from the external to the internal."[9] Yet, if we don't develop properly, we will undoubtedly face problems in the future.

The feelings of incompetence and worthlessness that are at the root of an unhealthy self-esteem are similar in every person. However, every individual learns and develops different methods to deal, or not deal, with these feelings during their developmental years. Fortunately, many children who choose to behave in irresponsible ways in their attempt to deal with an unhealthy self-esteem, later also choose to change their perspective of life. They mature and finally develop the healthy self-esteem they deserve. Others simply learn to deal with an unhealthy self-esteem through behaviors, such as being a workaholic, a sex-aholic, a spend-aholic, or an overeater.

This book isn't about these people. It's about the minority of us who choose to behave extremely irresponsibly - those who choose to commit crimes. While not everybody who has an unhealthy self-esteem chooses to commit crimes, all criminals have an unhealthy self-esteem. The reasons an individual develops errors in thought and perception are as numerous as the reasons why a person doesn't develop these errors in thought and perception. The complexity of the human mind and diversity of variables in human behavior make it impossible to pinpoint one experience or genetic

---

8 Branden, Nathaniel, "THE SIX PILLARS OF SELF-ESTEEM" (New York: Bantam Books, 1994) pp. X.V.

9 Branden, Nathaniel, "THE SIX PILLARS OF SELF-ESTEEM" (New York: Bantam Books, 1994) pp.279

trait that would definitely cause an individual to develop a criminal point-of-view.

The key is, however, that all criminals have common errors in thinking and perception that combine to create a point-of-view that is conducive to criminal thought and behavior. How and why we developed these errors is something which must be dealt with on an individual basis. Although some of these errors in thought and perception can be attributed to an already unhealthy self-esteem, many others are simply erroneous beliefs which have been cultivated and now serve to skew our moral compass.

Criminal Thinking

As I talked with other criminals, I noticed that many of us followed the same path in life. We weren't born criminals. We developed the errors in thinking and perception that ultimately lead to irresponsible and criminal behavior. A criminal mind doesn't just happen - it is planted, cared for, fostered, and grown to full bloom.

Early in life we developed erroneous thoughts and perceptions that led us to make a series of choices to live a life that we soon found exciting; a life in which we were determined to do whatever we wanted; a life where we ignored the restraints and morals taught to us by our family and society. As children, many of us were extremely energetic and adventurous. We had an iron-will and often insisted on taking charge. We would become angry or upset when others didn't do as we expected. We took risks. We became entangled in lies and difficulties, and then demanded to be bailed out and forgiven when we were caught.

As teenagers, our image was everything. Many of us were involved in gangs. Our friends were much more important than our self, so we often did stupid things in an attempt to be liked and accepted. As a teenager, I can recall many times when I did things that I knew I shouldn't do in an effort to be liked. I shoplifted a dozen cigarette lighters so that my friends and I could each have two. I started smoking so that everyone would think that I was cool. I stole an expensive bracelet and gave it to a girl I was trying to impress. And each time that I did one of these things to boost my self-image, it was at the expense of my self-esteem.

As we grew older, our errors in thinking and perception increased as they fed on themselves. We've already covered the fact that we all have a tendency to seek awareness of the things which support our thinking while avoiding the awareness of things that contradict our thinking. As criminals, this tendency is increased because of our erroneous self-perceptions and the distortion of reality. Thus, the further down the criminal path we go, the more regularly criminal thinking takes place and the easier it becomes to choose to commit crimes. Criminal behavior is not impulsive. We don't just commit crimes out of the blue. In our thinking, there is always a precedent for the crimes we commit.

At the height of our criminality, our mind is actively engaged in criminal thoughts. We're plotting so many crimes that there's little opportunity to act on them all. Many of us have experienced insomnia - the result of our minds racing with thoughts of potential criminal opportunities. We may even have to turn to drugs and alcohol to get some sleep. I feel that this extreme mental activity is, in part, a consequence of our increasingly unhealthy self-esteem. Our unhealthy self-esteem must be avoided through the distraction of excessive mental thoughts which, for us, are criminal in nature. The extreme workaholic and extreme over-eater would have similar problems. It's just that their thoughts would be about work or food rather than crime.

Naturally, our specific thoughts vary from criminal to criminal and from situation to situation. So the crimes that each of us commit are very different. Our behavior is simply a manifestation of our thinking. For example, a violent criminal is most likely to have recurring thoughts about proving themselves and regaining control through violence when they are offended or disrespected; a property or white-collar criminal usually dwells on making money and being in charge, while a rapist's thoughts are generally full of deviant sexual fantasies and control. In time, this way of thinking becomes habitual. And, once our mind has formulated a reservoir of criminal ideas, we begin to scan our environment looking for the opportunity to act upon these thoughts and desires.

At this point I would like to reiterate that although we all have much the same errors in thought and perception, we all vary in the degree to which these errors come into play, and thus the degree of our criminality. Furthermore, the extent to which an individual's thinking errors come into play in any specific choice process can vary from situation to situation depending on the type of crime. Thus, although I will be talking in extremes when discussing the errors in thought and perception that we all possess, we are not all as extreme in our thinking. In fact, some of the errors in thought and perception may only play a subtle role in our criminality. However, I believe that these errors must be present, to some degree, for us to choose to commit a crime. And, I firmly believe that all of these errors in thought and perception must be eradicated before we can experience a true and lasting change.

Another point I would like to make is that even though our errors in thinking and perception have a tendency to increase and decrease depending on our circumstances, the rate and extent of change also differs from criminal to criminal. Thus, some of us spend our whole lives behaving irresponsibly but only get involved in petty crimes. Others choose to commit increasingly serious offenses. For the most part though, as we become more irresponsible and involved in crime, our self-esteem becomes unhealthier, our thinking errors become more extreme, and our conscious awareness becomes more unrealistic. This all contributes to more outrageous crimes and more irresponsible behaviors.

In the end, crime is not caused by the environment, external circumstances, genetics, or drug addiction. Crime is a choice. A responsible person won't commit a crime because of what he watches or reads, or because of the people he associates with. Crime will only happen if the criminal thoughts and perceptions are already in place. And, even though criminal thoughts and actions may become habitual, our crimes are not impulsive or compulsive. Sure, at times we may not be realistic in our thinking, but we are solidly in touch with reality. Most of us are not mentally insane or psychopathic with no ability to control our own actions. Even though we may act impulsively in other areas of our life, we know that certain impulses lead to arrest, so we are constantly scanning our environment in order to get away with our crimes.

To some extent, our past choices and experiences have a tendency to influence our present thoughts and behavior. And, the more we become automatic or habitual in our decision-making, the greater this tendency becomes. However, past choices and actions do not have to dictate future ones. With each and every choice, we have the ability to reverse our present direction and choose to start anew. As human beings, we all have the capacity to focus our conscious awareness on what is right and on the consequences of our actions, or we can choose to endlessly justify and debate our choices within our minds. We can choose to overcome our past and do what is right. We can make the choices that lead to personal happiness and freedom. And if this is too difficult for us to do on our own, we can choose to seek help.

CHAPTER 3

The Cloak of Self-Image

Throughout our lives, our perceptions of ourselves and our environment have been full of contradictions. At times we can be self-assured, arrogant, and self-centered to the point of narcissism. Yet because this self-image is only a façade intended to conceal our unhealthy self-esteem, we can be quickly reduced, by the slightest provocation, to feeling unworthy, inferior and depressed.

More than half a century ago the noted psychologist, Alfred Adler, observed that, "With criminals it is different; they have a private logic, a private intelligence. They are suffering from a wrong outlook upon the world, a wrong estimate of their importance and the importance of other people."[1]

Much of the time we perceive ourselves as unique and superior to others. We feel that we are a "cut above the common herd" and we regard the world as our own personal playpen. The feelings, beliefs, and freedoms of others are less important than our own, because we are special. Some may say that we have too much of an ego or too much self-esteem. However, according to Nathaniel Branden, "It would be hard to name a more certain sign of poor self-esteem than the need to perceive <others> as inferior."[2] By focusing on the inadequacy of others to build ourselves up, we are attempting to avoid the awareness of our own feelings of inadequacy and self-doubt.

We are pretentious. There is usually an extravagance to everything we do and we often demand distinction and merit for doing

---

1   Samenow, Stanton E., Ph.D., "INSIDE THE CRIMINAL MIND" (New York: Times Books, 1984) pp.20

2   Branden, Nathaniel, "THE SIX PILLARS OF SELF-ESTEEM" (New York: Bantam Books, 1994) pp.12

even the most trivial things - things that we should be doing anyway. We seek praise and recognition from others in an effort to gain the inner sense of worth and worthiness we lack because of our unhealthy relationship with ourselves.

We are perfectionists. However, our perfectionism depends entirely upon what we value. And, if for some reason we aren't perfect, then we are likely to give up and quit. Most of us, at one point or another, have told ourselves that if we can't be good enough, then there is no use in even trying. The problem is that, for us, being good enough means being perfect - or at least better than everyone else.

Early in life we gravitated towards this unending quest for perfection in order to help defend against our unhealthy self-esteem. In essence, we led ourselves to believe that, for one reason or another, we had to prove ourselves. Unfortunately, because we are human, we can't be perfect. We can strive for perfection, but perfection is for God alone. It is when we fail to realize this that we become the confused person for whom nothing ever seems good enough. Every accomplishment, no matter how impressive, always falls short and leaves us feeling inadequate.

Since our quest for perfection always falls short, we are dreamers not doers. In our dreams and fantasies, we often see ourselves as invincible and almost superhuman. We dream of being in control of everything. We may fantasize about being a pro-football star, a multimillionaire businessman, or even some kind of magician with God-like abilities. Yet because we rarely, if ever, do what is necessary to reach our dreams, they exist only as frustrated yearnings. And, when we are immersed in crime, we often fantasize about the "one big score", the final crime, after which we will have it made and be able to live a rich lifestyle forever. However, this too, is only a fantasy, because the more we have, the more we inevitably want. Our appetite, once fuelled, is insatiable.

We are full of pride. It is not, however, a pride based on a proper sense of value or a satisfaction taken in achievement. Our criminal pride is more of a conceit that generally has little or no valid basis. Our pride is usually based on the delusion that we are without flaws. As criminals, we simply don't realize that authentic pride has nothing to do with bragging, arrogance, or being better than others. It is not intended to cover feelings of emptiness and inadequacy, but to reward the soul for a job well done. True pride is not about proving yourself, it is about enjoying yourself.

We crave power, but it is power for power's sake and rarely for the benefit of anyone but ourselves. Since we lack an internal sense of control and self-esteem, we attempt to fill this inner void by controlling others. Ultimately, this quest for power and control can be seen in all that we do. It is at the very root of all criminal behavior.

Rape, murder, burglary and all other criminal behavior can be attributed, at least in part, to cravings for power. The murderer exerts power over his victim; the drug dealer over his clientele; the rapist over his victims. The lyrics of "Captive Honor" by the heavy metal rock group Megadeth, demonstrates the power element that controls the thinking of young people who are involved in crimes like drive-by shootings: "Kill a man, you're a murderer; kill many, you're a conqueror; kill them all and you're God."

The proceeds from property crimes also play an important part in our thirst for power. We usually throw the money or "loot" around to impress others, gain influence, and bolster our self-importance. Throughout our lives we have learned that if we leave large tips and lavish our friends with extravagant gifts, we will be regarded as someone important and special. Everyone will want to hang out with us. Thus, the proceeds of crime simply become a tool for increasing our self-image (our sense of how others see us) and our sense of self-importance. Through crime we seek an external boost to our self-image – a temporary rush that comes from having power over others and being in control.

For most of us, the conquest and power element is what is most important in crime - not the proceeds gained or harm done. Our intent is rarely to victimize, but rather to gain, or regain, control and to promote a sense of self-worth. There is rarely any malice to crime. Rather, the victim and his rights simply aren't considered. If we were to empathize with the victim, few of us could do what we do.

The Put-Down

As criminals, we use a variety of different methods to get what we want. Some of us lie, cheat, steal, or even put on a façade of respectability, while others are mean and rely more on fear and intimidation to get what they want. There are also times when we will switch tactics if we think it will help us achieve our goals. However, regardless of which method we use, we are usually trying to just maintain our sense of power and control in an attempt to avoid the reality of our unhealthy reputation with ourselves (our poor self-esteem).

Our perfectionism, thirst for power and need for praise, are simply desperate attempts to cover for our lack of confidence and true feelings of self-doubt and unworthiness. And, because our self-esteem and self-image are not in harmony with each other, our self-image is very fragile. We have a sort of glass jaw when it comes to criticism from others. We can dish it out, but we can't take it.

We are also vulnerable to our own imperfections. Put-downs may be imagined whenever our behavior or achievements do not conform to our lofty self-image. In fact, anything that is not in line with our inflated self-image can be seen as a put-down, which can instantly transform us from being arrogant and self-assured to feeling inferior and depressed.

From our distorted perspective, we often find the evidence of rejection where none exists. We perceive slights and put-downs even when none are intended. So, we are often slighted, because we define failure as being anything less than an overwhelming success. For example, I remember feeling put down when I was picked last in sporting activities, because it didn't conform to my self-image of being a good athlete or sustain my view of myself as being important and better than others. I also remember feeling put down when I had to ask questions or ask for help, because I thought that it showed ignorance and made me look weak.

Put-downs are such a threat to us as criminals, because they can shatter our unrealistically inflated self-image. When this happens, our self-opinion totally collapses and we inevitably feel like a big zero. We lose all sense of self-confidence and self-worth. And we believe that everyone around us also sees us as being a zero and that this will last forever. These feelings of nothingness may last for minutes, hours, or even days during which time there may be thoughts of suicide and complete despair. However, there are also usually thoughts of how we may rebuild our deflated self-image and re-establish our self-worth – which, for us, often includes irresponsible behavior and crime.

We have learned through experience that the antidote to a put-down is to re-establish our control over others through power plays, lying, and exaggerating. We may get angry with the person we feel is responsible for the put-down and lash out verbally or physically. We also may just walk away, bottle-up our feelings, and attempt to rebuild our self-image by seeking to prove our superiority and power over others.

Many of us try to isolate ourselves from certain situations or people in order to avoid potential put-downs. If someone makes us feel uncomfortable or in some way poses a threat to our self-image, we avoid them. If we feel that we can't be the best at something, then we don't even try. We feel as though we should be a cut above the rest in everything we do, and we have found that the easiest way to maintain this unrealistic image of ourselves is through crime and irresponsible behavior.

It's a paradox. We go from one extreme to another, getting knocked down every time something doesn't go our way, only to build ourselves back up again, usually at the expense of others. And, what is even more frightening for us is our fear that these feelings of inadequacy will last forever if we don't do something quickly to build ourselves back up.

Ultimately, we must learn to understand that these self-perceptions are false. "In their thinking there are no gradations between being tops and being nothing; criminals usually assess a situation in extremes, perceiving it to be better or worse than it actually is."[3] According to Nathaniel Branden, this type of thinking is

---

3 Yochelson, Samuel, and Samenow, Stanton E., "THE CRIMINAL PERSONALITY - VOLUME ONE: A PROFILE FOR CHANGE" (New Jersey: Jason Aronson Inc., 1976) pp.266

common among people with low self-esteem. "In tests, low self-esteem individuals tend to underestimate or overestimate their abilities; high self-esteem individuals tend to assess their abilities realistically."[4]

The Development of a Criminal Personality

It is important to understand that we can't blame our criminality on anyone or anything other than ourselves. I believe that crime is solely the result of choices that we make. Focusing on outside forces can be counterproductive to lasting change, because it can provide excuses to allow us to see ourselves as the victim instead of the victimizer. It may also tempt us to focus on past events, instead of the real problems and our need to change our erroneous thoughts, attitudes and perceptions.

So, while we shouldn't look to our past to place blame for our problems, we should learn from our past so that we can make changes to our present course. Only with some realistic insight as to how we arrived at our present position can we do something to permanently change our direction. If we don't understand what the problem is and what caused it, we can't fix it.

This reminds me of a story about a student who, after spending hours typing a research assignment on his computer, discovered that the printer wouldn't print. Undaunted, he carefully re-entered the print commands into the computer, checked to make sure it was plugged in and pressed enter, again. Still it wouldn't print for him. After several more unproductive attempts, he picked it up intending to smash it to the ground. Only then did he discover the cause of his problem - it wasn't properly connected to the computer.

In my research, I managed to trace these feelings of inadequacy and hypersensitivity to others' opinions back to early childhood. Even as children, few of us felt like we really fit in. And, because we felt unable to live up to our own and others' expectations, we didn't feel comfortable enough to open up to those who may have

---

4   Branden, Nathaniel, "THE SIX PILLARS OF SELF-ESTEEM" (New York: Bantam Books, 1994)

been able to help us. We didn't like or care about ourselves so, we reasoned, how could anyone else like or care about us. Even those of us who came from seemingly stable families felt awkward, intimidated and unlikable. Often, there was a parent, sibling or peer who we felt would never accept us or whose expectations we could never live up to. As children, most of us downgraded our self image and felt as though we were ugly or uncoordinated - even if it wasn't true. Our image of ourselves was often a deception.

An example of how these feelings can be traced back to childhood is given in this autobiographical paper, written for a college course, by a convicted rapist.

Just after turning 12 years old, I progressed from grade school to junior high. The fear of not being able to follow in the footsteps of my older brother, Warren, overwhelmed me. My athletic ability had not developed as fast as Warren's had when he was at age 12. Warren was not only athletic, exceptionally smart and popular at school; he was also praised at home.

Upon entering junior high school, I quickly realized my teachers, peers, and family had built up the expectation that I would naturally follow my older brother's path. I was not as adept athletically as Warren and because of this I was not as popular. My academic status was much lower than Warren's, resulting in great disappointment from the school, heckling from my peers, and punishment from my parents. I felt I could never be good enough.

I tried my best to do well in school. No matter how hard I tried, I could still not earn the grades that Warren had earned. I always did well in sports, but never achieved the superstar status that Warren had attained.

I finally came to the realization that even if I did as well as Warren in all things, I would not experience the degree of admiration he had received from others and would always be a disappointment. It was at this point in my life that I decided if I could never be good enough, then nothing really mattered anyway. (Used by permission)

As children, many of us had the tendency to give up when things didn't go our way. We often wondered why we should even try because, from our unrealistic point-of-view, we thought that we would never be good enough or live up to the outrageously high standards which we had set for ourselves (and which we believed everyone else had set for us). In fact, not trying is a recurring pattern in most of our lives, because if we don't try, we don't risk failure. And because of our unhealthy self-esteem, we were also unable to properly confront or even open up about our problems, questions, or concerns about life. With our distorted perspective, talking about these things would have made us feel vulnerable and caused us to feel even more inadequate. Therefore, we usually kept everything bottled up.

Ultimately, many of our errors in perception and thinking have already come into play and perpetuated themselves by the time we reach our pre-teen years. While we are still young, we learn and then perfect the ways in which to maintain a positive self-image. The only difference between a potential criminal and another child who may have the same erroneous self-perceptions is that the potential criminal learns to deal with his low self-esteem through irresponsible behavior and crime. Others either grow out of this stage with the help of those around them, or learn to deal with their poor self-esteem in more "socially acceptable" ways.

Beginnings

So, where may these errors in thought and perception come from? In the book *High Risk Children without a Conscience* by Dr. Ken Magid and Carole A McKelney, the authors contend that "the foundation laid down during the first year of life develops the strength and stability of the personality."[5] The authors suggest that

---

5   Magid, Ken, and McKelvy, Carole A., "HIGH RISK CHILDREN WIHTOUT A CONSCIENCE" (New York: Bantam Books, 1989) pp.101

if proper bonding does not occur, a child will develop a distrust of others, a deep-seated rage, and a negative self-image. A lack of bonding with parents may also explain why the criminal, as a child, is unable to bond with others and pick up their responsible morals and values. The same authors go on to say that:

> Among the list of suspected culprits for unattached and dangerous children are: marital discord; physical, sexual and psychological abuse or neglect; overly harsh or inconsistent discipline; genetic influences; poverty and social disadvantage, the position in the family, the child's individual temperament and poor child-rearing abilities.[6]

The environment begins to have an impact in the development of self-esteem and emotional competence at the time of birth. Although emotional abilities such as self-awareness, empathy and the ability to delay gratification continue to develop throughout the childhood and teenage years, "<the> emotional abilities children acquire in later life build on those of the earliest years. And these abilities…are the essential foundation for all learning."[7]

The first few years of life are when a child's brain grows and evolves in complexity at an astonishing rate. During this period, the brain develops in response to its environment. The impact of experience on the still developing brain of an infant was explained in the groundbreaking work by Nobel prize-winning neuroscientists Thorsteon Wiesel and David Hubel.

> They showed that in cats and monkeys there was a critical period during the first few months of life for the development of the synapses that carry signals from the eye to the visual cortex, where those signals are interpreted. If one eye was kept closed during that period the number of synapses from that eye to the visual cortex dwindled away while those from the open eye multiplied. If, after the critical period ended, the closed eye

---

6 Magid, Ken, and McKelvy, Carole A., "HIGH RISK CHILDREN WIHTOUT A CONSCIENCE" (New York: Bantam Books, 1989) pp.32-33
7 Goleman, Daniel, "EMOTIONAL INTELLIGENCE" (New York: Bantam Books, 1995) pp.193

was reopened, the animal was functionally blind in that eye. Although nothing was wrong with the eye itself, there were too few circuits to the visual cortex for signals from that eye to be interpreted.[8]

So, consider the emotional and psychological foundations being laid for the infant who wakes up hungry and starts crying. His mother, who has been asleep in the next room, comes into the baby's room, lovingly picks the baby up out of his crib and holds him affectionately, singing lullabies to him as he nurses. After 20 minutes or so, the baby, content in sensing his needs are being fulfilled, that he is loved and that he can rely on others, falls back to sleep in his mother's arms.

Now consider the foundations being laid for another baby whose mother is aggravated at being woken up in the middle of the night. She storms into the room, roughly picks up the baby and impatiently sits down, telling the child, "Hurry, let's get this over with." As the baby begins to nurse, the mother becomes lost in thoughts about something upsetting that happened the day before. The baby, sensing that his mother is upset, tenses up, squirms and stops nursing. The mother, who is even more annoyed now, looks at the baby and says, "If that's all you wanted, I could have just stayed asleep!" Then she roughly puts him back and leaves, letting him cry himself back to sleep with the impression that people cannot be trusted or relied upon; that he really doesn't belong and that no one really loves or cares about him.

Of course, most babies get at least a taste of both kinds of interaction, but to the degree that one or the other is typical of how parents treat their child over the years, basic emotional lessons will be imparted. These lessons will inevitably impact on how secure a child believes he is in this world and how dependable he thinks others are.

An early traumatic experience, such as an illness or accident that causes extreme pain or suffering, can also leave a lasting barrier to the emotional and psychological development of a child.

---

8   Goleman, Daniel, "EMOTIONAL INTELLIGENCE" (New York: Bantam Books, 1995) pp.224

This is because the infant may perceive his parents or others as the cause of his pain and anguish, and come away with an intense impression of not being wanted, loved, or cared for. Consequently, he is apt to lose all trust in others. The youngster may also build a shell around himself by pruning or sculpting his brain so that he is able to avoid any further pain and suffering, leading to an increased ability to shut-off or hide his emotions and avoid conscious awareness.

With the absence of an appropriate emotional and psychological base, a child can be handicapped when it comes to developing positive relationships with themselves and others. Then, as the child develops, the errors in thought and perception that are the basis of unhealthy self-esteem and emotional illiteracy are cultivated and reinforced through selective attention. By this point, the actual way in which the child is being treated doesn't matter as much as the way he perceives that he is being treated.

This means that most of the time, a child who is treated with love and respect will tend to perceive that he is loved and respected. He will internalize that love and respect, and then treat others with love and respect. However, another child who is treated with the same amount of love and respect can twist his perceptions of reality so that he imagines indignities and abuse in neutral or even loving behaviors towards him. If his parents punish him, he feels it is because they don't love him. If they don't punish him, it is because they don't love or care about him. If his parents try to spend time with him, the child may feel it is because they don't trust him or respect his privacy, and if they don't spend time with him, it is because they don't love or value him. For the child with an unhealthy self-esteem it really doesn't matter how his parents or peers treat him, because he perceives the worst in any situation. These children also tend to exaggerate and quickly recall the few indignities that are a part of life while belittling true acts of love and respect. Since the child doesn't feel lovable, acts of love are not internalized.

Similarly, although a child who is abused may tend to internalize contempt for himself and others, this also doesn't have to be the case. Just as one child can perceive indignities in the best situations, others somehow find a sense of love, respect, and belonging in the most abusive situations. A child is capable of

67

avoiding the conscious awareness of abuse while actively seeking the awareness of any love, respect and belonging that may slip through the cracks into his life. Circumstances don't defeat people, their inner perceptions defeat them.

It is a person's inner point-of-view that allows him to do the best of things in the worst of times, or the worst of things in the best of times. This partially explains why some children who are raised in positive, loving environments can develop an unhealthy self-esteem and become utterly irresponsible or even criminal as adults. It's also why children who have been abused and come from extremely dysfunctional families can grow into responsible, loving adults.

It is important to understand that an unhealthy self-esteem and an unrealistic self-image are not the only characteristics that allow us to choose crime. There are many other psychological mechanisms and errors in thinking that also play a part in our choices and irresponsible behavior. Therefore, the potential causes for an unrealistic self-image do not, in and of themselves, cause criminal thinking. They do, however, help to create an unrealistic perception of self, which is at the very foundation of our criminal thinking and point-of-view.

Genetic Factors

I don't believe that there is a criminal gene that causes people to commit crimes. However, certain genetic and psychological characteristics may have an influence on the development of a criminal point-of-view. These genetic influences on behavior may also serve to partially explain why people develop differently in similar conditions - why children who are raised in the exact same environment inevitably grow up as unique individuals.

As children, we seek out our environments. We determine them almost as much as they determine us. Even as a newborn infant, the way we behave often influences the way we are treated. All mothers of more than one child can attest to the fact that from the time of birth, every infant has a unique individual temperament - some are active and loud while others are more quiet and timid.

Some like to be held and cuddled and others don't. In fact, it has been theorized that "about 50 percent of measured personality diversity can be attributed to genetic diversity".[9]

Some scientists believe that certain chemicals in the brain affect our need for excitement. "In studies of psychopathic brains it was found they have low levels of a mood-altering chemical called serotonin ... It is possible this may explain their constant desire for kicks which are often criminal in nature. These people must live on the edge ... <and> test themselves and others regardless of future consequences."[10]

Harington (1972) concluded that early experiments that injected adrenaline (which excites most people) into psychopath's bloodstreams caused them to temporarily stop searching for criminal excitement and feel more at peace. [11] More recently, "sensation seeking has been proposed to be related to the activity of catecholamine neurotransmitter systems in the brain."[12]

However, even though genetic factors may influence our thirst for excitement, genetics cannot explain what type of situations will ultimately trigger these feelings. They don't explain why one person is thrilled and excited in certain situations, while others would feel only shame or sorrow. And, having a thirst for excitement is not only a criminal characteristic. Many responsible people also have a thirst for excitement and quench this thirst in responsible ways.

A genetic connection to violence has also been made in recent studies. In the article <u>Violence triggers in brain located: research reveals genetic connection</u> the author writes:

> ...the most profound discovery, so new that parts of it have yet to be published formally in scientific literature, is that genetic

---

9   Konner, Melvin, "WHY THE RECKLESS SURVIVE AND OTHER SECRETS OF HUMAN NATURE" (Middlesex: Penguin Books, 1990) pp.226

10 Magid, Ken, and McKelvy, Carole A., "HIGH RISK CHILDREN WITHOUT A CONSCIENCE" (New York: Bantam Books, 1989) pp.194

11 Magid, Ken, and McKelvy, Carole A., "HIGH RISK CHILDREN WITHOUT A CONSCIENCE" (New York: Bantam Books, 1989) pp.331

12 Konner, Melvin, "WHY THE RECKLESS SURVIVE AND OTHER SECRETS OF HUMAN NATURE" (Middlesex: Penguin Books, 1990) pp.232

defects produce abnormal levels of serotonin and noradrenalin, two potent brain chemicals that researchers have successfully manipulated to make animals more violent.[13]

A later article by the same author goes on to explain that, "serotonin is the brain's key chemical modulator of primitive drives and emotions, including sex, appetite, mood, sleep and aggression".[14]

Noradrenalin is the brain's master alarm switch. It gets turned on when the brain perceives a threat, preparing the mind to deal with impending crisis and preparing the body to fight or flee. Not surprisingly, this genetic predisposition towards aggression and violence is believed to be environmentally triggered. In fact, several studies suggest that;

> Threatening environments can trigger imbalances in genetically susceptible people, laying the biochemical foundation for a lifetime of violent behavior. Such ominous trends as the collapse of the family structure, the surge of single parenting, persistent poverty and chronic drug abuse actually can tip brain chemistry into an aggressive mode.[15]

However, although chemical imbalances may influence a propensity for violence, they don't pre-determine what will actually trigger the violence. There are responsible outlets for aggressive behavior - football, weightlifting, boxing, jogging and a variety of other physical and mental activities. The decision for us is to choose the outlet.

Certainly many of the individual traits or errors in thinking that we associate with criminals can also be found in non-criminals. For example, you may have a boss who is a perfectionist. Your next-door-neighbor may be pretentious and egotistical. And, you

---

13 Kotulak, Ronald, "VIOLENCE TRIGGERS IN BRAIN LOCATED - RESEARCH REVEALS GENETIC CONNECTION" (The Denver Post: Sunday, January 2, 1994): 19A

14 Kotulak, Ronald, "VIOLENCE TRIGGERS IN BRAIN LOCATED - RESEARCH REVEALS GENETIC CONNECTION" (The Denver Post: Sunday, January 2, 1994): 19A

15 Kotulak, Ronald, "VIOLENCE TRIGGERS IN BRAIN LOCATED - RESEARCH REVEALS GENETIC CONNECTION" (The Denver Post: Sunday, January 2, 1994): 19A

probably have a responsible friend who always seeks excitement. Even though these individual traits can be found in all criminals, they don't, by themselves, steer people to habitually choose to behave irresponsibly or commit crimes. The key is that to think the way we do, and to continually make the criminal choices we do, all of the foundational characteristics must, to some extent, be present. It is the combination of these traits, psychological mechanisms and errors in thought and perception, that create what I call a criminal point-of-view. A point-of-view that is conducive to committing crime.

CHAPTER 4

Concealing Consciousness: the Destruction of Deterrents

A nother characteristic that all criminals share is the ability to shut off our emotions, which allows us to eliminate internal deterrents to irresponsible behavior, such as fear and guilt, and disregard lessons learned from experience. This defensive mechanism is the cornerstone of our lifestyle. Without this ability to avoid conscious awareness, we couldn't continue to choose to commit crime.

> Nature has given us an extraordinary responsibility: the option of turning the searchlight of consciousness brighter or dimmer. This is the option of seeking awareness or not bothering to seek it or actually avoiding it. The option of thinking or not thinking. This is the root of our freedom and our responsibility.[1]

For us, the avoidance of conscious awareness has become habitual and has developed to the point where it can destroy rationality and common sense. This shut-off mechanism allows us to eliminate any pangs of conscience, or fears of capture, when we're thinking about or participating in crime. It also enables us to shut-off any lessons we might have learned previously, and to eliminate any sense of guilt we may feel after a crime.

Internal and external deterrents usually keep most people from committing crimes. Internal deterrents include a person's morals, values, belief in God, fear, guilt, empathy for a victim, and pangs of conscience. External deterrents are the ones outside the individual that are usually reinforced by society. These include any

---

1 Branden, Nathaniel, "THE SIX PILLARS OF SELF-ESTEEM" (New York: Bantam Books, 1994) pp.31

legal consequences, including fines and prison, as well as potential ostracism from our social circle, and the loss of trust and respect from those around us.

As criminals, we are not devoid of emotion or incapable of learning from experience. We feel fear, guilt and shame. It's just that we have developed and enhanced our ability to avoid the awareness of these things when they interfere with what we want to do. But, even though this shut-off mechanism can become habitual and automatic, it is still a mental process that is totally under our control. We can choose whether to avoid awareness or not.

For the extreme criminal, this shut-off mechanism can be triggered instantly to eliminate any possible deterrents to his actions. Some extreme criminals reach the point where they don't even recognize any deterrents to crime until they are caught. However, for others, this shut-off mechanism is usually preceded by an erosion of deterrents.

The erosion of deterrents is a mental process in which internal and external deterrents are slowly eliminated as a deterrent to crime. We usually do this with excuses and justifications. Eventually, the desire to behave a certain way or commit a criminal act outweighs the deterrents to this action. Then the desire can be acted upon. Basically, these erosive thoughts and perceptions can be likened to drops of water that, over time, can wear away the rock of deterrents to crime.

An example of how easily an individual's morals and values can be eroded is vividly illustrated in a story I once heard about some frogs that were calmly boiled alive in a cauldron of water. Why didn't they resist? Well, when they were put in the cauldron, the water was lukewarm. Then the temperature was raised, little by little. The change was so slight that the frogs accommodated themselves to each temperature increase until it was too late. The point is that we are all more likely to accept evil as long as it is not thrust upon us abruptly. We are more inclined to do something that is morally wrong if it is only a shade more wrong than something we are already accepting as right. When I started doing drugs, I didn't start with marijuana or cocaine. I started smoking cigarettes. And when I started stealing, I didn't start by breaking into houses and businesses. I started by shoplifting and stealing money from my mom's purse.

Excuses

When I started smoking cigarettes, I first had to overcome the values against smoking taught to me by my family and others. I also had to shut off the medical warnings about the dangers of smoking and the fear of getting caught. I did much of this through excuses and justifications. My justifications went something like this:

- "I don't care what they say, smoking can't hurt <u>me</u> - nothing will ever happen to <u>me</u>."
- "Everyone I know smokes - so it can't be all that bad."
- "Smoking isn't that bad – it's not like I am doing drugs."
- "Smoking will make me seem older and cooler."
- "If I get caught smoking I will get grounded for a few days – no big deal."
- "I'll just try it out - I can stop whenever I want to."

It wasn't long before I was addicted. And the longer I smoked, the less excuses and justification I needed. I began to see myself as a smoker so I didn't need to excuse my actions. I simply avoided awareness of any deterrents to smoking - bad breath, wasted money, and the possibility of lung cancer - and continued smoking. Like many other irresponsible behaviors, smoking became more and more habitual until it eventually became just a way of life.

Another example of the erosion of deterrents can be seen in the story of a criminal who decided to change and get his life back on the right path. He got a job at a convenience store near his home and was determined to stay out of trouble. One day, however, he looked at all the money in the cash register and thought, "If I had all this money I could buy a new car – I hate riding the bus everywhere." He quickly dismissed any ideas of taking the money, partially because he knew it was wrong, but mostly because he didn't want to get caught and punished. At that point, he decided to start saving and started thinking about the type of car he wanted. Over the next few weeks, he was even able to save a couple hundred dollars for his new car.

However, as is common among criminals, he was impatient and had an inability to delay gratification. He wanted his new car now – not next month or next year. So, again, he thought of ways to get the money – including taking the money in the cash register. These thoughts, however, were quickly dismissed as he reminded himself of the potential consequences of stealing.

The following week, he noticed a man about his age driving a nice car. This reminded him of his desire for a new car...and the cash register, except this time he started to feel upset and put down because he didn't have a car. He felt like everyone else also saw him as a loser because he always had to ride the bus. He told himself that he had been doing well in his life and that he needed a car – he deserved a car. At this point, his internal deterrents started eroding. The moral implications of stealing began to have less of an impact on his thinking. Fear and the sense of wrongness of stealing were replaced with frustration and anger that he had no car. However, the external deterrents - the possibility of getting caught and punished - were still there.

From this point forward, thoughts of stealing the money to get his car took over his mind. In time, he was able to shut off all internal deterrents to stealing the money. He did this with his own private logic in which he trivialized the moral issues with thoughts such as, "It isn't that big of a deal – insurance will replace the money." "No one will ever know." "I am such a loser – I don't even have a car." And, "What's the point in always doing what's right if I can't even buy a car?"

Now, all that stood between him and the money were the external deterrents. So he started to scheme how to circumvent them. Finally, he concluded that he couldn't take all the money without being caught, but if he limited himself to $5 or $10 a day, he would get away with it and end up with his new car sooner. As he thought of excuses to explain the missing money, the external deterrents continued to erode and were eventually shut off and replaced by an extreme optimism that he could get away with his scheme. At this point, his desire for a new car outweighed the deterrents to taking the money, so he chose to steal the money. Interestingly, he never did get his car. Five dollars a day soon became $20.00 and then $100.00 as he became more and more brazen. In the end, he was arrested for theft and sent back to prison.

In this example, some of the excuses or justifications he gave himself were that:

- He deserved the car
- He would be seen as less of a person without a car
- He was powerless without a car
- Insurance would cover the cost of everything he took
- He would have more friends if he had a car
- He couldn't wait to have a car – if he didn't get one now he never would
- He could get away with stealing the money and circumvent any negative consequences.

However, there are many other justifications and excuses he could have given himself. These include:

- I can be forgiven for this
- I will just do it this once
- My life would be so much easier if I had a car
- I can't expect to be perfect all the time.
- Everyone else is just out for themselves so why shouldn't I be, too
- I had better take this chance for it may never present itself again
- I'm weak and scared if I don't do this

Some of the common excuses I have heard for other crimes are:

- For date rape - "This woman really does want me and is

just playing hard to get."

- For drug dealing - "I am not forcing anyone to do drugs – it is their own choice." "I'm not really hurting anyone."
- For murder - "This person disrespected me so if I don't do something about it, I will be a nothing and people will continue to view me as a nothing and disrespect me forever."
- For property crimes – "I'm not really hurting anyone. It is just stuff, and the insurance company will replace it." "I'm just taking from the rich and giving to the poor like Robin Hood."

If we are already involved in crime or have already been in trouble, then it's easy to use justifications and excuses like, "I'm already in trouble, so it won't make much difference" or "Everyone already thinks I'm bad so I might as well act that way." In fact, almost any insane justification or excuse may be used in the erosion of deterrents.

In the less extreme criminal or one who is just starting to commit crime, deterrents are usually eroded through this cycle and then finally shut off to permit irresponsible or criminal acts. However, once we have become immersed in crime and our thinking has become more habitual, we are usually able to shut off many of these deterrents without the justifications, excuses, and cajoling required to erode them. Thus, a less extreme criminal may contemplate and debate a criminal act before he chooses to do it while the extreme criminal is able to quickly eliminate any deterrents from his thinking and act.

Again, as criminals we don't just commit crimes out of the blue. We think and fantasize about our crimes first. We may have even told ourselves that we weren't going to proceed on these thoughts because it was wrong and we didn't want to go to prison. However, because we continue to allow ourselves to think about our crimes, these thoughts continue to wear on our mind to the point where our desire to commit the crime overrides the deterrents. In essence, what starts out as a passing thought becomes the seed that, through the process of erosion, ultimately leads to a crime. For example, most violent criminals have violent thoughts and fantasies whenever they are disrespected or put down for years before they finally commit their crime.

After we've committed the crime, we often have feelings of guilt and a fear of getting caught. As a habitual burglar, there were even times when I felt bad and told myself that I was going to give the money back. I wondered what had made me do the messed up things I did and promised myself that I'd never steal again! However, I was ultimately able to erode and shut off these thoughts and feelings, often with the help of drugs and alcohol. So, these pangs of conscience didn't stop me from committing further crimes.

Awareness

We all have the ability to choose to focus our conscious awareness in order to search for truth and reality. On the other hand, we also have the free-will to drop to a lower level of consciousness to avoid and shut off the truth. "In a situation in which our emotional feelings are overwhelmingly painful or unpleasant, we have the capacity to anesthetize ourselves."[2] And even though most people would find it almost impossible to shut off their conscious awareness of the deterrents to criminal behavior, the avoidance of consciousness can be seen in many irresponsible behaviors.

Paradoxically, even a hero usually has to shut off the awareness of the potential consequences of his actions. To be able to run into a burning building or jump into a raging river to save someone else, you must first somehow avoid the awareness that you could be killed. Not everyone has the ability to do this.

For us, once the deterrents to crime are finally shut–off, they are usually replaced by an extreme optimism. Although we may admit that we could eventually get caught if we continue in crime, we believe that this time we'll be safe. And our experience usually supports this optimistic view. Most of us have gotten away with so many irresponsible acts and crimes that we know our chances of

---

2   Peck, M. Scott M.D., "PEOPLE OF THE LIE: THE HOPE FOR HEALING HUMAN EVIL" (New York: Simon & Schuster, 1983) pp.227

being caught are very low. Each success reinforces our optimistic thinking, so our optimism is generally high. According to Daniel Claster, "'Delinquents have a 'greater belief in ability to evade arrest' than do non-delinquents." Claster's questionnaire study provided quantitative evidence of what he called "the 'magical immunity' mechanisms outlined in psychoanalytic ego psychology. The perception of immunity was found even among boys who were repeatedly apprehended and confined."[3] Ironically, because this optimism isn't based on the realistic appraisal of a situation, but instead on our own unrealistic and prejudiced assumptions, we usually don't realistically evaluate our schemes or plan for contingencies, so this optimism is often what gets us caught.

Fortunately, most people in society are incapable of, or unwilling to, completely shut off the deterrents to criminal behavior. However, it is apparent that the avoidance of consciousness is easier for children than for adults. Children are usually not as reality oriented as adults. If a person develops properly, their thinking becomes more and more reality-oriented. This is an important evolution of the mature adult mind. Unable to continue depending on others for guidance and support, adults must learn to utilize increasingly realistic thinking in order to survive and be productive. As criminals, however, I believe that we didn't learn to become more realistic in our thinking because it would force us to confront our own inadequacies and hinder us from doing the exciting things we want to do.

Developmental and environmental factors can also have a tremendous impact on someone's ability to avoid, or focus on, conscious awareness. For example, if someone has been brought up in an environment that opposed or undermined conscious thought, or encouraged the avoidance of certain feelings or emotions, then that person may never develop the skills necessary to appropriately focus their mind.

I believe that our enhanced ability to avoid conscious awareness

---

3   Yochelson, Samuel, and Samenow, Stanton E., "THE CRIMINAL PERSONALITY -
     VOLUME ONE: A PROFILE FOR CHANGE" (New Jersey: Jason Aronson Inc., 1976) pp.420

80

may actually be founded in our early developmental years. As children, we learned to subvert consciousness and build a wall around ourselves to avoid discomfort. This defensive ability was developed and perfected through practice so that, in time, we could eliminate any unwanted feelings and emotions. If we didn't think about them, they would seemingly go away. And this worked well for us - as children.

As a child I was fat and, like many overweight children, was picked on unmercifully by other children. In time, I learned to anesthetize myself to the feelings this teasing triggered. My parents would tell me to ignore it and not let it bother me. But it did bother me – I just learned to hide this awareness from myself.

> (W)hen we are young we may experience a good deal of hurt and rejection and develop a policy in "self-protection", to reject others first. This policy does not make for a happy life. And yet its intention is not to cause suffering but to reduce it.[4]

In time, anesthetizing myself became an habitual way of life. Sadly, this avoidance of reality actually served to further damage my self-esteem.

> If we do not bring an appropriate level of consciousness to our activities, if we do not live mindfully, the inevitable penalty is a diminished sense of self-efficacy and self-respect. We cannot feel competent and worthy while conducting our lives in a mental fog. Our mind is our basic tool for survival. Betray it and self-esteem suffers.[5]

By the time we reach our teenage years, our ability to avoid consciousness has become very efficient and increasingly habitual. It also expands into other areas of our lives. We learn that we can use this shut-off mechanism to avoid any unwanted thoughts,

---

4   Branden, Nathaniel, "THE SIX PILLARS OF SELF-ESTEEM" (New York: Bantam Books, 1994) pp.268
5   Branden, Nathaniel, "THE SIX PILLARS OF SELF-ESTEEM" (New York: Bantam Books, 1994) pp.68

feelings or emotions we want to. It also allows us to avoid the reality of our unhealthy relationship with, and lack of confidence in, ourselves (our self-esteem). From this point on, our life becomes a vicious cycle in which we behave in increasingly irresponsible and self-destructive ways in a misguided attempt to boost our self-image and conceal our increasingly unhealthy self-esteem. This combination ultimately has devastating effects on us and society as a whole.

In his book *The People of the Lie*, Dr. Peck writes:

The capacity for emotional self-anesthesia obviously has its advantages. Undoubtedly it has been built into us through evolution and enhances our ability to survive. It allows us to continue to function in situations so ghastly we would fall apart if we preserved our normal sensitivity. The problem, however, is that this self-anesthetizing mechanism seems not to be very specific. If because we live in the midst of garbage our sensitivity to ugliness becomes diminished, it is likely that we will become litterers and garbage strewers ourselves. Insensitive to our own suffering, we tend to become insensitive to the suffering of others. Treated with indignity, we lose not only the sense of our own dignity but also the sense of the dignity of others. When it no longer bothers us to see mangled bodies, it will no longer bother us to mangle them ourselves.[6]

Another devastating effect of the avoidance of internal feelings and emotions is that it can sabotage the development of emotional intelligence. It is our emotional intelligence that allows us to recognize and understand those emotions, in ourselves and others, that provide the foundation for our relationships with ourselves and others. And, without adequate awareness of our own emotions, we cannot possibly learn or develop any of the more advanced emotional abilities that combine to form emotional intelligence. Abilities such as:

---

6 Peck, M. Scott M.D., "PEOPLE OF THE LIE: THE HOPE FOR HEALING HUMAN EVIL" (New York: Simon & Schuster, 1983) pp.221

- responsibly managing our feelings and emotions
- motivating ourselves and focusing our emotions into the proper channels in order to reach our goals
- emotional self-control (which influences traits such as perseverance and the ability to delay gratification)
- recognizing emotions in, or empathizing with, other people
- responsibly handling relationships (which requires an ability to effectively deal with emotions in others)

Not surprisingly, a lack of emotional intelligence can also serve to do additional damage to our self-esteem because:

...children who can't read or express emotions well constantly feel frustrated. In essence, they don't understand what's going on...such kids end up feeling no sense of control over how other people treat them, that their actions have no impact on what happens to them. It leaves them feeling powerless, depressed, and apathetic.[7]

Shutting-off, eroding deterrents, and the disruption in emotional development can also result in a corresponding lack of moral development. Leading theories on moral development suggest that, similar to emotional development, "Ideas about morality and justice develop in regular, predictable stages as a person passes through certain various stages in childhood."[8] According to Jean Piaget, a noted psychologist, the development of morality begins at birth and proceeds in an orderly fashion until at least the age of 12. And, it seems that the development of morality requires an appropriate foundation of emotional awareness. In the first stage of moral development, children usually show what is termed a heteronymous morality or obedience based solely on a fear of punishment (a fear which can be, and usually is, successfully shut off by us criminals). Realistically, without a sufficient mastery of

---

7   Goleman, Daniel, "EMOTIONAL INTELLIGENCE" (New York: Bantam Books, 1995) pp.122
8   Bartollas, Clemens, and Dinitz, Simon, "INTRO TO CRIMINOLOGY: ORDER AND DISORDER" (New York: Harper and Row Publishers, 1989) pp.144

this rudimentary moral guide, we are simply incapable of developing more advanced moral concepts, such as autonomous morality, or obeying rules because of a recognition that they serve the best interests of both the individual and society (which is often viewed as the final stage of moral development).

For most of us, <u>any</u> obedience to rules or regulations is based in the first stage of moral development - the desire to avoid punishment or not be caught. With our own emotions shut off, we are unlikely to give any thought to anyone else's feelings or best interests, or even to the true extent of our wrongdoing, until we are caught. Until then, we usually don't feel sorry or even think about our irresponsible or criminal behavior, because to do so would force us to come face to face with our own wrongness. Thus, we must continually pretend that we are doing everything right in order to avoid any confrontation with our inner self and maintain our perfectionist self-image. Actually, even when we are caught we usually feel sorrier about being caught than about the irresponsible or criminal behavior itself.

Of course there are times when we are forced to face the evil nature of our behavior. When this happens, we're likely to experience feelings of fear, guilt and sorrow - feelings that we desperately try to avoid through excuses, distraction, lies and drug abuse. We do have a conscience, but due to our ability to anesthetize ourselves it is not fully operational. According to Dr. Peck:

> The essential component of evil is not the absence of a sense of sin or imperfection but the unwillingness to tolerate that sense. At one and the same time, the evil are aware of their evil and desperately trying to avoid the awareness. Rather than blissfully lacking a sense of morality, like the psychopath, they are continually engaged in sweeping the evidence of their evil under the rug of their own consciousness.[9]

And because we haven't properly dealt with these feelings,

---

9   Peck, M. Scott M.D., "PEOPLE OF THE LIE: THE HOPE FOR HEALING HUMAN EVIL" (New York: Simon & Schuster, 1983) pp.76

their energy often lurks in our subconscious mind and builds up until we explode in a rage of anger and emotion. It's similar to what is likely to happen if we constantly throw things into our junk closet at home without ever taking the time to clean it out. For a time it may seem convenient to just throw everything into this closet. It may even become habitual for us to use this closet in order to keep our house tidy. However, the time will eventually come when this closet becomes full - so full in fact that it takes all of our strength just to get the door shut. So, what happens the next time we open it to throw our junk inside? It explodes in our face as everything we have ever stuffed into it comes flooding out. By shutting off our emotions we, in effect, put them into a closet in our mind. After time, any perceived problem has the potential to become "the straw that broke the camel's back". Any little thing can open this door and release these concealed emotions - resulting in an eruption of violence and rage.

The Role of Drugs and Alcohol

Finally, I believe that drug and alcohol abuse not only contributes to crime, but that it can also be a consequence of crime. While it's easy to recognize that drugs can lower inhibitions, eliminate deterrent emotions, and help us gain the false courage to commit our crimes, many of us also use drugs just so that we can live with ourselves.

Since the ability to shut off emotion varies from person to person, many of us are not totally able to shut off the pangs of guilt and sorrow that are the result of our wrongdoing. So we use drugs to help anesthetize ourselves. We also use them to help us avoid the awareness of our unhealthy reputation with ourselves as well as the regrets and emotions which would otherwise compel us to behave responsibly.

It is important, however, to recognize that drugs and alcohol do not put the thoughts of irresponsible or criminal behavior into our minds. Drugs help us to erode and even shut off the deterrents to crime, but drugs don't cause crime – criminal thinking causes crime. So, any attempt to excuse criminal behavior by blaming it on drug use is just that – an excuse. Ultimately, it was a choice to use drugs in the first place – and we weren't on drugs when we made that choice.

Drugs also help to eliminate the boredom we loathe. We thirst for excitement and hate the notion of the routine, dull, mundane. Drugs often provide the charge or kicks we crave at those times when we feel our life is moving too slowly. They also help us to avoid the conscious awareness of our boredom.

Regardless of how it is accomplished, the ability to erode and shut off the deterrents to crime is a fundamental part of our criminal perspective. Without this ability we simply couldn't continue to commit crime. It allows us to do the evil and irresponsible things we do - and continue to live with ourselves.

CHAPTER 5

Convicts Without Convictions

nother characteristic that I have found to be common among us criminals is our capriciousness. Capriciousness is the term I have found that best describes the "Dr. Jekyll and Mr. Hyde" personality that we all display to some degree. It is characterized by inconsistencies in thought, attitude and behavior.

Due to our shifting states of mind, and our ability to shut-off and erode deterrents, we can switch from "loving and kind" to "mean and selfish" in almost an instant. We may go to church at 9:00 and then be involved in a crime at 10:00. Or, we may talk about getting our life together one minute only to do something extremely irresponsible or criminal the next.

We all go through phases where we are good and make responsible decisions. At times, we can be the most obedient child, honest employee, or giving person. However, these temporary phases inevitably give way to irresponsible thoughts, behaviors and crime as we search to build up our self-image. Thus, we become an enigma to all who know us, often showing a kindness and helpfulness that are as genuine as our selfishness and destructiveness.

We are like chameleons. Since our primary objective is to build ourselves up, we will often do whatever the situation calls for. If we are around responsible people, we will usually act and talk responsibly. We will tell them whatever we think they want to hear. Yet, when we are around irresponsible people, we will act and talk irresponsibly. And when we are alone, we will do just about anything that is exciting or will help to build up our self-image.

I believe that our capriciousness is due to the fact that we lack a stable moral foundation on which to base our decisions. Without this moral foundation we simply don't have the consistency of thought and desire required to live responsibly each and every day.

Our mind and soul are in continuous debate between what we know we should be doing and what we feel driven to do in an effort to prove ourselves. We know we should be good, but it feels so good to be bad.

Our capriciousness can best be described as a state in which we are continually changing our mind about what we actually want out of life. As criminals, we simply don't have a consistent purpose. At times, we may convince ourselves that we know exactly what we want out of life. The reality, however, is that what we want changes from moment to moment.

For example, when I was younger there were many days when I resolved to study harder, do better at school, and quit partying so much. Sometimes I would even succeed – for a little while. I would do great until my friends called and asked if I wanted to go to a party. At that point in my life, going to a party was simply more exciting than studying for school.

And when I got out of prison the first time, I resolved to never commit another crime. I vowed that I would never go back to prison. However, this pledge didn't guide my choices and less than two years later, I was back inside. I lost sight of what I really wanted in life. I gave up my freedom for the proof of power and excitement I craved at the moment.

A sense of responsibility and honesty may also appear sporadically and in a variety of different situations. For example, I once shoplifted hundreds of dollars worth of merchandise from a store and then walked all of the way back to the store the next day in order to return a few cents of excess change the cashier had given me. Many times I also stole money from one person only to turn around and blow much of the money on others in an effort to play the big shot.

Without a stable moral base, most of our decisions are based on feelings and desires which can change from day to day, hour to hour, and even minute to minute. Our fragile self-image only aggravates this inconsistency, because our glass jaw makes us more susceptible to life's ups and downs, not to mention that we often choose to shut-off our feelings – often leaving us slaves to our desire for excitement and power.

The problem is that we don't keep a consistent focus on our responsible goals and objectives. We also tend not to think about the future or consider the consequences of our actions. We simply do what we want to do, or feel like doing, at any given moment.

Due to our unrealistic self-image and our ability to shut off and erode emotions, it isn't difficult to understand why we haven't developed a stable moral base. A moral foundation is usually developed in adolescence as a child integrates the morals and values learned from his family, church, school, and society into his life. If developed properly, these morals and values are molded into a personal set of standards to live by. Ideally, these standards are used to guide all decisions. However, because we have retained our childhood tendency to avoid reality, and often choose to shut off the morals and values we have been taught, a stable moral foundation never developed.

To a certain degree, capriciousness can be seen in many people. It is characterized by impulsive and erratic behavior. And it can be seen in the competing thoughts and desires that sabotage any type of goal or resolution. For example, it is demonstrated when a person resolves to go on a diet one day only to go on an eating binge the next. A capricious person may even go on a diet and exercise program which lasts for days or weeks. But eventually, their thinking and desires will change (usually with the help of excuses and justifications) and they'll revert back to their old unhealthy ways of life. This can happen even when they have been told by their doctor that this could kill them. Some people may call this a lack of will power, but I will call it what it really is - a lack of conviction; a conviction for a healthy way of life. Similarly, we as criminals have a lack of conviction for a responsible way of life. And, just like some people spend their lives on and off of diets, many criminals spend their lives in and out of prison.

Criminal Equivalent Motives

As criminals, even when we are behaving responsibly, our thinking usually minimizes the good in our actions. Due to the selfish motives behind our actions, responsible behavior often becomes an equivalent to crime in building up our self-image. When we are kind and helpful, it is often selfish - in that we expect something in return. We don't just help to be helpful; we expect praise, recognition and indebtedness. Criminal equivalent behavior, although not criminal in nature, provides the same sense of power and excitement - the same boost to our self image – that we get from criminal behavior.

Due to our distorted point of view and the ulterior motives behind most of our behaviors, many of our thoughts and actions play the role of criminal equivalents. Basically, whether or not a thought or behavior is a criminal equivalent depends on its motive. If it is self-promoting or self-serving, then it is a criminal equivalent in that it is solely intended to boost an unrealistic self-image or quench a thirst for power and excitement.

Criminal equivalent behaviors can be seen in all aspects of our lives. When we are not involved in crime, they become the only way we can maintain our self-image and quench our thirst for power and excitement. They are demonstrated in our pretentiousness, our perfectionism, and in our desire to always be in charge. They can be seen in the way we give up when things don't go our way. They are illustrated in our humor, which is often at the expense of others. In fact, even doing something special for someone is often a criminal equivalent in that it is self-serving and often done for ulterior motives.

Working as a policeman, a minister, a psychiatrist or a lawyer (positions which many criminals can, and do, attain) is a criminal equivalent if the position is used solely as a way to satisfy a thirst for power and self-aggrandizement instead of being performed for the benefit of others. Actually, any of the responsible behaviors, projects, or jobs that we are involved in can be termed criminal equivalents if they are done solely for self-serving purposes.

Since many of us are very bright and energetic, we don't find it hard to impress others and receive the recognition and praise we need to boost our self-image. We often do very well in anything that we do. However, it doesn't usually last for long. The problem is that everything we do is intended to enhance our self-image. So, when our responsible actions get to the point where they fail to impress others and invoke praise, and when they quit being new and exciting, we inevitably look for other ways to find the recognition, praise, and excitement we crave.

The problem with criminal equivalent motives is that they serve the same purpose for us as crime does. Thus, they help to perpetuate all of our errors in thinking and perception – even when we are not involved in crime. And because we are still susceptible to put-downs and are still compelled to prove ourselves, we risk returning to our past criminal ways at any moment - regardless of our current beliefs or desires.

The Cycle of Crime

Once criminal equivalent behavior no longer provides the necessary boost to our self-image, a return to crime is inevitable. Usually, the path from criminal equivalent behavior to crime isn't automatic or immediate. Our thinking and behavior proceed through several stages as we become more and more irresponsible.

At first, we usually start making wrong and irresponsible choices without actually returning to crime. We will also attempt to maintain our appearance of responsibility, and circumvent any problems which our irresponsible behavior may cause. Thus, we are forced to become increasingly deceptive and secretive. At this point, we are even likely to tell ourselves things like:

- It's just a little white lie; I will never go back to the way I was before,
- I just want to have a little fun,
- I am not really hurting anyone.

But, this is a dangerous deception which takes a toll on our self-esteem, and further weakens our desire to live responsibly.

If we are a drug-user we will usually go back to drugs in order to help relieve our boredom and to consciously avoid the damaging effects our irresponsible behavior is having on our self-esteem. However, this is a fatal mistake, because the use of drugs only

91

helps to advance the erosion and shut-off of any deterrents to crime that may still be in place.

At this point, our errors in thinking and perception become increasingly extreme as our psyche attempts to counteract the impact of our irresponsible behavior on our self-esteem. Again, our self-esteem and behavior are reciprocal. They each influence, and are influenced by one another. Thus, our lives can become a vicious cycle. The more we behave irresponsibly, the lower our self-esteem becomes. And, the lower our self-esteem becomes, the more we crave a sense of worth and power. And we often choose irresponsible and criminal behaviors to quench our thirst for power, because they provide an easier, quicker and more intense feeling of power and excitement than most responsible behaviors.

Finally, because our self-esteem deteriorates with each irresponsible and criminal act, success in one crime actually necessitates more extreme crimes. Much like a drug addict must have a higher and higher dose in order to obtain the same effect, we must commit more crimes, or more extreme crimes, in order to get the kicks we need to maintain our unrealistic self-image and quench our thirst for power and excitement.

By the time we again become immersed in crime, so many criminal thoughts are passing through our minds that there is no chance of us acting on them all. Many of our schemes are dismissed due to their risk factor. And some are dismissed out of a sentiment not to behave some way. For example, we may talk about committing a bank robbery which might require killing a guard, but not act upon it due to a strong sentiment against hurting or killing someone. Or, we may see some money lying on the counter at home and think about taking it, yet not act on these thoughts because we have a sentiment against stealing from our family. The problem, however, is that as criminals even our sentiments have the potential to change. As we become increasingly immersed in crime, our errors in thought and perception become more extreme. Thus, as we travel down the criminal path, we have the potential to become more and more evil - to the point where we participate in crimes which we would never have imagined committing before.

Once we have started committing crimes, we will usually continue to until we are caught and deterred from further crimes. Even a close call usually is not good enough to deter us for long. If we don't stay properly focused, we will eventually erode and shut off the deterrent effects of this close call. Furthermore, being bailed out of trouble or getting away with only a "slap on the hand" can actually increase the likelihood of returning to crime. It reinforces the belief that even if we get caught, nothing will happen - which can later serve as an erosion to deterrents.

By the time we have decided to commit a crime, all of the deterrents have been totally shut off and our mind is focused solely on the task at hand. During the commission of a crime, we are usually full of energy and feel like we are on speed or amphetamines due to the adrenaline rush. This is much like the sensation the body experiences as it prepares for fight or flight. Rather than a sense of fear (which has also been shut off by this time), we simply feel excited, powerful and in-charge. Our heart begins pumping faster, our palms become sweaty, our senses become more acute, and we become more on edge. Finally, during the commission of the crime, it is often as if the events aren't real but instead some sort of dream. The shut-off mechanism we use to eliminate our emotions and the deterrents to crime numbs us to the point that it distorts reality.

After the commission of a crime our energy output usually remains high. There is often a sense of relief at the successful completion of the crime, but many times there is also a recurring fear that something is out of place, something which could possibly lead to our discovery and arrest. For example, we may think that someone saw us or our car, or that we left something at the crime scene that could connect us to the crime. This fear, I believe, is caused by a transient surge of the deterrents that were shut off during the crime. However, this fear is eventually shut off again (often through drug use) and replaced by an extreme optimism of success.

Most property criminals will celebrate after a crime. We may go out on the town with our friends or even take our spouse to an extravagant restaurant and throw around the proceeds from the crime in order to play the role of a big shot. Even the excuse for having lots of money can be exciting and self-image boosting. We may tell those around us that we got the money as a bonus from work for doing such a good job. Or we may tell them that we won the lottery and are thinking about taking a vacation to Europe in an effort to impress them (I will talk more about this in the section on lying.).

If we are a drug-using criminal, then drugs usually play a part in our celebration. Not only can drugs heighten the thrill of the moment but, as I said before, they also help eliminate any fears or pangs of conscience which we may still have.

However, regardless of what form our celebration takes, our thirst for excitement and power continues. Once the celebrating is done and the proceeds from the crime are gone, we invariably start planning our next conquest in an effort to maintain our inflated self-image and quench our thirst for excitement and power. One irresponsible behavior or crime almost always leads to another which is more exciting, more daring, and more extreme – until we are caught and the cycle begins again.

CHAPTER 6

Errors in Thinking: The Framework of Crime

I n addition to the characteristics that I have already discussed, I have found that as criminals we also possess many other, often interrelated, errors in thinking and perception. Again, these errors have the potential to distort reality to the point where irresponsible or even criminal behavior seems justifiable, excusable, acceptable or even necessary. Yet, because we tend to believe that everyone else thinks the same way we do, and because these errors in thinking usually confirm themselves, we are not likely to recognize them in ourselves without some help.

As we journey down an irresponsible path towards crime, these errors in thinking and perception tend to become increasingly extreme and more habitual. They become more ingrained and perfected with practice. And, by the time we are fully immersed in crime, they have become the building blocks of our criminal point of view.

It is important to note that many of these errors may only play a subtle role in our thinking and behavior. Also, not every one of these errors in thinking is present during the commission of every crime and irresponsible behavior. Different errors distort reality in different ways and thus contribute to different behaviors.

It can also be easy to identify certain errors as being more prevalent in ourselves (which may serve to explain why we become involved in some crimes but not others). However, I believe that if we are honest with ourselves we will acknowledge that most, if not all, of these errors in thinking have come into play and distorted our perceptions of reality at some point in our lives.

1. <u>We tend to think concretely and not conceptually.</u>

Although we may seem to conceptualize in some areas of our lives, we have not learned to, or are unwilling to, recognize the connections between similar situations. We tend to look at specifics instead of seeing the big picture. I once knew a criminal who had been sent to prison for selling "meth" (methamphetamines) on the streets. He vowed never to sell it again, but started selling cigarettes while he was in prison (which was against the rules) – and then failed to recognize any connection when he was caught and punished again!

Due to our concrete thinking, we tend to assume that being responsible simply entails singular acts of responsibility and not a life-long commitment to it. For example, we may do some volunteer work at a nursing home and feel all proud of ourselves for being a humanitarian and helping others, even when we are immersed in irresponsible behavior and crime. Or, we may simply pay all our bills on time and feel like we are basically a very responsible person – even if it is the first time we've paid all of our bills in months.

On the other hand, we may be doing very well at work or school, have one bad day, and consequently convince ourselves that we are worthless and then give up. Or, we may miss a few easy shots on our basketball team one game and feel like a total loser. Unable to view our individual imperfections in context, we view them concretely (as put-downs) and often end up feeling put-down, regardless of the true circumstances or past history.

This lack of conceptualization can really be seen in the way that many of us cry unfair and complain when someone else gets preferential treatment, yet when we get preferential treatment it is because we are special. And if others complain or say that this treatment is unfair, then they are viewed as crybabies or snitches who have nothing better to do than interfere with things that are none of their business.

Finally, most of us are unwilling or unable to conceptualize our own or others' experiences in order to learn from them. Thus, we rarely learn from others' mistakes. In fact, we often don't even learn from our own. We do the same things over and over again, each time expecting a different outcome. We see others' lives turned upside down because of drugs, alcohol, and crime, yet we do the same type of things. Many of those around us wonder if we will ever learn. And without improving our ability to conceptualize, we never will.

2. We do not see ourselves as criminals - even when we are participating in crime.

Even though most of us have committed literally hundreds of crimes, we are deceptively able to maintain a view of ourselves as being good and responsible because of our concrete thinking and the shut-off mechanisms we use. In our minds, we are able to selectively focus on all the good things about ourselves and shut off the thoughts and moral implications of our irresponsible acts and crimes. For most of us, this happens automatically. If it didn't, our narcissistic self-image of perfection would be shattered and we would not be able to live with ourselves.

Realistically, most of us have redeeming qualities and many of us have even done some good in our lives. Many of us have strong sentiments against hurting the young, elderly, or women, while others may have a total respect for life and wouldn't even squash a bug. A few of us even harbor deep sentiments against stealing or using drugs. And it is these kinds of sentiments, along with other singularly good deeds and responsible acts (such as giving a dollar to a homeless person or doing well on a test in school), which are the concrete details that we often focus on in order to sustain our view of ourselves as basically good people and not the victimizers we really are.

As criminals, we also tend to create our own set of morals and values which help to sustain this view of ourselves. For example, a thief or burglar may view a rapist, child molester or murderer as being despicable and the real criminal, whereas a rapist or murderer may have a strong sentiment against stealing. Each one, then, carries the belief that the other is more criminal and that they are not the real criminals or threats to society. In effect, each of us actually builds up our opinion of ourselves by emphasizing what we would not do and thus lessening the effect of our own irresponsible actions.

This can be further exemplified by the way that we usually feel the slate has been wiped clean and that we are entitled to one little slip-up whenever we have been acting responsibly for any period of time. And when we are caught, we are likely to hearken back to our good deeds, thinking that they will somehow make up for all of our misconduct.

As criminals, we do what we feel like doing at any given moment. And if this happens to be contrary to what we know to be right, then we avoid the reality of the situation. We simply can't be wrong. In my estimation, this unwillingness to conceptualize a realistic view of our behavior is one of the traits most counterproductive to change, because if we are unable to recognize that something is wrong, then we are unlikely to make any effort to change.

3. <u>We are unwilling to ask for help in responsible decision-making.</u>

To have to ask for help would show ignorance or stupidity, which could be viewed as a put-down and shatter our unrealistic self-image of being better than others. So, we often make choices and decisions in areas we know nothing about. However, because of the way we are, we are incapable of consistently making responsible choices without the help and guidance of a responsible individual.

While working for a prison industry in Minnesota many of my co-workers filed for the Earned Income Credit on their taxes and received hundreds of dollars extra back on their tax refund – until the IRS found out (which made me even more thankful that I didn't file for it). Most of them were honestly under the assumption that they were doing nothing wrong, because they never thought to ask. They just filed for the credit because everyone else was doing it. Yet, it didn't matter that they didn't know when the IRS found out, they all had to pay back the money and pay huge penalties.

4. We fail to fact find or consider alternatives in decision-making.

This error is related to the last one. As criminals, our tunnel vision and fragmentation inevitably leads us to make decisions based on our own assumptions and perceptions. However, as I have said before, these feelings and perceptions are often unrealistic and unreliable. Sadly, our decisions are rarely based on things such as the possible consequences, or even our own morals and values, because we are able to erode and shut off these things. Regardless, for us to even admit that we needed to fact find would show ignorance, and to consider other alternatives would imply that we weren't so perfect in the first place. Thus, it is often considered as a type of put-down for us to do these things.

Ironically, this error in thinking often leads us to getting caught. Without fact finding or considering possible alternatives, we are likely to make many mistakes during our exploits. This also leads to shows like "The World's Stupidest Criminals". I have heard of criminals who were caught because they were stuck in the window of the warehouse they planned to burglarize simply because they had failed to measure the window. Similarly, the reason that I got caught for burglary was because I took one of the items that I had stolen just a few days earlier to a local repairman who recognized it as belonging to the victim. I didn't think to do a little fact finding in order to determine whether or not this repairman knew my victims.

5. We fail to be self-critical; however, we are quick to criticize others.

We can identify all the bad or evil traits in others, but we often fail to recognize these traits in ourselves. It is not in our nature to find fault with ourselves, because this would undermine our fragile self-image. And by finding faults in others, we serve to unrealistically boost our own self-image by establishing that we are better than them. Anyone who has ever played sports in prison has undoubtedly seen many examples of this error in thinking. Guys will often yell and talk bad about anyone who makes the slightest mistake, even if they have already made numerous errors themselves.

Due to our unhealthy self-esteem, even a single admission of error or imperfection can be extremely painful for us. In *The People of the Lie,* Dr. Peck explains that:

> The evil are pathologically attached to the status quo of their personalities, which in their narcissism they consciously regard as perfect. I think it is quite possible that the evil may perceive even a small degree of change in their beloved selves as representing total annihilation. In this sense, the threat of self-criticism may feel to one who is evil synonymous with the threat of extinction.[1]

Unfortunately, self-criticism is an essential component of any personality change or self-improvement. Without self-criticism there can be no personal acknowledgment of a need to improve and, without this acknowledgment, no reason to make the consistent effort necessary to grow.

6.   We fail to put ourselves in other people's shoes.

We seldom think about how our actions can, and do, affect others. Although we usually want every consideration for ourselves (especially when we are caught), we fail to take into account what others feel, think and expect. This is partially due to the fact that we lack the empathy which builds on self-awareness. Not only does this allow us to maintain our unrealistically high self-image, but it also allows us to do what we want without the deterrent effects which putting ourselves in another's place might have.

Even on those rare occasions when we do try to put ourselves in another's shoes, our preconceived notions, unrealistic perceptions, emotional illiteracy, and concrete thinking make it almost

---

1   Peck, M. Scott M.D., "PEOPLE OF THE LIE: THE HOPE FOR HEALING HUMAN EVIL" (New York: Simon & Schuster, 1983) pp.74

impossible for us to truly understand a responsible person's perspective on anything.

7. We fail to consider other's points of view.

From an early stage in development, we are sure that we know best. And, for the most part, we are also very anti-authoritarian. We maintain that it is our life and that we are above listening to what others (especially parents and those in authority who think they are better than us) have to say, or doing what they tell us to do. Thus, we have a tendency to approach many situations and choices with our minds already made up. So, although we may pay lip service or agree to certain morals, ideas and opinions in order to maintain a respectable front, we all tend to utilize selective listening and decide for ourselves what is important while disregarding the rest.

When I was 17, my father thought that it would be a good idea for me to join the military. It had helped him to settle down when he was younger and he advised me that it may also help me to settle down. Well, I didn't take his advice, because I thought that I knew better – so I ended up going to prison instead. I don't know if time in the military would have helped me turn my life around, but I do know that I would have had a much happier life if I would have been better at following the advice of my parents.

8. We have an unrealistic view of pain and suffering in others.

Due to our inability to empathize with others, as well as our augmented ability to shut off and erode painful emotions, we usually do not feel as though we've hurt anyone unless we have drawn blood. During the commission of a crime, empathy is typically and tragically nonexistent. This is due to the fact that we are only thinking of ourselves, not the victim.

According to Daniel Goleman, author of the book *Emotional Intelligence:*

A psychological fault line is common to rapists, child molesters and many perpetrators of family violence alike: they are incapable of empathy. This inability to feel their victim's pain allows them to tell themselves lies that encourage crimes.[2]

Ultimately, these "lies that encourage crime" are the same lies which serve to erode the deterrents to crime and help to diminish our sense of wrongdoing during and after the commission of a crime.

Even on those rare occasions when we do think about the victims of our crimes (usually only after we have been caught), we tend to downplay the true extent of the harm we have caused. We only recognize the concrete damage which we have done (such as the amount of money we have stolen, physical damage we have done, or bodily harm we have inflicted). We fail to recognize the true extent of the harm we have inflicted on the victim, because we are unable or unwilling to conceptualize the feelings of fear, anger, frustration and vulnerability the victim usually feels. (Not to mention their family, their friends, our own family, and society in general.)

While still in prison there were numerous times that I would catch myself arguing that I got way too much time for my crimes, because I felt that I really didn't hurt anyone – no one died or was physically hurt; I just stole their money. It took a while for me to fully realize the extent of my crimes and the pain I inflicted on everyone, including my own family.

9. <u>We feel that we are not obligated to anyone, but others are obligated to us.</u>

Our obligations to others are only recognized when they fall in line with what we want. When there is a conflict, we simply fail to recognize the obligation or come up with excuses. However, if the table is turned and another person fails to fulfill their obligations to us, we are likely to feel put down and get angry. When I first

---

2   Goleman, Daniel, "EMOTIONAL INTELLIGENCE" (New York: Bantam Books, 1995) pp.106

started doing time in prison I saw a guy who owed someone else almost $500.00 stab and kill another inmate because he owed him $5.00 – it was crazy. And how can we ever expect to be forgiven of our own crimes if we can't forgive others?

10. We see a potential criminal in everyone.

Since we all believe that everyone thinks and feels like we do, we tend to think that everyone else is also out for themselves and capable of committing crime. In fact, a common saying in prison is "the only difference between us and them is that they haven't been caught." Many criminals also believe that those who choose not to commit crimes only do so because they are weak or scared. This error also makes us suspicious of 'good Samaritans' and skeptical of other people's actions toward us.

This view of other people, I believe, can be attributed to the mechanism which psychiatrists call projection. In *The People of the Lie,* Dr. Peck explains that "Since they must deny their own badness, they must perceive others as bad. They project their own evil onto the world. They never think of themselves as evil, <so> they consequently see much evil in others."[3] Basically, we must view others as being criminal in order to maintain our own self-image as being responsible. What a paradox!

And because irresponsible and criminal behavior is so pervasive in society today, it usually isn't hard for us to find some bad or criminal in many of the people we see. If you could have heard all the guys in prison talking about President Clinton during his sex scandal, you would have thought they were a bunch of saints!

11. We have an inability to see responsible effort in others.

Since we tend to project our own evils onto others, we usually feel that everyone basically acts the same way we do. Thus, we often believe that most accomplished people achieve their status or

---

3   Peck, M. Scott M.D., "PEOPLE OF THE LIE: THE HOPE FOR HEALING HUMAN EVIL" (New York: Simon & Schuster, 1983) pp.73

worth through mainly immoral, irresponsible and criminal means. And again, our perception is reinforced, because we tend to associate with other irresponsible and criminal people.

For example, as criminals we are unable to accept the fact that a self-made millionaire may have earned his money through hard work and effort. Instead, we are sure they used underhanded means to achieve their wealth (stealing, bribery, cheating on taxes). Likewise, we would like to believe that most politicians achieved their rank and position at the expense of others. Basically, these erroneous beliefs serve a purpose in that they help us to justify our own underhanded and irresponsible tactics to achieve our desired status and self-worth. "If everyone else is doing it then why shouldn't I?" One criminal I talked to even went as far as to use this error to explain why he hadn't been a total success yet – "maybe I'm just being a little too nice."

Additionally, because of our inability to recognize responsible effort in others, we don't consider the work and effort necessary for others to earn what they have. So, to us, stealing these things usually isn't that big of a deal. "Why should it be," we tell ourselves, "they can get it all back from their insurance."

12. <u>We are untrusting.</u>

We are often considered paranoid due to our extreme distrust of others. In fact, many criminals say that trusting people is foolish. Basically, this distrust is simply a mixture of the projection of our own inability to be trustworthy as well as the suspicious nature which is required for a criminal way of life. Again, our lack of trust may also be partially due to the fact that we associate with others who are untrustworthy and thus we have often been let down. And realistically when it comes to trusting responsible people, our outlook and objectives are usually so different from theirs that we can't very well trust them to understand us or our secret way of life.

13. We refuse to be dependent on anyone.

We are undependable so we can't expect others to be dependable. Realistically, dependence is the antithesis of the control which is so important to us criminals. And admitting that we are dependent on anyone could destroy our fragile self-image. Consequently, we are usually exploitive rather than dependent. We simply fail to realize that a mutual dependence is a necessary part of living responsibly.

14. We are never satisfied.

The more we have, the more we want, and even the best isn't good enough much of the time. Due to our pretentiousness, perfectionism and narcissistic view of ourselves as being better than others, we are always looking for something more or something better than we already have (and better than everybody else). For us, the grass is always greener on the other side of the fence. We are never truly happy with where we are at or what we've got. Thus, we spend most of our time looking for something bigger and better rather than simply enjoying what we have.

This inability to be satisfied is very apparent in the prison setting. As inmates we complain about everything from cell searches to food, even though most of us eat better in prison than we did when we were out in society. If we are given special privileges, we inevitably want more. Regardless of where we are incarcerated, we complain that we would be better off at some other facility. Once we are transferred, however, we complain that we were better off where we were before. And, even when our grievances are handled the way we want, we will usually find something else to complain about. We are never satisfied regardless of what we get or are offered. Thus, for us, life often becomes an endless quest to simply be satisfied.

15. We lack a proper perspective of time.

Most of us live our lives for today, never thinking of what the future may hold or considering the consequences of our actions. Truthfully, many of us don't even think we will live long enough to reach old age, let alone plan for it. Combined with our emotional immaturity, this lack of a realistic time perspective also makes it difficult for us to have patience or to delay gratification. We want everything <u>now</u>.

We also have a difficult time setting and reaching responsible long-term goals. There may have been times in our lives when we have set and reached goals, but for the most part they have not been up to our potential. And if we don't instantly reach our goals, we tend to feel put down. We get angry and blame others, and then we convince ourselves that we really didn't want whatever it was anyway.

In *The Criminal Personality,* the authors note that "the criminal is a sprinter and not a long distance runner". [4] Our abilities and potential can be astounding at almost any task until we get bored, discouraged, or simply change our mind. Built the way we are, we don't have the moral foundation or convictions necessary to stick with a task for long. We may do great for a while, but we don't endure. Many of us have gotten jobs and been promoted in a matter of weeks, only to be fired a couple of months later.

I am not trying to say that we can't set and reach goals. Many of us develop very complex schemes and set goals when it comes to our criminal exploits. And if it is something very important to us, we can have the patience of Job. The problem is that if we can find a way to bypass waiting, we will - even if irresponsible means are required. So, we take shortcuts in life. Instead of working for our money, we steal it; instead of working through our problems, we run away from them; instead of studying to do well we cheat. But in the end, these shortcuts usually don't end up being what we expected. My shortcuts led me to a 30-year prison sentence.

---

4   Yochelson, Samuel, and Samenow, Stanton E., "THE CRIMINAL PERSONALITY - VOLUME ONE: A PROFILE FOR CHANGE" (New Jersey: Jason Aronson Inc., 1976) pp.257

16. We fail to show effort in responsible pursuits.

Effort refers to doing something that is contrary to what one prefers to be doing. And as I have said before, we usually only do what we want to do. We usually have an extreme amount of energy and persistence when we are doing what we want to do. But, give us something we dislike doing, or don't want to do, and we will fail to make any effort whatsoever. When required to do something contrary to our desires, we tend to either give up or complete the task in a slow, complaining and inefficient manner.

Parents, educators, and other members of the community commonly find themselves exasperated and in despair over the unrealized potential of many a delinquent youngster. We have pointed out that these are children of promise. They are energetic, generally of average or above average intelligence, and in many cases talented and creative. Unfortunately, at least from the standpoint of society, the promise is never fulfilled. Owing to competing interests the criminal child does not acquire the skills and knowledge needed to progress in the responsible world, nor does he cultivate his talents in any disciplined manner so that he can utilize them.[5]

If forced to choose between the easy way and the right way, we will choose the easy way every time. **As criminals we want to be the best, not to do our best.** The difference is that one requires effort while the other only requires our unrealistic perceptions. Our choice not to make an effort is very sad, because many of us are very bright and talented, and could do just about anything we wanted to do if we just tried.

Sadly, our true talents and intelligence are most likely only to surface in the prison setting. In prison, we are in a structured environment, we have an abundance of free time, and we are deterred from seeking out more exciting activities. In prison, many of us

---

5   Yochelson, Samuel, and Samenow, Stanton E., "THE CRIMINAL PERSONALITY -
VOLUME ONE: A PROFILE FOR CHANGE" (New Jersey: Jason Aronson Inc., 1976) pp.393

actually spend time developing our talents and work on bettering ourselves. However, it usually isn't long before we get bored, or become discouraged and quit. If we feel that we aren't better than others, then we are likely to give up. Others simply ignore prison programs, such as the hobby shop or educational classes, because to get involved would mean the risk of failure. Thus, many of us have talents and an intelligence that is likely to remain hidden from ourselves and society forever.

The fact is that the prison system is full of talented and intelligent young men who could, except for their erroneous thoughts and perceptions, be almost anything they ever fantasized about. I guess it is just easier and less risky to fool ourselves into believing that we are a gifted athlete, artist, or author, than to endure what it takes to actually become one.

17. We fail to endure adversity.

We don't endure adversity because our unrealistic, egocentric self-image maintains that we shouldn't have to. Adversity means suffering, and we think that suffering is for losers. For most of us, it is considered a put-down when things do not go the way they were planned. So, while responsible people usually deal with adversity in responsible ways, we are likely to complain, quit, or not even try.

There are times when we may deal with adversity as a way of scoring points, maintaining a facade of responsibility, or boosting our self-image. But, we are bound to make sure that everyone is aware of our suffering. In this way, our adversity becomes another criminal equivalent meant to enhance our self-image. However, because dealing with adversity requires effort and may expose us to failure, we will usually try to avoid it in any way we can.

18. We tend to gravitate towards irresponsible activities.

I believe that, as criminals, we tend to stray from responsible behavior and actually seek out irresponsibility for several reasons.

1) Responsible behavior requires a purpose, effort, and an ability to recognize consequences – three things which we lack.

2) Since we do not really know how to consistently act responsibly (we've never really tried), trying to live responsibly has the potential to make us appear ignorant or to risk failing.

3) Responsible actions seldom offer anything immediately concrete enough for us. There are usually no immediate prizes for responsible living. There is no rush of gratification. Nobody is going to praise us for just doing the things that we should be doing in the first place. Responsible actions also usually require the individual to put the consideration of others, or the future, before the immediate consideration of self. However, because we must continually maintain our self-image, we are unlikely to do these things.

4) Irresponsible people are usually easier to impress than responsible people and will tend to accept us regardless of our fragmented states. Responsible people will rarely tolerate irresponsible behavior while irresponsible people are willing to accept occasional responsible behavior.

5) We find an irresponsible way of life, a life of living on the edge, more exciting, fun and daring than responsible living. In fact, many of us actually build ourselves up through irresponsible behaviors by perceiving responsible people as being scared or weak because they are not willing to do the things we do.

6) Although we usually end up paying for them later, irresponsible behaviors are more likely to provide immediate rewards without all the consistent effort and sacrifice (or delaying gratification) which is necessary to succeed responsibly. In other words, because it usually takes time and

effort to reap the rewards of responsible behavior, irresponsible behavior seemingly provides an easier and quicker boost to our self-image than responsible behavior does.

7) Many of us do not believe that we can live up to our own, or others', expectations of us in a responsible way, but see the possibility of reaching these expectations through irresponsible and criminal behavior. Although it is difficult to finish school, work your way up the corporate ladder, and eventually find a job that pays more than $100,000 a year, it is easy to make that much money by selling drugs or committing burglaries.

8) The forbidden entices us. When someone tells us not to do something, we feel like we lose control of the situation, but when we do it anyway, it puts us back in control. It gives us the sense of power we crave.

19. <u>We don't take responsibility for our actions.</u>

Although we may pay lip service to being responsible for our actions so that we can score points, boost our own self-image, or reach some other exploitative objective, deep inside we rarely take full responsibility for anything. Taking responsibility for our faults would require us to deny our narcissistic self-image and would shatter our good opinion of ourselves. Thus, even though at times we may accept partial responsibility for things that go wrong, we are more likely to blame others, or circumstances beyond our control, whenever things don't go our way. Even when caught and held accountable we usually blame our behavior on everything from drugs, to friends, racism, the government, the system, the environment or even the victims themselves. In *The People of the Lie*, author M. Scott Peck, MD writes:

A predominant characteristic ... of those I call evil is scapegoating. Since the evil, deep down, feel themselves to be faultless, it is inevitable that when they are in conflict with the world they will invariably perceive the conflict as the world's fault.[6]

This victim stance is not only an integral part of our criminal thinking, but also one of the biggest enemies of change. It prevents us from taking responsibility for our own actions, which is a prerequisite for change. And, it can also serve to justify or excuse further irresponsible and criminal behavior. When everything that goes wrong for us is seen as somebody else's fault, then it is easy to get caught up in the mistaken idea that "everyone else needs to change – not me."

One of the criminals that I knew, a man with a life sentence for murder, actually blamed the murder on the victim's father. When the father refused to pay a drug debt, he kidnapped his son and told the father that if he didn't pay, he would kill his son. The father didn't pay, so in this criminal's mind it wasn't his fault that the man's son was dead.

Personally, I had a tendency to blame others and circumstances beyond my control whenever I got into trouble. Years after I was sentenced as a habitual criminal I felt that I was the victim of reverse discrimination and the political climate. So, instead of focusing on what I did to get myself into prison, I focused on how unfairly I was treated. It wasn't until I took responsibility for going to prison that was I able to take responsibility for doing what I needed to do to get, and stay, out.

20. We think we own everything.

None of us are very good at sharing. If we want to use the telephone and someone else is using it, we are likely to demand that the other person get off "our phone." If we are working out at the gym and the machine we want is being used, we get mad and feel put down that someone has the audacity to use "our weights" when we want to use them. And nobody better ever sit in "our seat" in

---

6   Peck, M. Scott M.D., "PEOPLE OF THE LIE: THE HOPE FOR HEALING HUMAN EVIL" (New York: Simon & Schuster, 1983)

the chow hall. In fact, while I was in prison I saw numerous fights over someone using someone else's weights or sitting in their seat in the chow hall.

This sense of ownership also carries over into our relationships where we usually feel that the control and power should be one-way instead of being an equal two-way give and take association. In our minds, our rights transcend the rights of others (we are special) so we must be the focus in all relationships. Thus, we expect most of the effort and sacrifice to be done by the other person. And if we are dating or married, we usually expect our girlfriend or wife to be completely faithful and obedient even though we feel that we are free to do whatever we choose.

This sense of ownership is simply an extreme form of control, which serves to boost our unrealistic self-image of being special and superior to others. "Instead of being nothing and having nothing, the criminal functions as though he is 'somebody' and owns everything."[7]

21. We easily become bored.

Our boredom usually stems from an inability to find excitement. Being responsible rarely provides the thrill we seek, so the boredom of responsibility often affects our decision-making process. As we discussed in the first chapter, there is reason to believe that we require more stimulation than the average person. This may result from genetic factors, or it may simply be the result of our own thrill-seeking choices which have fed an addiction to excitement - an addiction which, like any other addiction, grows with each exciting choice we make. Thus, each thrill increases our thirst for excitement as well as the amount of excitement which it takes to quench this thirst.

Due to this internal need for excitement, the lack of heightened stimulation or excitement can lead to extreme boredom, a state which is very intense and discomforting. I believe that we also tend

---

7   Yochelson, Samuel, and Samenow, Stanton E., "THE CRIMINAL PERSONALITY - VOLUME ONE: A PROFILE FOR CHANGE" (New Jersey: Jason Aronson Inc., 1976) pp.385

to become bored quicker than the average individual. Even though we are often initially excited and enthusiastic about new jobs and possessions, once the learning phase has passed, the newness is gone and repetition sets in, so does our boredom.

I believe that this boredom is one of the main reasons why many of us slip back down the criminal path. Although there are many responsible ways for us to find excitement and stimulation, responsible living in and of itself entails a large degree of repetitious, mundane, and boring behaviors. Going to work each day, paying bills and mowing the lawn are not normally considered exciting, but they are a necessity of daily life. Often, we cannot tolerate this boredom, so we turn to drug use, irresponsible behavior, or even crime in order to help relieve the tension. However, it is important to understand that everyone must learn to overcome this occasional boredom in order to reap the rewards of responsible living.

22. We are prone to magical thinking.

Magical thinking in its extreme form is the belief that our thinking may cause events to happen (or not happen). It is common among young children, but is usually discarded as a child matures and develops more realistic thinking. However, as criminals, we retain our ability to think magically for several reasons. First, it allows us to view ourselves as unique and superior to others without all the effort. Second, it reduces the need for us to prove ourselves through external activities. Finally, it helps us to overcome and avoid put-downs.

With the help of our magical thinking, we can become a big shot, a gifted artist, or a special person who is better than anyone else simply because our thinking makes it so. And by simply thinking that we are the best, then we don't actually need to try and risk failure. For example, we may go to a concert to hear a band, and then convince ourselves that we could do better than they did if we wanted to, even if we had never sung or played an instrument before. We may never even try to play an instrument. The important thing is that in our thinking we have convinced ourselves that we could be the best, which temporarily enhances our opinion of ourselves. Or, we may go to an art gallery and see a beautiful painting. And even though we have no formal experience or training as an artist, we convince ourselves that if we really wanted to we could paint one as good or even better. In fact, we may even start bragging about these imagined abilities to those around us. In the prison setting you often hear criminals say, "I could do that if I really wanted to" or "He isn't that good, I could do better." However, you rarely see them make the effort to do it. And if they do start making the effort, it is often short-lived.

Another great example of magical thinking is illustrated in the way that we as criminals believe we will never get caught. Although we may admit that we could eventually get caught if we continue to commit crime, we simply cannot visualize ourselves getting caught "this time." And because we can't imagine it happening, we truly believe it won't happen. Even the fact that we may have been caught in the past doesn't help to dim our belief that we won't be caught. Ironically, this belief unrealistically reinforces us with an extreme optimism, which allows us to shut off the external deterrents to crime and puts us in jeopardy of being caught.

Magical thinking also enables us to play the expert, even in situations where we have no basis for expertise. For us, simply reading a book or talking with someone who is knowledgeable about something like weight-lifting or computers, can become the foundation for our expertise. And we seem to think that we can learn in weeks what it takes others years to learn. For us, effort is replaced by magical thinking, because it is so much easier to simply think of ourselves as experts than to exert the time and energy required to become one.

23. <u>We have a distorted view of personal strength, inner strength and compassion.</u>

For most of us, having a heart means being fearless in asserting our power over others. It has nothing to do with compassion, or the inner-strength associated with acting on moral convictions. In fact, many of us view compassion as a weakness, unless we are the recipients of it. As criminals, we tend to believe that if a man has heart it means that he will stand up to, fight, or even kill anybody who disrespects him in any way. Conversely, a man is viewed as weak - or as having no heart - if he does not assert his power by standing up for himself and dealing with his own problems. While most people would applaud the ability to turn away from confrontation or go to the authorities to get help with problems, we consider this cowardice. For example, if an inmate who is robbed and assaulted by another inmate goes to the authorities, he is tagged as a snitch and a punk. In our eyes, he has no heart. In the same situation a criminal with heart would be expected to confront the offending individual and either fight or, in the extreme, kill him to retrieve his property.

As criminals, we also believe it is a weakness to be afraid or to show fear. Regardless of our true fears, we will almost always put on a front of fearlessness. If we are hanging out with criminal associates who want to rob a convenience store, we are likely suppress our fears of being caught or having something go wrong, and join in rather than be labeled as scared or weak. Once again, this emphasizes the fact that our biggest fear is of being put down or being seen by others as being a nothing. For us, being scared or weak is the same as being a nothing. In fact, many violent crimes are the result of our perceiving (often mistakenly) that we are being put down or disrespected because someone thinks we are a "punk" (scared and weak). Our concept of personal strength often requires us to deal with put-downs and disrespect by asserting physical power and saving face.

As criminals we also have a tendency to misinterpret kindness. Instead of recognizing kindness as generosity, we often perceive it as submissiveness. This is because much of the time our own kindness is usually employed for some exploitive purpose. As criminals we will typically be nice or kind to any person we want something from. On the other hand, we will rarely be very kind to any individual whom we perceive as inferior, or weaker than ourselves, unless we are trying to build up our self-image, score points or achieve some exploitive objective.

Due to our distorted view of personal strength, many of us actually feel the world should be an exciting Mad Max style society where only the strong survive. And, because of our magical thinking, we are able to convince ourselves that we would inevitably be one of the powerful, surviving few. We believe that nothing really bad could ever happen to us because we are special and destined to be great. It is our birthright. (Even though we keep getting caught and sent to prison) So, in much the same way that society says they have no use for us as criminals, we often tell ourselves that we have no use for the weak and scared of society.

I believe this erroneous perception of kindness, personal strength and character in others is a defensive mechanism that enables us to take the focus off of our own weaknesses and fearfulness. In essence, we project our own intense, but carefully concealed, fears onto others, because to admit our fears could potentially shatter our narcissistic self-image, revealing the fragile image of ourselves that we fear the most.

24. <u>We have a "me against the world" attitude.</u>

Throughout this book I have described the selfish nature of criminal behavior. The sad fact is that many of us actually believe that we have the right to do as we please and that no one has the right to stand in our way. This selfishness develops in us from an early stage in life and can be partially attributed to our error in thinking that people are against us and want to prevent us from being successful (the "everyone hates me" syndrome). This thinking error then serves to distort our perceptions of reality to the point where it seems justifiable or even necessary to fight or bend rules in order to grab our fair share and prevent others from taking advantage of us.

Since we have an unrealistic self-image, there are often discrepancies between the way we believe we should be treated and the way we are actually treated. Consequently, we often believe we are being picked on or put down even when it is not intended. And because it is so difficult (if not impossible) for us to live up to our perfect self-image, we often become angry at ourselves for our own mistakes and then we project this anger onto the world around us. In essence, we get mad at others for our own inadequacies, blaming them for our failures and cursing them whenever they excel at things we feel that we should be the best at.

25. We pride ourselves at being slick.

As criminals we all lead secret lives and revel at being slick enough to fool everyone around us. We believe that we are smarter, faster, shrewder, and superior to others and that because we are who we are, we are destined to have a trouble-free life, never getting caught up in any problems or difficulties. We think that we are so slick that we will never get caught. And even if we do get caught, we believe that we will be able to talk our way out of it.

Getting away with irresponsible or criminal behavior simply reinforces this arrogant self-image. For us, it is actually a boost to our narcissistic self-image to be able to get away with our crimes and get over on others. When we get away with our schemes, it makes us feel like we are better than the "common herd". And if we are caught, we simply use excuses, blame others for our failures, and shut off the awareness of our own un-slickness in order to maintain our illusion of being slick and superior to others.

In prison, we often talk about how slick we are when we get over on someone, especially the staff. And much of the criminal talk that goes on is about our past successful criminal exploits and how slick we were at not getting caught.

26. We scorn responsible living, and often look down on responsible people.

As criminals, we have convinced ourselves that responsible living is for suckers. Because we have never made the consistent effort necessary to reap the rewards of responsible living, we incorrectly assume that a responsible way of life is boring, uneventful, and simply full of such mundane and repetitious things as work, bills, taxes, rules, and eventually death. We want to "eat, drink, and be merry", yet the responsible way of life often entails restrictions, worries, duties, and working to overcome problems - things which we despise. We often view responsible people as slaves or pawns who follow others' rules simply because they are too scared or weak to stand up for themselves, do what they really want to do, and make the most out of life.

While I was on parole, my parole officer told me about a young man on his case load that had been increasingly breaking the rules. When threatened with a return to prison, this criminal replied, "That doesn't scare me – if you really want to scare me then threaten me with a 9 to 5 job every day, bills, taxes, responsibility and a boring life."

27. We have polarized thinking

As criminals, we usually think in extremes. Things are often perceived as either black or white, good or bad. We believe we have to be perfect or we are a failure. We must have the best or we want nothing at all. Through the lens of this distorted perspective, others are viewed as either for us or against us. They either love us... or they hate us. Because of the way we are, there can be no middle ground. Simply being average or ordinary is antithetical to our perfectionist self-perception. Deep down we are scared that without this perspective we may become lost in the ocean of mediocrity and, in effect, be relegated to a state of "nothingness" along with all the other "nobodies" in the world. Thus, we are often likely to decide that if we can't be the best, then we won't even try and by default we will be the worst at whatever we do.

28. We are impulsive

As criminals, we are consistently driven by a thirst for excitement and a craving for instant gratification. We are also able to shut off the consideration of the potential consequences of our actions. Thus, we are often propelled to follow our first impulse and worry about dealing with the consequences later. In fact, because of our impatience and lack of a responsible time perspective, we often convince ourselves that we must act on our first impulse or risk losing the opportunity forever. We fear that if we don't immediately take advantage of all our opportunities - opportunities to party, have sex, steal, get back at someone, take advantage of others, or in some way build ourselves up - that life will simply pass us by and we will never get the opportunity again. So, we usually jump at any chance we get to do these things without much consideration of our options or the potential consequences of these actions.

This impulsiveness has manifested itself many times in my life, but never more so than the time I decided one day to take a road trip to Las Vegas – while I was on parole. I didn't think about the consequences...and I didn't care if there were any. I was supposed to be working and going to school, and had been doing well for a while, so I felt like I deserved a vacation. I had just received some money from a school loan and decided that instead of applying it towards school and books, I would use it for my vacation. I asked a couple of friends to come along (who were very excited at the prospect of an all expenses paid vacation), and we left the next day. I returned two weeks later, after missing a couple parole meetings and many days at work and school, and was left frantically trying to avoid the consequences of my impulsive decision. I had piled up some debt, but was able to talk my way out of everything, and returned to work and school the following week. However, it wasn't long before I was in trouble again for burglary – and this time I wasn't able to talk my way out of it.

29. We have a tendency to blow things out of proportion.

Through the process of selective awareness, we usually filter out only the details of sensory information which serve to confirm our own distorted perception of self importance. Thus, we tend to make mountains out of molehills. This is because we imagine that the events that are taking place in our lives are somehow more important, or more significant, than anything that may happen in anyone else's life. When we do anything which is the least bit good or positive, we often perceive it as being better and "of greater value"

119

than anything anyone else may do. Conversely, when we make a mistake or fail at anything, then we are likely to perceive ourselves as a nothing who did worse than anyone could ever imagine. However, this feeling of nothingness usually only lasts until we take a victim stance and blame our failure on others.

On the other end of the spectrum we also make "molehills out of mountains." "Nobody was hurt," we tell ourselves. "Why is everyone making such a big deal out of it?" Or we complain that our sentences were disproportionate to our crimes. Since we are unable to recognize the true extent of the harm that we cause, we often convince ourselves that the crimes we commit aren't really that big of a deal.

An example of this tendency can be seen in my thinking the last time I went to prison. While sitting in jail waiting to go on trial for felony theft by receiving, I truly thought that I would be out in a year or two. I convinced myself that I hadn't really hurt anybody. I had only stolen someone's art collection – and they had gotten everything back. In my thinking I couldn't envision myself going to prison for long, so I felt sure that I would be out soon. The reality of my situation didn't hit me until the day I was sentenced to 30 years as a habitual criminal.

30. We believe that we can read minds.

At times we believe that just by looking at someone or hearing about a few concrete details about their behavior, we know what that person is all about. Because of our belief that everyone thinks like us, and our tendency to form stereotypes based on concrete characteristics and events, we often think that we can tell what others are thinking, what their motives are, and what they are going to do next. In particular, we believe that we know exactly how others feel towards us, what they think about us, and why they act the way they do towards us.

Most of the time, however, these perceptions are erroneous. Due to our tendency to take others' actions and behavior personally, and our inability to think conceptually, we are usually even worse than the normal person at judging others. For example, if we pass by a person we know in the hall who doesn't say "hi", or even look at us, we are likely to imagine that this is because they are upset with us, or they think that they are too good to talk to us. We don't consider the fact that they may just be having a bad day or may not have even seen us. Instead of simply communicating with this other person in order to find out the true reason why they didn't say "hi", we will usually convince ourselves that we already know what they think. In fact, we are even likely to get mad at them and to start feeling put down because of these false assumptions.

While in prison, I was working as a Para-pro for the music program and was put in charge of making sure that everyone got a chance to practice. We only had a few guitars, yet we had a lot of people that wanted to use them. I often had problems when I told guys that they could only practice for ½ an hour. One day in particular, I got what I thought was a bad vibe from one of the guys when I told him that he could only practice for ½ an hour. When his ½ hour slot was up, I told him to give the guitar to someone else and he said, "Okay essay," in a way that I perceived as negative. I wasn't sure what essay meant, but I was sure that it was disrespectful and I was ready to fight...until I was told that essay meant "friend" in Spanish.

31. <u>We have developed a concrete image of how everything should be.</u>

We have our own personal list of ironclad rules about how we, and others, should act, and about how things are supposed to be in life. When things don't turn out the way we think they should, or when people don't conform to our idea of the way things ought to be, we get angry. If we have to work late and miss something we planned, we get upset. If for some reason we don't get what was scheduled for dinner, we get mad. And if we don't live up to our own expectations of how we should be, we feel put down. We feel that everything should go perfect in our lives. Everything should work out for us and others should fit in line with our idea of how life is supposed to be. And because in this imperfect world things seldom ever go the way they really should, we are often let down and end up feeling angry, frustrated, depressed, and put down.

32. <u>We have a tendency to take things personally.</u>

Because of our egocentric view of the world, we often believe that everything is some type of personal reaction to us. If someone disagrees with our opinion, we take it as a personal affront. If they see things from a different point of view, we are likely to feel put down and get upset. If someone does something that we don't like, such as talk to our girlfriend or use our things at work, we think that they are doing it with the intention of disrespecting us. And if we notice someone telling a secret or laughing we often think that the secret or laughter is somehow about us. We believe that the world revolves around us, so we typically think that everything somehow pertains to us.

33. <u>We always have to be right.</u>

We often feel that we are on trial to prove that our ideas, opinions, and beliefs are correct. So, we are likely to argue a point forever, even if we aren't really sure that it is right. And if someone proves us wrong, then we are likely to feel angry and put down.

Being wrong is unacceptable. So, we will go to almost any length to prove that we are right. Our perfectionist self-image must be maintained at all costs. Admitting that we are wrong has the potential to destroy our self-image and make us feel like a nothing.

CHAPTER 7

Lies

T he reason I have decided to devote a whole chapter to the role of lying as a criminal characteristic is because of the way it pervades our lives. Lying and deception have a tremendously negative impact on our self-esteem, and consequently on our capacity for criminality. In fact, I believe that if we could simply learn to be honest with ourselves and those around us, we would find it almost impossible to commit crimes.

From a very early age we found that lying could be beneficial. Not only did it help us circumvent the possible consequences of our irresponsible behavior, but it was also useful as a way of increasing our own self-image. By lying we could portray a glorified image of ourselves to others, thus influencing the way they perceived and reacted to us. For example, in order to be liked and viewed as cool, we often told other children that we had things we didn't really have, had been places we hadn't really been, or had done things we hadn't really done. We discovered that by simply lying, we could be viewed as the "cool" kid who played the guitar in a rock band, had traveled all over the world, and had parents who owned a Ferrari. Similarly, in order to keep our parents happy, we would tell them whatever we thought they wanted to hear. For example, we may have told them that we really enjoyed church or school and learned a lot, when truthfully we hadn't even been there.

As we got older, we usually discovered that our lying could, and often did, lead to problems. But instead of learning to tell the truth, we choose to become more adept liars by learning to scan our environment and remembering what lies did and did not work. In time, lying became a way of life that was almost as imperative and automatic as breathing. Ultimately, being a criminal necessitates lying, not only in situations where we may want to keep our criminal exploits secret, but also in order to help us maintain an inflated self-image and the illusion of power and control we crave.

However, even though our lying may become habitual, it is still completely under our control. We know when we are lying and in fact, are constantly scanning our environment and others' behavior in order to better anticipate their reactions to our lies. And even though we may consciously try to block the self-awareness of our lies, we cannot fully hide them from ourselves. For the most part, we are not psychopaths. We may be unrealistic in many situations, but we are always in touch with reality. And we do know the difference between wrong and right, and between the truth and lies. Even though we may avoid the conscious awareness of our lies, or convince ourselves that our lies are justifiable; we simply cannot be indifferent to the consequences of these lies on our self-esteem.

The Absence of Truth

Our lying takes many forms. There are lies of omission, diversion, exaggeration, distortion and circumlocution. We assert, manipulate, con and feed people what we believe they want to hear. As criminals, we are also very secretive. An open channel of communication is antithetical to our way of life, because it could leave us vulnerable to others. And because we lie so often and engage in so many secretive acts, we are also very distrustful and suspicious of others. We project our own criminal characteristics onto others, so we believe that everyone lies and 'stretches the truth' to some extent. Thus, even though we see nothing wrong with lying in certain situations, we feel that we are justified in being suspicious and not trusting others.

There are basically four reasons why we lie:

1. To hide irresponsible or criminal behavior
2. To build ourselves up or maintain an inflated self-image
3. To maintain a respectable front
4. To exploit others.

For us, lying is always purposeful. Although our lying may become habitual and ever more pervasive in our lives due to the increasingly tangled web of lies which we weave, it never becomes compulsive. Each time we lie, it is a choice. It may not be a fully-conscious choice based on a total awareness of reality, but it is still a choice.

Secrets – Hiding Criminal Behavior

It is not really difficult to explain why it is necessary to keep our criminal exploits secret. If we didn't, we would run the risk of being caught and having to face the consequences of our actions. Although we may sometimes tell an individual about our crimes, it is usually only if we feel that we can trust that person and believe that confiding in this person will achieve some objective, such as proving we are more daring and thus better than they are. For the most part, however, we have discovered that it is much more advantageous to keep our criminal exploits secret.

As criminals, even when we are caught red-handed at something, we will usually lie in one form or another about the full extent of our culpability. When questioned, we are likely to:

- downplay our role or involvement in the crime
- minimize the extent of damage done
- blame our actions on external factors, such as drugs
- try to deny all knowledge of the transgression

However, we rarely, if ever, admit to the full extent of our wrongdoing. In fact, as soon as we think that we might be caught, our minds race as we attempt to formulate a lie which is not only believable, but also minimizes our culpability as much as possible.

Lying to Ourselves

Because of who we are, not only do we lie to others when we are caught, but we must also lie to ourselves in an effort to maintain our inner sense of goodness and perfection. Once caught, we are forced to face our own wrongdoing and sense of worthlessness. So, we must try to rebuild our deflated self-image in order to avoid our unhealthy self-esteem and overcome being a nothing.

Most of the time, we do this by convincing ourselves that we are the victim and not necessarily the victimizer. Or we somehow justify and excuse our behavior. Realistically, this isn't hard for us to do. It simply requires us to shut off the awareness or thoughts of our criminal acts, and then focus our conscious mind on those things which we feel support our victim stance or our excuses. This strategy also enables us to circumvent the feelings of guilt, remorse, depression, and worthlessness that could potentially lead to thoughts of suicide (which are common in the nothingness state). I believe that subconsciously our psyche does what our self believes will best help it to survive - create an unrealistic self-image... create a lie. Whereas an individual with a healthy self-esteem would be able to recognize their wrongdoing, identify why it occurred, and then change whatever they needed to in order to correct it, we find it is easier to hide behind excuses and lies. Our self-esteem simply isn't strong enough to endure the possibility that we might have been wrong, so we create a perceived reality in which it isn't us but others, or other things, which are wrong.

This self deception, however, doesn't just start when we are caught. As criminals, we regularly lie in order to maintain and boost our unrealistic self-image. Because of who we are, we must inevitably lie about ourselves, our accomplishments, and our abilities in order to portray an image of being somebody special.

Much like when we were children, we often end up telling others that we've done things that we haven't done, or that we have things that we don't have. And we pretend to be people that we really aren't. It's simply much easier that way, at least for the short term. By lying, we can instantly become a somebody - a millionaire, a college graduate, a drug kingpin, a player with the ladies, a good student, a decorated veteran, or even some type of spiritual guru. Depending on who we are talking to, we can become whoever we want. We imagine that by lying we can cause others to view us as special and important people. In turn, this misperception helps us to sustain our unrealistic self-image. In essence, we convince ourselves that if others think we are special and important, then we must be special and important. Thus, lying becomes just another way for us to assert our power and superiority over others. And also allows us to maintain our self-image as being better than others.

Lying to maintain and boost an unrealistic self-image can take many forms and come in a variety of degrees. Not only do we lie in order to impress others, but we also lie in an effort to conceal any truths which may damage our perceived self-image in the eyes of others. For example, we are unlikely to tell any of our bro's that we are scared of the dark – or that we cried when we saw "Where the Red Fern Grows". It is an image thing. And if we happen to get fired from our job, we are unlikely to tell anyone that we are not forced to tell. If we must tell them, we are sure to come up with some excuse or lie, such as, "I wasn't fired - I quit!!" Another common response, much like the victim stance used when we are caught, would be to blame being fired on external factors, such as our boss, our car, or anything that we can think of. This form of lying is intended not only to take other peoples' focus off the real reasons for being fired, but also to justify our own ordinariness and imperfection to ourselves.

Ironically, however, this is one of the biggest reasons why our self-image is so fragile and so susceptible to put-downs, because it is not built on the rock of truth but on the quicksand of lies. We lie in order to impress people and influence their perceptions of us, but we fail to realize the tremendously negative impact that these lies have on our perceptions of ourselves. We simply don't understand how they increasingly damage our self-esteem or how harmful it can be to create a reputation with ourselves as liars. On a very basic level, the relationship between our unrealistic self-image and our lying is reciprocal. They are both a cause and effect of each other. The more we lie, the more damage we do to our self-esteem. And the more we damage our self-esteem, the more unrealistic our self-image must become in order to compensate for it. In turn, the more unrealistic our self-image becomes, the more we must lie to ourselves and others in order to sustain it. In the end, we must increasingly lie to sustain the lies that were created by our lying in the first place.

When taken to the extreme, our lies can also allow us to actually create distorted or unrealistic memories, which can then be used as a personal proof of power, achievement and ability. Since our lies are usually based on reality, it can be easy for us to twist them to form our own reality. The more we tell our altered stories, the more apt we are to distort our actual memories of these events to the point where even we can't remember where the reality ends and the lies begin. In essence, our lies become our memories. Personally, I believe that all people are capable, to some extent, of distorting their memories of certain events, especially painful memories. However, because our way of life is dependent upon our ability to lie, I believe that we are even more capable of living our lies than other people.

A simple example of this distorted memory can be seen in an individual who goes on a fishing trip and catches a fish, which is actually ten inches long. Yet, when he returns home and tells his friends about his wonderful trip, he exaggerates the size of the fish he caught and tells everyone that it was actually 15 inches long. At first, when the memories of his fishing trip are recent, he may realize that he is, in fact, lying. However, he does so because he wants to make his story more exciting or to impress people. With each subsequent telling of his story, the fish may even get longer until it becomes 20 inches long. Now, as this individual's actual memories of his fishing trip fade, the true size of the fish he caught may be forgotten and then replaced by the distortions he has made up about his experience. Due to of the repetitious nature of his tall stories, they can partially become his memories and he may actually remember catching a 20-inch long fish. Even if he does happen to remember that he had exaggerated the size of the fish, he is unlikely to remember the actual size of the fish. So, instead of remembering the actual fish as being the 20 inches which he has told people, he is likely to recall the fish as being closer to 15 inches, which was the length of the fish in the first lie, not the actual length of the fish.

Truthfully, these distorted memories can only happen if we allow them to. First, they require a lie as a foundation. Next, they require us to actually eliminate the conscious awareness of the memories that are based on reality. Finally, we must allow these lies to permeate our own reality. They involve a series of choices; they don't just happen.

By the time we are an adult, we have usually become a master at sizing up others, and our environment, in order to recognize which lies work and what impact they will have on different people in different situations. We are then able to edit our lies and become a different person in different situations. This trait not only shows that we are aware of our lying, but also that we know the difference between right and wrong, and the truth and our lies. Without this awareness, our lies could not be edited to suit our purpose or to maintain our unrealistic self-image. For example, if we decide to call in sick to work and go out bar-hopping with friends, we are likely to tell different stories about our actions to different people. We may tell other irresponsible people an exaggerated story in which we called in sick to work and had the best night of our life. However, we are likely to tell a responsible person (other than those at work) that we were at work all night and that our job is going well. This doesn't even include the lies that we must tell our boss and peers at work in order to explain away our absence, or the lies we must tell a girlfriend, wife, parole officer, or mother. Our lying often becomes very confusing. With this one incident I have described several different lies which we must stay aware of in order to keep from getting caught. It isn't hard, then, to see how we often start confusing our lies, and how we confuse them with reality. It reminds me of a saying my mother used to tell me: "Oh, what a tangled web we weave when first we practice to deceive."

Ultimately, due to so much lying, sneaking, and secrecy, there is usually an enormous communication gap in any type of relationship we may develop with others. Even our closest friends and lovers usually don't know the whole truth about us, what we think and how we feel inside. We keep our deep dark thoughts and secrets to ourselves, because we are afraid of what others may think if they knew the whole truth about us. Furthermore, a trusting, mutual relationship with full disclosure would demand the acknowledgment of all our faults and weaknesses. This would leave us naked and defenseless, something our unhealthy self-esteem and fragile self-image just couldn't, or more precisely, doesn't want to handle.

Sadly, even when we do something extremely special or worthwhile, we have a tendency to exaggerate or downplay our actions depending upon the situation and the audience. For example, we are unlikely to tell our criminal associates or irresponsible friends that we received special recognition for something at church or earned an award in Boy Scouts. Yet we are likely to tell our parents, or other responsible people, a distorted version of our accomplishment, which exaggerates our success. Realistically, no matter how special our accomplishments are, we never feel that they are enough or that we are enough. Because we believe that we must be perfect, we never really experience a feeling of satisfaction or completion from the things we do. So, our personal need to prove ourselves is never fully satisfied. Thus, we often feel a need to exaggerate our accomplishments. For example, we may graduate from college and still lie about the grades we received (A's and B's rather than C's) or the type of degree we earned (a Master's degree rather than a Bachelor's degree). We may also get a promotion at work and still feel as though we must lie about the amount of raise we got or the actual title of the job we received. For us, nothing is ever enough. The more we have, the more we want. Yet sadly, the more we try to "prove" our worth through lies and deceit, the more we actually convince our inner selves that our worth is in question, and we end up feeling that we must prove ourselves even more.

Lying to Maintain an Image of Respectability

When discussing our desire to be viewed as respectable, it is important to note that what is respectable for one person may not be for another. For example, most criminals don't respect a person who walks away from a fight, even though it is the responsible thing to do. But most responsible people in civilized society respect this. And although most people respect responsible behavior, I do not want to confuse these terms. While responsibility is an objective term in that it is associated with ideals that are fixed, respectability deals more with an individual's subjective perceptions. Thus, what an irresponsible or criminal person respects may be vastly different than what a responsible person respects. So, when I say that we seek to create an image of respectability through lies, it does not mean that we will always act responsibly or try to create an image of responsibility; it simply means that we will do whatever we believe that the person, or people, we are around will respect.

We recognize that it is necessary to tell different versions of our lies in order to portray different images of ourselves, depending on who we are talking to. We want responsible people to respect us as much as, or even more than, irresponsible people. We know that it is more difficult to impress responsible people, but we also recognize that gaining the respect of responsible people can be useful in achieving certain objectives. So we lie around them in order to maintain a "respectable" facade.

When we are around responsible people, we put on a mask and act responsibly, almost to the extreme. We talk about being responsible, ask questions, feign interest and work hard, but only if we feel that someone is watching us so we can receive recognition. On the other hand, when we are around irresponsible people our lying and actions are designed to portray an image which, although much different than the one we portray to the responsible person, is still intended to impress them.

In *The People of the Lie,* Dr. Peck explains that "The words 'image', 'appearance' and 'outwardly' are crucial to understanding the morality of the evil. While they seem to lack any motivation to be good, they intensely desire to appear good. Their 'goodness' is all on a level of pretense. It is in effect a lie. This is why they are the 'people of the lie'.[1] For us image is everything, because it helps us to avoid the painful awareness of who we really are.

I saw this need for an outward appearance of respectability in

---

1   Peck, M. Scott M.D., "PEOPLE OF THE LIE: THE HOPE FOR HEALING HUMAN EVIL" (New York: Simon & Schuster, 1983) pp.75

myself throughout my life. When I was younger, I usually assented to such activities as going to school, doing chores, going to church, and participating in respectable pursuits (such religious and educational activities) in order to maintain an appearance of respectability. I learned that I was much more likely to get away with the other things we wanted to do if people believed that I was participating in responsible activities. And I also discovered that it was easier not to "rock the boat" by refusing to be involved in the activities my parents viewed as important. Yet, because most of the time I didn't really want to be doing these things, I learned little from these activities. And although I often paid lip service to the values and morals which I was taught in the home, these lessons were usually eroded and shut off. My parents used to say that it seemed that everything they said "went in one ear and out the other".

As I got older and left home, I continued to maintain a respectable front as much as possible, which I usually did through lies. When I had contact with responsible people (family, old employers, parole officers), I was likely to tell them just about anything to portray an image of respectability. For example, I once told my parents that I had a job when I didn't. I told my parole officer that I had insurance for my car when I didn't. And, I told an old employer that I wasn't drinking or doing drugs anymore when I was. Throughout my life I have been utterly dedicated to preserving an image of respectability - at the expense of respecting myself.

Since we often get caught up in our lies and irresponsible behavior, it is difficult for us to maintain an appearance of respectability for long. When we do lose the respect of others, we get angry, and then we struggle to repair our shattered self-image. To do this we come up with excuses and justifications. Then we shut off any feelings of shame and worthlessness by simply not thinking about these painful feelings or the behaviors that caused them. Finally, we try to do or say something respectable which, because we think concretely, helps to restore our self-image of respectability again.

Because of our tendency to think concretely, we do not view

human traits such as honor, honesty, and integrity as a way of life. Instead, we see them only as the direct consequence of certain behaviors. Therefore, we are able to regain and maintain our self-image of respectability and perfection through concrete acts which we perceive to be honorable, respectable or perfect. We then use much the same method to restore our respectable reputation with others. If we can, we will cover up our actions through lies or, if possible, by simply not letting anyone know. If we can, we will also avoid anyone who is aware of our imperfections, or we will downplay, or outright deny, everything. Then, if it is necessary, we will admonish that our actions were "not a big deal", highlight our previous respectable actions, and then act respectably for a while. We usually feel that this should be enough to make them respect us again. We may also use diversionary tactics if we have to, such as changing the subject or referring back to the irresponsible behaviors of others. Regardless of how it is accomplished, our self-image of respectability must somehow be repaired , because without it we are likely to end up feeling like a nothing.

Lying to Exploit Others

Finally, we lie in order to achieve any exploitive objective we may have, or in order to "score points", which we may later exchange for something we want. For example, we may tell our parents we got an A on a test or that all our homework is done in order to convince them to let us go to the movies on a school night. Or, we may tell someone that we like them if we see an opportunity to exploit it later. In fact, if we see that someone is good at math and could be useful somewhere down the line, we may tell that person that they are one of our best friends and be extra nice to them, even if we really don't like them. Basically, we lie in order to get over on other people and to get whatever we want.

As I have said before, we believe that we are entitled to whatever we want. And if getting what we want involves a little lying, then so be it. Most people are aware of the lying that is involved in criminal behavior. They have heard about the con artist who, by sleight of hand, can give a cashier a $10.00 bill and get change for

$100.00 bill, or who sells someone property or services which turn out to be fantasy. In fact, most property crimes are based on lies. The counterfeiter lies every time he uses his fake money; the check forger lies when he cashes checks and claims them as his own; and the thief lies every time he takes something that isn't his. Most people are not aware, however, of the full extent to which we con, exploit, manipulate, fabricate and lie in order to get what we want.

As children, most of us discover the exploitive benefits of lying and we begin lying in order to achieve objectives that range from seemingly responsible to totally irresponsible. Many times we benefit from our lies, even if we get caught. For example, I once told my parents that I had to go to work so that I could use the family car to go partying with our friends. And even though I got caught, at least I still got to go partying. I also lied to get money from my parents by telling them I needed it for a science project, and then used it to buy drugs. And, I forged my parents' signatures on excuse notes many times so that I could skip school.

As adults, our lies are endless and can change from moment to moment, and situation to situation, according to our objectives and desires. Our lying takes many forms and happens extensively. We conceal much, and what we do reveal is often distorted, exaggerated or in some way edited in order to suit our own purposes. At times, even we can't understand why we are lying. We know that we are lying, but because it has become so natural, so habitual, we can't understand the purpose behind some of our lies.

Sure, we can understand the lies used to exploit another person in order to get what we want and the lies we use to cover up our irresponsible acts and criminal behaviors, but the lies which solely serve to boost our self-image and maintain our respectability happen so quickly and so naturally, that we often can't understand why we lied; why we were driven to exaggerate or edit our version of reality in a way which presented a better image of ourselves. We tell ourselves that we don't really care what others think about us, yet the lies intended to impress them continue to happen. Eventually, lying becomes a way of life that feels more natural than telling the truth.

The Consequences of Dishonesty

Regardless of the reason, every time we lie it has a tremendous impact on our self-esteem. Lies serve to undermine our confidence and tarnish the relationship we have with ourselves. As much as we may try, we simply cannot exempt ourselves from the knowledge of right and wrong, or from the moral consequences of our actions. Although we may try to conceal our dishonesty, at some level it inevitably influences us. Our thoughts, choices, and actions always leave either positive or negative feelings about ourselves. Even though we may try to conceal our lies from others and downplay their effect on our self-esteem, we can never really hide them from ourselves.

As Nathanial Branden explains in his book *The Six Pillars of Self-Esteem:*

> One of the great self deceptions is to tell oneself, "Only I will know." The implication is that my judgment is unimportant and that only the judgment of others counts. But when it comes to matters of self-esteem, I have more to fear from my own judgment than from anyone else's. In the inner courtroom of my mind, mine is the only judgment that counts. My ego, the "I" at the center of my consciousness, is the judge from whom there is no escape. I can avoid people who have learned the humiliating truth about me. I cannot avoid myself.[2]

When we lie, cheat or steal, we create a reputation with ourselves as a liar, cheater or thief. And no matter what others may think about us, we can't hide the truth from ourselves. With each lie, we solidify the reputation with ourselves as liars. So, even if we forget the content of our lies, we remain a liar as far as our inner-self is concerned. And because deep down we already see our-

---

2   Branden, Nathaniel, "THE SIX PILLARS OF SELF-ESTEEM" (New York: Bantam Books, 1994) pp.146

selves as liars, we are more likely to lie in the future.

Ultimately, the more that lying pervades our lives, the more irresponsible we will become. Consequently, our capacity for criminal thoughts, choices and actions will increase. And the more irresponsible we become, the more we will inevitably lie. In fact, we must lie in order to continue living in a way which is contrary to truth and reality. It can become a vicious cycle in which we have the most to lose.

SECTION II
THE DYNAMICS OF CHANGE

CHAPTER 8

Reprogramming Our Minds

I n order for us to truly change, we must eliminate all of our errors in thinking and perception, and replace them with more responsible ways of thinking and viewing the world. We must totally reprogram our minds. As Albert Einstein once observed, "The significant problems we face cannot be solved at the same level of thinking we were at when we created them."[1]

Now that we better understand these errors, we must learn to apply this knowledge in our lives. Everything we have learned so far must become operational in our struggle to change and live responsibly, or else it is worthless. Changing lifelong thinking patterns is an active process – it will not happen magically. We must struggle each day to discover and implement the necessary truth and insight required to think and live responsibly. True change takes time. It requires learning through experience and maturing through practice. Even though our newly-acquired knowledge can help to facilitate change, we are still faced with a choice. We can either consciously use this knowledge in order to grow and develop, or we can avoid the awareness of this knowledge through the self-deception of our excuses and lies. As a warning, the excitement and newness of our decision to change will quickly fade. That is when the real work, and true potential for change, will begin.

I Think I Can

The best place for us to overcome irresponsible choices and behavior is in our thinking. If we can destroy the seeds of irresponsible behavior and crime, then the plant will never grow. If instead of

---

1   Covey, Stephen R., "THE 7 HABITS OF HIGHLY EFFECTIVE PEOPLE - POWERFUL LESSONS IN PERSONAL CHANGE" (New York: Simon & Schuster, 1989) pp.42

thinking about stealing we think about how we can responsibly earn the things we need, then we are less likely to steal – and more likely to be creative, productive and happy. If we learn to humble ourselves instead of thinking that we are special and superior to everyone else, then we will be less likely to behave selfishly and hurt others - and more likely to be successful. If we don't allow ourselves to think that "others" are to blame for our problems and instead take responsibility for ourselves, then we will be more likely to learn from our mistakes and empower ourselves to grow.

However, in order for this to work, we must fully accept that we are not victims of the kind of thoughts which pass through our heads. We can, and do, have control over our own thinking. Our thoughts are not intruders in our mind over which we have no control, but instead a result of our own conscious focus and programming. Even though we may sometimes give up control over our thinking, we are always capable of focusing our mind on certain objectives and seeking reality if we so desire. If we want to study for a math exam, then we can focus our thinking on our notes and textbooks. And, if we want to do well at work, then we can focus our thinking on the task at hand. In the past, we have often controlled our thinking when it came to irresponsible and criminal objectives. So there is no reason why now we can't learn to responsibly focus and control our thoughts in order to change our point of view. Realistically, we must first learn to control our thinking if we are ever going to learn to control our lives.

By simply learning to responsibly control our own thinking we can:

- influence our perceptions
- control our emotions
- overcome our fragmentation
- gain a better time perspective
- enhance our personal relationships
- overcome shut-off and erosion
- and eliminate all of our criminal errors in thinking and perception.

Learning to control our thinking is so important, because responsible living begins with responsible thinking. If, in our thoughts, we can learn to continually hold ourselves accountable for our own choices and behavior, then our actions themselves are much more likely to be responsible.

Our Mind

As human beings we possess an awesome bio-computer called our brain. However, we are not automatically experts at how to use it or program it correctly. Like any other ability, the ability to think must be learned and developed. And because thinking is an active process, it can only be improved through practice.

If we want to get better at free-throws in basketball, then what should we do? Practice free throws!! Similarly, if we want to improve our ability to think, then we must practice controlling our thinking. By simply reading this book you are practicing controlling your thoughts. Hopefully, right now you are thinking about the words that are written on this page. You are consciously focusing on something. Now, think about where you have been and where you want to go in life. Think about your purpose. Just think – use your mind.

Much like we can learn to control any computer, we can learn to better control our mind. With effort, we can become more efficient at controlling the focus of our conscious thoughts. We can eliminate irresponsible thoughts and think responsibly. We can apply ourselves instead of daydreaming. We can think through problems instead of giving up. And once we learn to responsibly control our thoughts, we can change who we are inside. We can actually reprogram our subconscious mind.

Our Subconscious Mind

Within each of us there is an infinite and powerful subconscious mind that quietly guides our thinking and perceptions. Our attitude, character, beliefs, values, habits, perceptions and many other personal traits are influenced by the lifelong programming of

141

our subconscious mind. Like the operating system on a computer, it defines who we are and how we deal with the outside world.

It is also the gatekeeper of our conscious awareness. Through the reticular activating system, it filters through all of our incoming sensory information and determines what, from the vast amount of possible information, will be permitted into the light of our conscious awareness. It is simply impossible for us to focus on everything that we see and hear in a given moment. It is our subconscious mind that helps us decide what is important for us to perceive and what is not. Thus, it quietly guides our thoughts, perceptions and behaviors.

However, just because our subconscious mind influences our thoughts and actions, it doesn't mean that we don't have a choice. Ultimately, our subconscious is still under our control. Our "subconscious mind does not think or act on its own volition or its own initiative. Its primary purpose is to achieve the goals that have been given to it by <our> conscious mind."[2]

For example, I usually never pay very close attention to the vast number of cars that I pass on the road each day. However, when I decided it was time to buy a new car, I consciously started paying more attention to all of the cars that I passed by. I was trying to figure out what type of car I wanted. After some further thought, I decided that I wanted a midsized SUV because my family was getting larger and I needed all-wheel drive due to the potential for snow here in Colorado. So, from that point on I only really focused when I passed by different styles of all-wheel drive SUV's. All other types of cars were again relegated to subconsciousness, because I had programmed my subconscious mind to be on the lookout for all-wheel drive SUV's.

Similarly, if we are always consciously telling ourselves to be on the lookout for excitement and proof of power, then our subconscious mind will help us to achieve these objectives also. It is our subconscious mind, then, that decides what - out of the tremendous mass of data going into our brain through all of our

2   VanFleet, James K., "HIDDEN POWER: HOW TO UNLEASH THE POWER OF YOUR SUBCONSCIOUS MIND" (West Nyack: Parker Publishing, 1987) pp.1

senses (sight, hearing, touch, taste, smell) - we should pay attention to. And although we can take conscious control of this process, it is an operation which will be left up to past programming if we do not appropriately focus our thinking.

Throughout our past way of life, we have irresponsibly programmed our subconscious minds with all types of lies, self-deceptions, selfishness and evil thoughts. It is no wonder, then, that at times irresponsible and criminal thoughts seem to just jump into our mind, and that we always seem to keep finding ourselves in irresponsible situations and criminal circumstances. Throughout our lives we have programmed ourselves to seek out those activities and environments which could help us to achieve our criminal objectives. And we have also programmed ourselves to withhold and eliminate any conscious thoughts and perceptions which could interfere with these goals and objectives.

However, because of our human abilities of self-awareness and self-examination, we are not simply the sum of our past thoughts, feelings and perceptions. We are not limited to, or bound by, our subconscious programming. We have the ability to stand apart from ourselves, examine our programming, and use our conscious awareness, imagination, and limitless potential in order to develop a new perspective on life. We can form new attitudes, beliefs and values. We can create new habits that are more positive and productive. We can think about our thinking, have feelings about our feelings, and even develop a perception of our own perceptions, but only if that is what we consciously want to do. We can only override all of the negative things stored in our subconscious mind, and rewrite our programming, if we make the consistent effort necessary in order to responsibly control our thinking.

As with any computer, the output of our subconscious mind will always equal its input. Thus, during our change process it is critical that we become extremely careful of what we allow ourselves to consciously think or fantasize about. Because it is our conscious input that will actually write or program the influential output of our subconscious mind. Personally, I have even gone as far as to quit listening to any music which may have any evil, irresponsible, immoral, or criminal lyrics, or which causes me to think or feel this way. And I have begun listening to more spiritually up-lifting music. I don't watch any television shows or movies that may promote criminal thinking. I also refuse to talk or listen to anyone whose vocabulary consists mainly of four-letter words. And I don't hang around anyone who suggests irresponsible or criminal behavior. I simply do not want to think about these things. I have a tough enough time without someone planting these thoughts in my head.

I believe we must continuously struggle to implement responsible thinking patterns in all areas of our lives. We should always try to think good, productive and purposeful thoughts. We should also concentrate on developing responsible and productive habits. And when those irresponsible and criminal thoughts do arise, we must learn to recognize them as undesirable - and opposed to our commitment to change. We should immediately eliminate these unwanted thoughts from our mind by replacing them with responsible thoughts of things such as our purpose, our goals, and our ultimate choice of total responsibility, or a return to crime and its consequences.

We shouldn't ever allow ourselves to think or fantasize about irresponsible objectives. Even non-criminal fantasies are danger-ous if they simply become our past pattern of unrealistically boost-ing our self-image or quenching our thirst for power and excitement. And even though they may seem to be all around us, we must struggle to mentally resist all the external influences of ir-responsibility, immorality and crime. When we see or hear these things, we should not allow them to remain in our thinking. If we do, then we risk the chance of them being negatively programmed into our subconscious mind.

Ultimately, if it becomes our conscious purpose to think re-sponsibly, then our subconscious mind will eventually figure that we are no longer interested in irresponsible thoughts or criminal objectives. In time, it will actually help to eliminate these irrespon-sible ideas and attitudes from our conscious thoughts and percep-tions, and help us to achieve our responsible goals and objectives. We will reprogram our mind and subconsciously become exactly what we consciously think about.

David O. McKay once said, "The thought in your mind at this moment is contributing, however infinitesimally, almost imperceptibly to the shaping of your soul, even to the lineaments of your countenance....even passing and idle thoughts leave their impression."[3] We should always strive to keep our minds so full of good, responsible and moral thoughts that there is no room for evil ones. Each and every thought we have should be weighed against reality, directed by our purpose and fortified by our desire to change.

Eventually, if we are persistent in our struggle to change, our countenance will begin to change. With each victory over an irresponsible thought or desire; with each correction of an error in our thinking and perception; with each responsible choice we implement; and with each responsible and productive thought, we will reprogram our mind - and transform the very essence of our character. Just as we developed our current subconscious programming through repetition, we can rewrite the programming of our subconscious mind through repetition also.

Replacing Bad Thoughts With Good Ones

For some time after our decision to change, our subconscious mind will continue to flood our conscious mind with exciting irresponsible, immoral, and even criminal thoughts. I believe that this may be in an attempt to replace, or somehow make up for, the excitement and proof of power which we are depriving ourselves of by deterring our irresponsible and criminal behavior. However, we must not ever savor or fondle these thoughts as we might a family pet. We must struggle to eradicate them as soon as we become consciously aware of them, or else we run the risk of them growing from a harmless pet into a dangerous monster which can destroy our lives and the lives of those around us.

Reprogramming our subconscious mind through positive thinking is much like growing a prized rose garden. Not only must we continually care for and nurture our roses, or responsible thoughts,

---

3   Kimball, Spencer W., "THE MIRACLE OF FORGIVENESS" (Salt Lake City: Bookcraft Inc., 1969) pp105

but we must also ceaselessly struggle to remove all of the weeds, or irresponsible thoughts and errors in thinking. If we don't, then they have the inherent potential to rapidly grow, choke out our roses, and infest the whole garden. Soon, what may have simply begun as one or two small weeds can, if neglected, grow and multiply. If we are not careful, this can undermine all of our efforts at reprogramming our mind and developing a new perspective on life. When our garden is infested with weeds, it tends to distort our whole perspective on life. It is only when our rose garden is flourishing and consciously being cared for that we can maintain a responsible and realistic perspective.

In order for us to effectively eliminate irresponsible and criminal thoughts from our minds, we must first learn to replace these thoughts with more responsible ones. When confronted with an irresponsible thought, we should teach ourselves to immediately think more responsibly by consciously focusing on things such as:

- the deterrents to these irresponsible thoughts
- our purpose
- our higher power
- our desire to change
- the people we love
- the responsible ways in which we could otherwise achieve our goals and objectives

It can also be extremely helpful to develop and continually use specific visualizations, ideas, thoughts, affirmations, or even childhood songs in order to help us redirect our thinking and replace irresponsible or criminal thoughts. When confronted with inappropriate thoughts, we can then use these replacements to automatically refocus our conscious thinking. We may choose to visualize ourselves responsibly achieving some long term goal, or to automatically think about our mother, our family, or God. We may even choose to personally create some positive affirmation - a statement such as, "I am a responsible individual and when I control my thinking, I control my life" - which is in line with reality, the principles of change, and our purpose in life. However, in order for these things to become fully effective in redirecting our thinking and reprogramming our subconscious mind, they must become automatic deterrents to irresponsible thinking - they must be programmed into our subconscious mind through repetition and become habits themselves.

Personally, whenever I catch myself thinking inappropriate or irresponsible thoughts, I have programmed myself to immediately think of, and quickly begin singing, a song which I was taught when I was a child, entitled, "I am a Child of God". In this way not only do I effectively replace my irresponsible thoughts, but I also cause myself to think about all those things that I associate with that song - my mother, grandmother, God, the value of following the teachings of Christ, and the joy that can come from living righteously. In this way, I am reprogramming my mind with the fundamental principles and values I want to instill in myself and my life.

I have also found that by putting a rubber band around my wrist and "snapping" my wrist every time I have an irresponsible thought, or allow myself to act in any way that is not fully in line with my purpose, I can redirect my thinking and reaffirm my desire to change. I can also remember each "snap" more easily at the end of the day when I am doing my personal inventory. Thus, I can more thoroughly examine each of them individually, determine what caused the thought or action to arise, and decide what I can, and should, do differently next time.

Being Proactive

The next step, as we grow and develop in a responsible way of life, is to learn to be proactive and preempt irresponsible and criminal thinking before it ever happens. To do this we must learn to recognize all the situations and environments which may lead to irresponsible thoughts, and then avoid them. We can also prepare ourselves by thinking through difficult situations and deciding beforehand how we plan to think and act if, and when, any of these situations come up.

As criminals, it is easy to recognize that we must avoid all of our old criminal accomplices and past hangouts. But our deterrents should go much further than that. I believe that from the outset we shouldn't watch irresponsible, immoral, or criminal movies, especially if they cause us to think about past crimes, sexual exploits, or irresponsible behavior - or to fantasize about future ones. And if simply passing by a bar or pharmacy causes us to think about doing drugs or partying, we should try our best to avoid all bars and pharmacies.

However, there is a good chance that we will eventually pass by a bar or run into an old irresponsible acquaintance. So, we should adequately prepare ourselves and already know what to think about and how to behave when that happens. By simply using our imagination, our future thoughts, choices, and actions can be evaluated before we are ever confronted with a difficult situation. Without all of the added pressures of the situation, we can better analyze the possible consequences of making the wrong choice. This way we can make a decision based on our goals and purpose instead of fleeting desires or peer pressure. And then, when we are confronted with a difficult choice, we will be better prepared.

Through preparation, we gain more control over our thinking. And when a difficult situation does arise, we can make the right choice instead of simply allowing our old, ineffective subconscious programming to shape and guide our lives. By learning to responsibly replace, anticipate, and preempt irresponsible thoughts and errors in thinking, we can begin the process of reprogramming our subconscious mind. And we can develop a more responsible point of view. We can pull enough of the weeds in order to allow our roses to grow.

Seeking Reality

If we want our change to last, we must do more than simply replace or preempt our errors in thinking with programmed thoughts and affirmations. To fully correct our errors in thinking, we must believe in what we are trying to do. We must actively seek to discover, critically analyze, and fully accept all of the relevant realities which contradict these errors and verify a more responsible way of thinking. Our thinking errors must be replaced with responsible reasoning. Then, we must train ourselves to think of these appropriate realities or correctives, at the right place and the right time, for all the right reasons.

For example, instead of simply thinking about our family, quoting some affirmation, or listing all the deterrents every time we think about getting high on drugs, we should actually believe in what we are trying to do. We should actively seek to discover, understand, and personally acknowledge all the reasons why we shouldn't get high, so that these realities can serve to guide our thoughts in a way that promotes and verifies a responsible way of life.

Trying to overcome an urge to use drugs through willpower alone is not enough. Instead of continuing to think of drugs as enjoyable, exciting, and "not that big of a deal", we should actually seek out and consciously stay aware of all the realities which contradict these errors in thinking. We may begin with the fact that drugs are illegal and thus can cause further legal problems, and the pain and sorrow associated with losing our freedom and being separated from the ones we love. Next, we could acknowledge the fact that drugs are harmful to the body and the mind, and curse everyone who touches them. They:

- diminish our ability to properly focus our conscious awareness
- distort reality
- decrease our productivity
- reduce our coordination
- lead to health problems
- waste money, time and potential
- reduce the amount of control we have over ourselves and our lives
- lower our inhibitions - leading to immorality, irresponsibility, and crime

Finally, as we continue to search reality, we will inevitably realize that not only do we hurt ourselves with drugs, but we also hurt all of those around us, especially the ones we profess to love.

Armed with these newfound realities to consistently correct our thinking, our point of view and attitude towards drugs will soon change. Instead of secretly desiring to use drugs and then, when the thoughts arise, simply trying to fight them through willpower alone, we will begin to abhor drugs and despise even the thought of them. Instead of envying the drug user who isn't being deterred from using drugs, we will pity them. We will begin to think of, and perceive, drugs realistically as the evil they are instead of continuing to be fooled by their charm.

Actually, the correctives to our errors in thinking are simply the same realities which any responsibly mature individual has already recognized and applied to their thoughts, choices and behavior. They are the foundation of all responsible patterns of thinking and decision-making. And yes, they are also the same realities which we had to avoid in order to behave irresponsibly and criminally. For many of us, the problem wasn't so much that we were unable to identify these correctives in reality, but that we failed to make the conscious effort and sacrifice necessary to properly implement them in our thinking and decision-making. We usually avoided these realities, through shut off and erosion, in order to make the easy irresponsible choices even easier.

Over time, we have become habitually accustomed to avoiding them. And we have also become mentally lazy when it comes to thinking responsibly. Thus, it is going to take an enormous amount of personal effort, spiritual guidance, and some outside help, in order for us to consistently stay focused on these correctives so that they become a part of our internal programming. Without consistent mental focus and effort, our thoughts will be habitually relegated to areas outside of our conscious awareness and guided by our defective subconscious programming. In essence, without a consistent effort to change and focus our thinking, we will continue to think, and thus behave, the same way we have in the past.

Again, it is only through the repeated exercise of properly implementing these correctives in our thoughts that we will begin to develop and habituate responsible patterns of thought and behavior. Again, knowledge without implementation is worthless. Simply knowing about these correctives isn't enough. They must become operational in our thinking. Through practice and experience, we must learn to implement these correctives at the right place and the right time for the right reasons. It is worthless to think of all the realities which contradict using drugs when we are confronted with a choice to rob a bank. And it would also be counterproductive to go from one extreme of trusting no one and never fulfilling obligations to the other extreme of uncritically trusting everyone and fulfilling every perceived obligation to the point where they begin to interfere with our responsible development in other areas of our lives. As changing criminals, we must not allow ourselves to simply return to our criminal equivalent pattern of going to extremes, or confusing good intentions with a responsible way of life.

No one on this earth was born totally responsible, knowledgeable, autonomous, and mature. These things must be learned and then developed through practice and experience. And developing these realistic and responsible traits isn't automatic, it represents an achievement. Everyone must struggle through a growth process in order to become more mature. And because we neglected to struggle in our earlier years, our struggle begins now.

<u>Finding Reality</u>

In order to be effective, the correctives to our errors in thinking should be founded on the personal discovery and acceptance of their pragmatic correctness and necessity for the common good of all people. We must actually believe these correctives in order for them to work. It is impossible to sustain the enormous amount of effort and dedication required to truly change ourselves simply because this book, or someone else, told us that our thoughts and perceptions were wrong and needed to be changed. And, we cannot merely assent to the realities of responsible living and then hope for them to become a consistent and lasting guide to our lives. These correctives can only serve to correct our errors in thinking if we truly believe they are correct.

In order for these correctives to be effective, we must critically think about them and analyze their importance and value in our life - and in fulfilling our purpose. And we must also strive to have a complete understanding of how responsible patterns of thought and behavior interrelate among responsible people in society. For example, how we all must depend on others, learn to control our emotions, be honest, and have empathy for others in order to live responsibly and be successful.

In the past, we searched out and selectively paid attentions to those things which supported and served to perpetuate our errors in thinking. We told ourselves that our drug use wasn't that big of a deal. We thought that we wouldn't get caught. That we weren't really hurting anybody. That even though drugs were dangerous, nothing would ever happen to us. Now we must learn to selectively focus our thoughts and perceptions on the correctives to this type of thinking. We should actively seek the realities which serve to verify and support a responsible way of life. We should remind ourselves that drug use is a big deal, and that we are likely to get caught. We should think of all the productive things that we can do instead of getting high. And, we should think of all the consequences of our drug use in the past.

To truly change, we must become open to the responsible realities around us while avoiding all criminal and irresponsible influences. We should focus our perceptions and our attitude so that these realistic correctives can be verified in our thinking. Instead of relying on others to convince us of the truthfulness and accuracy of the principles underlying a responsible way of life, it is up to each one of us to individually convince ourselves. For example, if we hear about someone robbing a bank and getting away with all the money, instead of focusing on the fact that the thief got away with this crime and thus unrealistically verifying that crime pays, we should selectively focus our thinking on the pain and suffering the thief has caused all his victims, as well as the lack of spiritual satisfaction inherent to this criminal way of life, and the inevitable consequences of his continued participation in crime. And instead of always attempting to justify and excuse our "little white lies" or "bending little rules", we must focus our thinking on all the inherent, and potential, undesirable consequences of such choices and behaviors. If nothing else, even if we don't get caught, it is these types of "little" irresponsible behaviors and decisions that eventually grow into larger ones - and can lead to our committing more crime.

Finally, it is impossible for us to uncritically hold onto any thought or perception that is not totally in line with reality and a responsible way of life, and still hope to endure temptations and continuously live responsibly. We must fully correct all of our errors in thinking - pull all of our weeds - before we can ever truly develop responsible patterns of thought and perception. We simply cannot believe deep down inside that we are the victim and everyone is picking on us, and still take responsibility for our life. We can't think that we are special and better than everyone, and still have empathy for others or be able to put ourselves in their shoes. And we can't think that it is really alright to cheat, tell a small lie, or break "little" rules because everyone else does it, and still develop a good reputation with ourselves. Willpower alone is not enough to overcome inconsistencies between our thinking and the realities of a responsible way of life. As a rule, whenever our core beliefs and our willpower are in conflict, our beliefs will always win out. Just like a small drop of water will eventually wear through solid rock, in time our thoughts and desires will wear down our willpower no matter how strong it may be.

Believe

To be successful, I feel that it is important to maintain the mindset that success is possible. We must believe in ourselves. Despair and doubt are the enemies of change. Although we should always remember the shame and suffering which we have caused, we must learn to visualize ourselves as being truly honest and responsible people. We should imagine ourselves changing and maintaining a totally responsible and purposeful way of life each and every day - and then we should persistently struggle towards this goal one step at a time.

Realistically, a responsible and productive life that is totally void of criminal thoughts and behavior is a very achievable goal. However, it will require time, effort, and determination to achieve - and then to maintain. We can change our patterns of thinking and reprogram our subconscious mind if we make the conscious effort to do so, but we must also be aware that this won't happen overnight.

In the past, when we weren't successful as quickly as we thought we should be, we often gave up and regarded the endeavor as impossible. However, in order to change lifelong patterns of thought and behavior, we need to endure and overcome. We must totally eliminate our cowardly pattern of thinking "I can't" when the going gets rough. "I can't" quit using drugs. "I can't" stop hanging around with old criminal and irresponsible associates. "I can't" properly focus my thinking. "I can't" humble myself. "I can't" live responsibly. For us, "I can't" just means we don't want to. It stems from a lack of willingness to exert the effort required to responsibly overcome the obstacles in life - not from a lack of ability. Often, this phrase can become such a habitual cop-out that we say it before we even truly think about the situation or try. As criminals, there actually isn't much that we can't do. And if anyone else ever told us that we couldn't do something, then we would most likely view this as a put-down, and then strive to prove that we could.

Another form of this "I can't" thinking which we must eliminate from the outset is "I need". "I need" a girlfriend! "I need" money! "I need" excitement! "I need" power - drugs – friends! "I need" is basically just another insane excuse for us to give in to our irresponsible and criminal desires, and to give up on our effort to change our irresponsible patterns of thinking and behavior.

Ultimately, any type of "I can't" or "I need" thinking is not in line with our objective of overcoming our errors in thinking and living a consistently responsible way of life. The only thing we truly can't do is live a responsible life, and also seek out the excitement and proof of power which irresponsible thought and action may provide. In order to overcome our errors in thinking and develop responsible patterns of thought, the "I can't" attitude must give way to the mental set of "I can" and "I must". "I can" replace and eliminate my errors in thinking! "I can" properly use the realistic correctives I have discovered in order to responsibly direct my thoughts, choices and behavior! "I can" eliminate these irresponsible and criminal thoughts from my mind! In order to change our old patterns of thought, perception and behavior, we must simply eliminate the excuses, make the effort, and prove to ourselves that we can.

Learning to Think Critically

To help us fully identify and overcome all our errors in thinking, we must learn to think critically. "Thinking is the way we make sense of the world; thinking critically is thinking about our thinking so that we can clarify and improve it."[4]

Learning to think critically will be very difficult for us. We are not in the habit of focusing on our thinking. In fact, our tendency is to shut off important realities in our thinking, and to avoid the awareness of our own faults and imperfections. As active criminals, our thoughts were the enemy. We lived life in a daze. If we had really been thinking, we probably wouldn't have done most of the irresponsible and criminal things that we have done. But, with some effort, we <u>can</u> overcome our habits and learn to think critically.

In order to develop our ability to think critically, we must first learn to consistently pay attention to what we are thinking. One of the ways that we can start doing this is by keeping a journal. In our journal, we should write about everything from our thoughts and goals to our concerns and fears. We should record all of our successes and examine our failures. We should practice being honest and open with ourselves by listing our imperfections and areas where we need to grow. We should keep track of our thinking and write down things such as whether or not our thoughts were in line with our purpose. Were they productive or unproductive throughout the day? Were we able to overcome any irresponsible thoughts?

---

4   Chaffee, John, "THINKING CRITICALLY: 4TH EDITION" (Boston: Houghton Mifflin Company, 1994) pp.51

Did we make progress in our choice to think responsibly?

We should also pay attention to the correlation between our thoughts and feelings. For this, it can be very helpful to write down what feelings certain thoughts provoked, as well as what thoughts certain feelings provoked.

Most importantly, we should make note of any particularly responsible or irresponsible thoughts, or series of thoughts, we had throughout the day. For any irresponsible thought or error in thinking, we should analyze:

- the circumstances and feelings which led to the thought
- the consequences of the thought
- our thoughts about the thought
- the appropriate "correctives" and "deterrents" to this type of thinking.
- as many alternative perspectives and responsible ways of thinking as we can imagine

For example, one day I felt put down and got angry because I thought that someone was disrespecting me. I even had thoughts of getting even by assaulting this person because they were always being so obnoxious. I had struck out in a softball game and he was laughing at me, making fun of me. I felt like a loser and thought that everyone else viewed me this way. I thought that there was no way I should ever strike out – I was better than everyone else. Worst of all, I imagined that I would never live it down. In my journal, I started by writing all of this down and analyzing what had happened. Then I identified my errors in thinking:

- Thinking that I should be perfect and never strike out
- Thinking that I was a loser just for striking out
- Thinking that everyone else viewed me as a loser
- Thinking that this self-image would never end
- Not viewing my strikeout conceptually (I had also scored two runs and made several great defensive plays in the game - and we ended up winning the game)

- Thinking of getting even through criminal means
- Not putting myself in other people's shoes
- Thinking that I was better than everyone else

Next, I wrote down all of the correctives to these errors in thinking that I could come up with. Correctives such as:

- I can't always be perfect; even professionals strike out.
- I must be weary of my sense of perfectionism.
- I am not a loser just because I struck out. In fact, I am actually pretty good at softball.
- I can't allow one isolated incident to have such a dramatic effect on my self-esteem and self-image – nobody will even remember it in a week.
- Thinking about assaulting someone isn't going to help anything, and isn't in line with my purpose and my goals in life.
- Thinking about assaulting someone is simply a reflection of my past pattern of criminal thinking and behavior.
- Because criminal thoughts lead to criminal actions, this type of thinking is very dangerous.
- Assaulting someone is a crime.
- I am not better than everyone. Actually, there are a lot of people better at softball than I am. But this isn't important. What is important is that I do my best and live a purposeful and productive life.
- If I allow myself to feel put down, get angry, or try to 'get even', I risk the chance of putting myself in a position to lose everything I have worked to responsibly gain.

Then, I listed more responsible thoughts I could have had when the incident occurred. I wrote things such as:

- Nobody was laughing at me – they were laughing with me. It was really was kind of funny.
- I should get out and practice my batting a little more if it is

so important to me that it makes me feel that bad when I strike out.

- Playing softball is supposed to be fun. I shouldn't allow anyone or anything to make me feel put down or angry and ruin my day, especially when the whole purpose behind my activity is to relax and enjoy myself.
- I have actually been doing pretty well this game.
- I will do better next time.
- Okay, so I hit like a little girl. Striking out isn't the end of the world.

Keeping a detailed journal of our thoughts on a daily basis is also a kind of psychological discipline. It is a spiritual practice that will, in time, help us to:

- enhance our personal awareness and insight
- overcome our errors in thinking
- develop emotional intelligence
- gain empathy for others
- bring a responsible routine and consistency to our lives
- develop more realistic and responsible perceptions
- change the way we think and talk to ourselves
- develop a better reputation with ourselves
- Identify criminal equivalent behavior

To truly recognize criminal equivalent behavior, we must first analyze our inner thoughts and motives. If our motives are wrong, then any behavior which they cause cannot be right. Even things such as helping the sick, feeding the poor, or being kind to our neighbor become vile and tainted when they are done for selfish purposes or ulterior motives. And, as changing criminals, we must be very careful when it comes to criminal equivalent behavior. Any behavior that is motivated primarily by a desire to impress others, boost our self-image, or prove ourselves has the potential to lead to irresponsible thoughts and behavior, and a return to crime.

As we gain a better awareness of our thoughts, it is also important that we learn to recognize all the different influences on our thinking. Our experience of the world is presented to us through our senses - sight, sound, smell, touch, and taste. However, our perceptions of these senses can vary significantly depending on what we consciously, or habitually (through our subconscious programming), decide to pay attention to. The circumstances, our beliefs, our values, and even our habitual errors in thinking and perception can all play a role in influencing our patterns of thought. So, it is important that we stay aware of both our thoughts and all the influences on our thinking. As I have said before, only when we learn to control our thinking can we gain control over the other aspects of our lives. And we can only truly learn to control our thinking when we become consciously aware of how our errors in thinking and perception can distort reality, and better understand how and why we made the decisions we did and how we can keep this from ever happening again.

Identifying the Errors

In order to get the most benefit out of keeping a journal, we should review our journal daily with our responsible guide. With the help of our responsible guide we can learn to identify errors in thinking and perception, and criminal equivalent behaviors, as they manifest themselves. Only by learning to fully recognize our errors in thinking can we effectively implement the correctives needed to overcome them.

When learning to identify our errors in thinking, it is helpful to understand that the same error in thinking can arise in many different situations and a variety of contexts. Additionally, one irresponsible thought, choice, or behavior can also be the result of a combination of many different errors. For example, not mowing the lawn or doing the dishes when it is our turn, not being on time for an appointment and speeding in our car, are all a manifestation of our failure to fulfill obligations. But, speeding is also the manifestation of many other errors in thinking, such as:

- our tendency to seek excitement (by going fast)
- a proof of power (by going faster than others)
- viewing ourselves as special and superior to others (the laws don't apply to us)
- magical thinking (in that we truly believe we won't get caught, or get into an accident)
- a lack of conceptual thinking (we fail to see the relationship between allowing ourselves speed and our tendency to always "bend the rules")
- shut-off and erosion (as changing criminals any time we allow ourselves to break any rule we must first consciously avoid the potential consequences)

As we write in our journal, we should also try to conceptualize our actions and thinking patterns. This means learning to use concrete thoughts and experiences in order to extract principles which relate to, and can be utilized in, other areas of our lives.

With the help of our responsible guide, we should work to develop our ability to conceptualize our thoughts and experiences. We must learn that there really isn't much difference between stealing a car and "borrowing" a pen from work with no intention of returning it. There also isn't much difference between wanting to be in control and proving ourselves when we are committing a crime, and always wanting to be in control and prove ourselves when we are playing basketball or developing relationships with others. And, conceptually, there isn't much difference between excusing the fact that we are breaking the law by littering or jaywalking than for us to excuse and justify the fact that we are breaking the law by committing an armed robbery. Ultimately, for us to truly live responsibly, it is these types of concepts, and the principles we derive from them, which must serve to direct our thinking, fortify our choices, and guide our lives.

As active criminals, our view of living responsibly had nothing to do with consistently thinking responsibly. It was based on misconceptions, concrete behaviors, and isolated thoughts and choices which we considered responsible. We couldn't be punished for our thoughts, so we believed any thought we had, no matter how irresponsible or criminal, was alright. However, in order to ever learn to live responsibly, we must learn to conceptualize our thinking. In the past our errors in thinking often combined to form a criminal perspective on life. Similarly, responsible thoughts and thought patterns are interrelated, and must be completely implemented and integrated in order to form a responsible perspective on life. So, if we truly want to change ourselves and live a consistently responsible way of life, we must think and act responsibly in all aspects of our lives.

We must always be wary of our inability to conceptualize and not allow ourselves to become so focused on one aspect of our lives that we default on other aspects. We can't become selectively responsible, or only struggle to grow and develop in certain areas of our lives. For us it is all or nothing. Because of the way we are, we can't just walk the line between being responsible and being irresponsible. We must always be moving forward in our lives or we will undoubtedly regress.

Asking Questions

Another important step in learning to think more responsibly is to develop our ability to ask questions about our own thinking and the thinking of others. "The ability to ask appropriate and penetrating questions is one of the most powerful thinking tools we possess, although many of us do not make full use of it."[5]

Through consistent practice and mental exercise, we should learn to habitually ask ourselves questions, such as:

- Are my thoughts consistent with my purpose?
- Are they realistic?
- Are they productive?
- What are the possible consequences of this type of thinking?

5

- What is the basis for my thoughts - what provoked my current thinking?
- Am I actively controlling my own thoughts? Or, am I still allowing other variables, such as my feelings, my subconscious programming, the circumstances, or other people's words and behavior, to control them?
- Are there any similarities or relationships between my current thinking and my thought patterns in the past?
- Can I speculate on the possible consequences of this type of thinking?
- How should I be directing my thinking - what should I be thinking about or focusing on right now in order to be successful?

In order to become effective in improving our thought processes, this type of mental questioning should be consistently exercised and valued as a discipline. It should be used repeatedly so that it becomes a habitual part of our thought patterns. At every opportunity we should question ourselves about our thinking with an open mind and an honest heart, so that we can make sure that our thoughts are always focused in the right direction.

In order to clarify our understanding of the differences between responsible and irresponsible thinking patterns, we should also ask our responsible guide about their thoughts in different situations, and then compare these thoughts and thought patterns with our own. Whenever we have the opportunity, we should ask them questions, such as:

- What do you think about what just happened, and what were you thinking when it happened?" (during a specific incident)
- What kind of thoughts pass through your mind in your spare time?
- What are the majority of your thoughts about?
- What would your thinking be if you were confronted with... (Any type of difficult decision)?

Then, in order to fortify these responsible concepts, ideas, and thought patterns in our own mind, we must openly and honestly discuss our own thinking and thought patterns in the same situations.

It is very important that we always maintain an honest and open channel of communication with our responsible guide. This is the only way that we can gain from their valuable knowledge, experience and insight. They have been living responsibly, so they are bound to have a more responsible and realistic perspective of the world around us.

By comparing and contrasting our own thoughts with those of our responsible guide, and with the fundamental principles and ideas which can be found in books such the Bible and the books in the suggested readings section, we can learn to develop the thought patterns necessary to be successful. It can also be helpful to compare and contrast our new thinking patterns, as they develop, with our old criminal patterns of thought and perception. Some may believe that future happiness requires us to forget the past. That the only way we can move forward in our lives is to put our past behind us and totally forget about who we once were. However, this type of perspective is selfish and dangerous. To forget our past can only lead to complacency in our struggle to live responsibly.

This does not mean that we should live in the past, or not forgive ourselves and look towards a responsible future, but only that we must always be consciously aware of where we came from, if only to keep us focused on where we are going and remind us of how far we have come. The purpose of exploring past experiences is not to affix blame for present situations or to provide excuses. It is simply intended to enable us to better understand ourselves, conceptually learn from our past mistakes, and to consistently give our change a responsible meaning and direction.

The practice of reflecting on our past experiences, conceptually learning from them and then applying these lessons to future thoughts, choices, and actions is an integral part of developing a more responsible and realistic pattern of thinking. As with our present thoughts, when exploring our past thoughts and behaviors, we should ask ourselves penetrating questions. Questions such as:

- Why did I do what I did?
- What were the excuses and justifications that I gave myself?
- What should I have been thinking of?
- What were the consequences of my thoughts?
- What were my patterns of thought?
- What did I think about myself?
- What did I think about others?
- Was there anything important that I shut off or chose not to think about?
- Was there anything I pretended not to see or know?
- Were there questions I should have asked myself but brushed aside?
- Any issues which needed to be confronted but weren't?
- What were my errors in thinking?
- Did these thoughts cause the consequences I wanted in my life?
- What should I think or do if a situation like this ever happens again?
- What can I do to make sure that it never happens again?

We should also discuss these questions with our responsible guide, pay attention to the lessons we can learn, and then properly focus on allowing these lessons to guide our lives. In developing our new patterns of thinking, this experience can be an awesome guide and extremely valuable in our struggle to change. Experience can give us direction and help stabilize our lives.

By learning to compare our thoughts and perspectives with others, discussing our own thoughts and ideas in an organized way and carefully exploring our thinking with questions, we will enable ourselves to identify and correct our broader errors in thinking and perception. We will also learn what it takes to think responsibly. And through the conscious exercise of comparing our thoughts and perspectives with others, we will gain more control over our thinking, and our lives.

Our Motives

When analyzing our thinking and behavior, it is very important to pay attention to our intentions and motives. The reasons for our thoughts and behavior can be more important than the consequences of the behavior. We shouldn't ever allow ourselves to judge our thinking based on the outcome of our behavior. By doing this, we may simply be concealing latent errors in our thinking and perception through justifications.

For example, if we decide to lie and call in sick to work because we would rather do something else more exciting, and then during our day off we discover that we have many productive things to do, we cannot excuse or justify our decision to call in sick to work simply because the day ended up being productive. In order to truly recognize and overcome our errors in thinking, we must analyze, question, and correct the thoughts that gave rise to our decision to call in sick. In this case, the decision was full of errors in thinking and perception, such as:

- failure to fulfill obligations to our employer
- failure to exert effort in responsible initiatives
- unwillingness to overcome boredom and routine
- seeking excitement
- inability to delay gratification until the weekend

Additionally, the decision was dangerous because it could have led to idle time and complacency, two things that have the potential to result in irresponsible behavior and crime.

Irresponsible thoughts and behaviors can often result in desirable consequences and, if we are lucky, few negative consequences. However, this doesn't mean that these thoughts and behaviors are proper, realistic or responsible. When we think and behave irresponsibly, we are not consciously causing the consequences we want in life. We are shooting blindly and hoping we hit the target, and eventually we are going to miss - big time. n the other hand, responsible thoughts and their resultant behaviors can easily bring unintended or unforeseen consequences. But this, too, doesn't change the fact that the thought itself was responsibly directed towards our purpose. And even though we may miss our target from time to time, when our thoughts are properly focused, we are more likely to cause the consequences we want in our life.

Responsible Decision-making

Responsible decision-making is a process, a process based on responsible thinking. In the past, we usually approached our decisions irresponsibly with concrete thinking, tubular vision, selfish objectives, prejudices, and pretentious assumptions. Our choices themselves were often based more on our feelings and misguided perceptions than on reason and intellect. Experience, knowledge, possible consequences, and moral considerations were conveniently eliminated from our thinking in order to enable us to do whatever we felt like doing at any given moment.

Many of us will have to begin from scratch in developing a responsible decision-making process. Not only will we need to fully eliminate our errors in thinking, but we must also learn to implement all the human abilities which enable us to choose correctly. Instead of avoiding the facts, we must seek reality. Instead of making assumptions, we must ask questions. Instead of living for today, we must think of the future and the consequences of our actions. For us, it is always better to make a late decision after a thorough review of all the facts than to make a hasty decision. Hasty decisions will almost always be based more on our feelings and our ineffective subconscious programming than on a responsible decision-making process. Finally, we have to learn to consistently live with the open-mindedness, self-awareness, and responsible focus, which enables us to learn from our mistakes and to use this knowledge in future decisions.

From the outset, it can be very helpful to identify all the steps involved in making a responsible decision. This way it will be easier to implement this process at the moment of choice. In order to simplify the process of responsible decision-making, I have broken it down into five steps:

1) Focus
2) Fact-find
3) Analyze
4) Implement
5) Review

The first step in responsible decision-making is to properly focus our conscious awareness. We should focus not only on all the relevant realities and circumstances surrounding our decision, but also on the fact that, no matter what, we always <u>do</u> have a choice. And that it is the choice we make right now which will inevitably decide the direction and momentum of our life. We create our life every day through the decisions we make. But if we don't recognize that we do have a choice, then we are more likely to allow our decisions to continue to be directed by our old ineffective subconscious programming.

The next step in responsible decision-making is fact-finding. This includes making a preliminary analysis of the situation. To make the best decision possible, we should seek out all the relevant facts by asking questions and actively searching for information in all the appropriate places. We should also conceptualize our past experiences and determine whether we have already encountered a similar decision in the past that could help guide our current choice. For example, if we were faced with the decision to buy a used car, we should:

- honestly question the necessity of buying a car in order to make sure that it isn't simply a criminal equivalent desire or founded on errors in thinking
- examine all of our past experiences with cars and our present desires (make, model, color, etc.) in order to guide our decision
- shop around to compare prices
- ask questions of people who are more knowledgeable about used cars than us
- refer to the blue book in order to determine average prices

- have any car we are considering buying examined by an experienced auto mechanic.

For us, asking the appropriate questions may not always be easy. But it is extremely important that we do ask questions because, realistically, we are not very experienced when it comes to making responsible decisions. Asking questions doesn't show ignorance or a lack of intelligence, but instead it indicates a true desire to seek reality and make a responsible decision. Without questions, we can never get the answers. It is also important to remember that all information requires verification. We must never allow ourselves to be gullible and simply take things at face value as we have done before. This doesn't result in responsible decisions, only foolish ones.

The third step to making a responsible decision is to analyze the decision by considering all our options. We should weigh each option against our purpose, our goals, and our priorities. Then we should use our imagination to anticipate the possible consequences of each option. Our goal is to learn to make responsible decisions, which are guided by a clear understanding of our purpose and our desired destination. It is important for us to know where we want to go with our decision so that we can realistically assess where we are, how far we have come, and how far we still need to go.

We must also analyze our decisions in order to identify their base influence or motivation. Responsible choices should be based solely on reality and our purpose, and motivated by responsible goals and objectives, not by a desire for power, a desire for excitement, a desire to prove ourselves, or for any other criminal equivalent purpose. We should also always think win/win when considering our options. We should strive to make choices and decisions in which everybody benefits.

In the past, our victories often came at the expense of others. And because we felt that we were superior to others, we didn't really care what happened to them as long as we came out ahead. Now, however, our decisions must be filled with empathy and our victories should be tied to the victories of others. For us, it is better to capitulate and let others win than to continue with our past patterns of behavior. Realistically, gains made at the expense of others are actually losses when it comes to our responsible growth and spiritual development.

When weighing the potential consequences of each option, it is important that we also try to anticipate any unexpected results or problems which may require even more decisions. We must always follow the rule that if anything can possibly go wrong, it will. Ultimately, if we learn to always anticipate the worst possible consequences of our decisions, then we are less likely to make irresponsible decisions in the first place.

The next step in responsible decision-making is to implement our decision regardless of any fears or lame excuses (criminal errors in thinking) that we may come up with. Personally, I have found that this is the most difficult part of the decision-making process. Although I often knew what the appropriate and responsible choice should be, I came up with many excuses not to implement it. I didn't want others to view me as a nerd or a geek, or think that I was scared. I didn't want to lose the respect of others. I didn't have time. I couldn't make it work.

I have been confronted with a lot of difficult decisions during my struggle to live responsibly. One decision stands out in my mind. I had proposed starting a Fantasy Football League to the recreation department at the facility where I was incarcerated with the intentions of providing an entertaining activity that could help pass the time for myself and other inmates. When the idea was shot down by the recreation department, I decided to take matters into my own hands. I wrote a spreadsheet program on the computer in order to keep track of all the statistics and team standings in the league and then, with the help of another inmate, formulated the rules for the league, which included paying an "activation fee" with "prizes" going to the winning teams each week. I had just recently made the commitment to do anything that was necessary in order to change, so I was relatively new to thinking and living responsibly. Once we started the league, however, I began to conceptually realize that the activation fee and weekly prizes were simply a form of gambling (which was against prison rules). I also recognized that by starting the league and being commissioner with the final say over all disputes, I was simply continuing with my past patterns of always wanting to be in control. After some further thought I identified many other errors in thinking, including:

- a failure to fact-find and follow a responsible decision-making process before I started the league
- a thirst for excitement
- a failure to conceptualize that not only was this league against the rules in prison, but it was also against the law and much like running a numbers racket or participating in illegal gambling on the streets
- a failure to be completely open and honest with my responsible guide. Although I had told my guide about the league, I had left out key information which would have dramatically altered their perspective of my actions, and their advice.

Yet, even after I had begun to recognize all these errors in thinking, I still didn't want to make the right choice and stop the league. Not only was the league exciting and fun, but I also didn't want the other participants in the league to get angry at me for quitting the league which I started, or to think that I was a quitter, a punk, or scared. So, I used every excuse and justification I could come up with in order to rationalize my irresponsible decision to continue in the league and not implement the responsible decision to quit. I told myself that because I had founded the league, I had an obligation to finish what I had started (however, as my responsible guide later pointed out, we can never be obligated to irresponsible behavior). I convinced myself that it wasn't really that big of a deal (until my responsible guide helped me to recognize how much trouble I could possibly get into if I was caught). I told myself that I had already made the irresponsible choice and that continued participation in the league was simply a continuation or consequence of this initial choice. I even convinced myself that I didn't have any further choice. I failed to recognize the fact that with each passing moment we are given the opportunity for a new choice - to behave responsibly or to continue behaving irresponsibly.

With the help of my excuses, I continued to run the league for several weeks after I had already recognized that doing so was irresponsible. I knew that I wasn't consciously causing the consequences I wanted in my life, and that the responsible decision would probably be to simply quit the league. But, I really enjoyed playing fantasy football. Although I avoided thinking about it as much as possible, something inside of me kept telling me that I wasn't doing the right thing. If I truly wanted to change myself and was sincere about my commitment to live responsibly, I needed to discuss this problem with my responsible guide, and then make the right decision, no matter how hard it may be.

In the end, I chose to make the right decision. I honestly discussed the issue with my responsible guide, and with her support and guidance, I was able to implement the responsible choice and quit the league. Many of the other inmates involved in the league were upset. But as my responsible guide reminded me, I wasn't there to impress them any way.

I would love to say that since then I have never had a problem implementing a responsible decision, but that would be a lie. The implementing part is still the hardest for me. However, I have learned that when the time comes to implement a responsible decision, it is helpful to focus solely on implementing it, and then shut-off any fears or excuses—much like we used to focus our thinking solely on our irresponsible and criminal objectives so that we couldn't be swayed from our decisions by fear, possible consequences, moral considerations, or anything else.

Making the right choice isn't always easy, but it is necessary if we truly want to avoid returning to our old way of life. Realistically, not implementing a responsible choice renders the whole decision-making process worthless. In fact, not implementing a responsible choice once it has been made is even worse than not going through the process of making a responsible choice in the first place. This is because it requires us to shut off the awareness of truth and reality, perpetuates our habitual lack of effort, and promotes doubt in our ability to responsibly control and direct our own lives.

Finally, even though responsible thinking patterns and decision-making will never lead to irresponsible choices, they may lead to unintended consequences. Thus, the process of decision-making is not over once the decision has been made. After we have implemented our choice, we should always review our decision and the decision-making process. We should analyze the outcome of our decision to confirm that it has led us in the right direction and make sure that we made no errors in the decision-making process. Then we should review our decision and its consequences in an attempt to uncover any conceptual lessons that can be added to our experience, and help us make more responsible decisions in the future.

Only through practice and experience can we truly enhance our ability to make decisions in a way which causes the consequences we want in life. This experience may come through personal lessons of cause and consequence, or vicariously through an examination of the consequences which result from the behavior of others. The important thing, however, is that this experience, once gained, becomes operational in our decision-making process. If we don't make the conscious effort to repetitiously analyze our decisions and the decisions of others, then these valuable experiences are likely to continue to get shut-off when they are needed the most, just like they have in the past.

Once we fully understand the decision-making process, we must learn, through practice, to implement it at the right time and the right place for the right reasons. In his book *The Seven Habits of Highly Effective People*, Stephen R. Covey illustrates that there is always a moment in time between a stimulus and our chosen response. There is a gap in time, no matter how small or unproductive we may allow it to be, between the moment when we are faced with a decision and the moment when we implement our choice. And, for us, the key to personal growth, happiness and success lies in properly using this moment to make the right decision. If we don't use this gap properly, then we are destined to be guided by our old ineffective subconscious programming, and we will continue to make decisions the same way we always have. But if we can learn to use this moment in time effectively, then we will empower ourselves to move forward and responsibly create the circumstances and consequences we want in our lives. [5]

Decisions, Decisions...

Although it is important that every decision we make is based on a responsible pattern of thinking, not every decision requires the same degree of time, focus and preparation. A decision on whether to have a hamburger or pizza for lunch will not require the same amount of fact-finding, analysis, and responsible reasoning as say a decision on whether or not to buy a house or go to a party. As we gain experience and grow in a responsible way of life, and begin to replace our errors in thinking with new patterns of thought, we will become more proficient in making responsible decisions. We will begin to understand when, and to what degree, to implement the decision-making process in order to efficiently and effectively make the appropriate decision.

At first, however, as we are just learning how to make consistently responsible decisions, we cannot simply decide for ourselves which decisions are important and which ones aren't. We are handicapped when it comes to making responsible decisions because of our habitual errors in thinking and perception. So, we are not yet capable of determining to what degree we should implement the decision-making process. Therefore, we should struggle to implement the whole process for every decision. Every choice, no matter how small or menial we may think it is, should be consciously focused on, questioned, analyzed, discussed with our responsible guide, implemented, and then examined once it has been made.

The problem is that because of our errors in thinking and perception, we are unable to truly recognize the patterns behind our

5   Covey, Stephen R., "THE 7 HABITS OF HIGHLY EFFECTIVE PEOPLE - POWERFUL LESSONS IN PERSONAL CHANGE" (New York: Simon & Schuster, 1989)

decision-making and the subtle consequences of our choices. For example, we may not view a decision to carelessly spend $10.00 on something we don't really need as being that big of a deal, because we fail to realize that the <u>pattern</u> of irresponsibly spending $10.00 is just the same as our old criminal pattern of frivolously spending $1,000.00 on something we don't really need. And although we truly don't intend to drink any alcohol, we may irresponsibly choose to go out to a restaurant and bar with our buddies after work, because we don't think that it is that big of a deal. We may consciously avoid our basic motivation of simply seeking excitement and not fully realize the potential consequences putting ourselves in this type of situation. Again, as we are struggling to change, we do not yet have the ability to truly decide what is important and what isn't. We simply do not have the experience necessary to consistently make responsible decisions, so we must always be completely honest and open with our responsible guide, and allow them to help and guide us in our decision-making. This may mean using our "moment in time" to talk to them before we make a decision.

At the beginning of our change process, we will undoubtedly continue to make hasty decisions full of errors and mistakes. We will not become perfect overnight. Many of our decisions will still be influenced by our errors in thinking and perception, and subconsciously directed by our old programming. Only after the decision has already been made, and we have properly analyzed it and discussed it with our responsible guide, will we be able to understand the problems with our decision and recognize the errors in thinking and perception that gave rise to it.

For example, while I was incarcerated I often decided to bend the rules when I was still hungry and go through the chow line twice in order to get extra food. Once I decided to change my life, I quit going through the line more than once, because I was intent on following all the rules and I had begun to conceptually realize that getting extra food in this way was just like stealing. However, I continued asking my "bro's" who were serving the food to fix me up and give me extra portions. In my mind, I thought that because I wasn't really breaking the rules that this was alright. I convinced myself that I was simply realizing my objective and getting extra food through another more responsible means. It wasn't until later, after I had started learning to properly analyze my decisions, that I realized asking to get fixed up was also the same as stealing in that I was asking my "bro's" to steal for me. It was the manifestation of many different errors in thinking including:

- thinking that I was unique and superior to others (that I should get special privileges and get more food than everyone else just because I was special)
- lack of empathy for others (if I was still hungry then others were too, yet they weren't all getting extra food)
- inability to understand the possible consequences (if I get extra food, then they could run out of food and someone else may have to go without)
- inability to conceptualize (that this was just like stealing)
- and a lack of responsible initiative (I could have made the administration aware of the fact that I felt I wasn't getting fed enough, bought a little extra canteen to help augment the portion size, or gotten a job in the kitchen where I could have eaten more).

Making the Most of our Opportunities

Once we recognize our mistakes, we must struggle to never again allow ourselves to do the same thing, or anything like it, again. Learning from our experiences is an essential part of the growth process. We are all going to make mistakes as we struggle to responsibly move forward in life. However, if used properly, our mistakes can actually become an opportunity for growth. In fact, we can often learn more from our mistakes and failures than we can from our successes. It is only when these mistakes and failures are excused or shut off, and not used as a guide for future choices, that they become useless, and even detrimental.

When we choose not to correct and learn from our mistakes, they gain power over us. They serve to perpetuate self-deception, and damage any trust or confidence we may have in ourselves. Thus, we compound our mistake with another even more damaging mistake and cause even deeper injury to ourselves. So, we must struggle to make sure that all the lessons we learn become operational in our decision-making process. If we don't, then we risk the chance of forgetting about them and making the same mistake again. Even little slip-ups or misunderstandings cannot be overlooked, excused or tolerated. For us, making a little mistake isn't so much the issue. Instead, it is our past pattern of making exceptions and excuses for our mistakes, failing to learn from them, and continually allowing one mistake or slip-up to lead to another, and another, and another.

In the end, the only way we can truly overcome our mistakes, correct our errors in thinking, reprogram our mind, and develop responsible patterns of thinking and decision-making is by actually **doing** these things. It is in the conscious struggle to learn from our experiences and make the correct choices, and through the effort and sacrifice necessary to implement these choices, that we are given the opportunity to grow and develop. Good thoughts, choices, and habits can only be developed and fortified in the same way that we developed and fortified our irresponsible thoughts and habits - through repetition. Thus, in order to grow, we must take action. We must implement all the lessons we learn and struggle to overcome all the habitual remnants of our past way of life. Our opportunities lie in the way we confront our difficult choices, bear our burdens, and struggle to transcend the habitual responses of our defective subconscious programming. Ultimately, it is this joyous challenge - the struggle to responsibly think, make decisions, achieve, and move forward in our lives - that will become the essence and reward of a responsible way of life.

CHAPTER 9

Consciously Seeking a Realistic Perspective

T hroughout our lives we have chosen to view ourselves and the world around us from a distorted, unrealistic point of view - a point of view which played a fundamental role in the way we lived our lives. Instead of consistently seeking the awareness of reality, we avoided it. We chose to focus on those things that allowed us to pursue and achieve our criminal objectives, and avoided the awareness of any deterrents. Now, we must learn to focus our conscious awareness more realistically. We must develop a new perspective on life - a perspective that is guided by fundamental truths and principles instead of unrealistic thoughts and beliefs.

What we see and do not see in life depends primarily on our point of view. And, our point of view depends largely on our programmed paradigms, or the "interpretations, evaluations, conclusions, or predictions about the world which we endorse as true."[1] In turn, it is these paradigms that, by helping us to interpret incoming sensory information, are the main tools we use to make sense of the world. They intrinsically guide our thoughts, perceptions and behavior. So, our point of view depends a lot on our internal explanation of reality.

However, because of our lifelong errors in thought and perception, these paradigms, or internal maps, are skewed. They are wrong. Thus, they serve to distort and misdirect our perceptions, and inevitably our thinking and behavior, by erroneously shaping how we interpret reality. For example, if we have never really tried to succeed by being honest and living with integrity, then it doesn't make sense that others could actually succeed in this manner.

---

1   Chaffee, John, "THINKING CRITICALLY: 4TH EDITION" (Boston: Houghton Mifflin Company, 1994) pp.205

Thus, we often don't see those who are successful as being honest and virtuous. Instead, we usually perceive them as being people who bend the rules and have achieved much of their success by underhanded means. As unique and superior individuals who are supposed to be perfect, it also doesn't make sense that we could fail or make a mistake. Therefore, when this happens, we actually perceive it as being someone, or something, else's fault. And as egocentric individuals who think that the world revolves around us, it doesn't make sense that things won't always go just the way we want them to. So when things don't go our way or go as planned, we take it personally, feel picked on, and perceive it as a put-down.

On a very basic level, the way we make sense of reality is wrong. So, no matter how hard we try, we will never be able to truly change until we correct these maps so that they can lead us in the right direction. No matter how far we may seem to progress, without the proper paradigms to guide our perceptions, we will still be misguided and subject to return to our past way of life. As Stephen R. Covey writes, "To try to change outward attitudes and behaviors does very little good in the long run if we fail to examine the basic paradigms from which those attitudes and behaviors flow". [2]

For example, it is much easier to eliminate drugs and alcohol from our lives if instead of simply staying away from them, we develop paradigms (thoughts, beliefs and attitudes) that oppose their use. And if it truly makes sense to us that we are special and better than others, then we are unlikely to ever have empathy or ask for the help that we need. By distorting our perceptions, any unrealistic paradigms will eventually get in the way of our progress. We could spend years trying to change our erroneous thoughts, attitudes and behavior externally through programs, education and sheer willpower, and not begin to approach the magnitude of change that occurs spontaneously when we simply begin to see things from a different point of view.

Ultimately, we can, and must, alter our own point of view

---

2   Covey, Stephen R., "THE 7 HABITS OF HIGHLY EFFECTIVE PEOPLE - POWERFUL LESSONS IN PERSONAL CHANGE" (New York: Simon & Schuster, 1989) pp.28

through effort, practice and experience. By learning to live consciously and properly focusing our awareness on the right thing at the right time for the right reason, we can develop a more realistic and purposeful interpretation of life.

Correcting the Errors

Because of the reciprocal nature of our thoughts and perceptions, a fundamental shift in either one can lead to tremendous change. By actively seeking reality and focusing on those things that contradict our errors in thinking, not only can we correct our errors in perception, but also the paradigms which influence how we make sense of these perceptions. In turn, developing more realistic perceptions will help us to correct our errors in thinking. Thus, a very basic shift in our thinking can have a dramatic influence on our whole outlook on life. And much of the time it isn't so much what we are looking at, but how we are looking at it that counts.

To correct our errors in perception, we should first learn to critically examine our perceptions at all times, much like we do with our errors in thinking. In order to do this, we should begin by becoming fully aware of our perceptions and how they can be distorted by our errors in thinking and unrealistic paradigms. We should always be consciously aware of our potential errors in thinking and perception. And, we should remember that the way we see things isn't the only way to see them. We must be willing to accept the fact that because of who we are, our perceptions and our interpretation of these perceptions are often likely to be distorted. "As long as we believe that the way we see things is the only way to see them, we will be unable to recognize when our perceptions are distorted or inaccurate."[3] Thus, we will be unable to correct them, and unable to grow.

As with our errors in thinking, we must always maintain a wide-open channel of communication when it comes to our perceptions. We should always be totally honest and open about our own

---

3   Chaffee, John, "THINKING CRITICALLY: 4TH EDITION" (Boston: Houghton Mifflin Company, 1994) pp.190

point of view so that our responsible guide can help us identify and correct any unrealistic paradigms or errors in thinking, and perception that may not be evident to us. Not only should we always verify our own perceptions by actively seeking other people's points of view, but we should also evaluate these different perspectives and balance them with our own point of view. This way we can identify anything that could be used to improve our own perspective and correct any of our unrealistic paradigms or errors in thinking.

Living Consciously

In order to overcome our habitual tendency to shut off important realities and gain the most realistic point of view possible, we must learn to always live consciously. "Living consciously implies respect for the facts of reality. This means the facts of our inner world as well as of the outer world."[4] When we live consciously, we do not always have to like what we see. In fact, not liking what we see can give us the primary motivation necessary to change. To live consciously we must only recognize that what is, is, and what is not, is not. Our first loyalty must be to the truth and reality, not simply making ourselves right through the self-deception of justifications and excuses.

By living consciously we can learn how our thoughts, feelings, beliefs, and subconscious programs influence our perceptions and distort our point of view. This way we don't allow ourselves to confuse reality with our own subjectivity. We overcome our childish idea that we are at the center of the universe and that everything revolves around us. And we realize that although we interpret our perceptions of reality in a way that makes sense to us, not everybody makes sense of things in the same way we do. Thus, we don't imagine that the way we perceive things is always the right way, the only way, or fully based on the truth and reality.

Living consciously not only means staying focused on the right

---

4   Branden, Nathaniel, "THE SIX PILLARS OF SELF-ESTEEM" (New York: Bantam Books, 1994) pp.71

thing at the right time for the right reasons, but it also entails being committed to actively seeking reality, and then behaving in accordance with this reality. When we live consciously, we move forward rather than retreat from life.

Living consciously, however, isn't easy - especially when we are unaccustomed to it. It will require us to overcome our habitual tendencies of shut off and erosion, as well as the stagnation and atrophy of desire, which can result from an unwillingness to sustain the effort required to live consciously. Instead of simply avoiding the undesirable facts of reality as we did in the past, we will have to:

- face our fears
- analyze potential consequences
- confront painful emotions
- accept our faults and imperfections
- take full responsibility for our lives (past and present)
- and recognize the awful truth about ourselves

Instead of allowing ourselves to continue to effortlessly drift through life in a mental fog, we must work hard to clear our vision, be guided by reality, and be directed by our purpose.

Living consciously won't be easy, but with courage and effort it is possible. Like any other human ability, we can develop our ability to properly focus our conscious awareness through consistent practice, exercise and experience.

In order to develop our ability to live consciously, we must first learn to consistently stay focused on the moment by fully experiencing, questioning and thinking about everything we do, think, see, hear or feel. Again, we can help ourselves do this and improve our conscious abilities by simply making the consistent conscious effort to keep a detailed journal. In the past we often thought, perceived, and did many things outside the light of our conscious awareness - out of habit. We also didn't think, didn't perceive, and didn't do many things out of habit. Once they became habitual, our errors in thinking and perception took control over our lives and perpetuated themselves without us even knowing it. This is the reason why habits are so powerful in defining who we are and why they are so difficult to overcome. Most of the time, these habits are manifested outside the realm of our conscious awareness. We simply do them without even thinking about it. However, when we learn how to live consciously and start properly focusing our conscious awareness, it will enable us to recognize and examine these habits instead of remaining unaware of them. It will allow us to see things more as they really are instead of simply how we habitually, or subconsciously, imagine them to be. Thus, it will empower us to overcome their constraint and, with conscious effort, to eliminate them from our lives.

When learning to live consciously, it can also be beneficial for us to visualize everything that everyone else does, says, or experiences as though we did, said, or experienced it ourselves. This can help us identify more responsible patterns of thought and perception, enable us to learn from others mistakes, and help us develop true empathy for others, which will allow us to see the world more realistically.

In the past, our tendency was to think the worst of others' behavior and words, while expecting them to view us in the best, most favorable, light possible. We also condemned others while always expecting compassion for ourselves, and got angry at others for doing much the same things we excused and justified doing ourselves. However, in order to become more realistic and overcome these habitual tendencies, we must learn to "use the same programming in perceiving and interpreting the actions and words of other people that <we> use in understanding <our> own actions."[5]

Living consciously is one of the most powerful methods we can use in order to overcome our habits and correct our errors in thinking and perception. It stands in the way of indulging irresponsible thoughts, feelings, and desires, because they contradict reality and are contrary to the consequences that we want to create in our

---

5   Keyes, Ken, Jr., "HANDBOOK TO HIGHER CONSCIOUSNESS:FIFTH EDITION" (The Living Love Center, 1975) pp.111

lives. "If we remain fully conscious, the contradictions stare us in the face, inhibiting our impulsiveness like a stop sign before a rush of irrationality."[6] As I have said before, it is very difficult to behave irresponsibly when we are consciously aware of all the reasons why we shouldn't behave that way.

Living consciously also enables us to grow and mature by learning from our experiences. When we live consciously, not only do we accept and examine all of our experiences, but we also become aware of these lessons at the right moment so that our experiences can help us properly guide our lives. In the past, our experience was often clouded by justifications and excuses, or shunned and perverted through the shut-off and erosion of awareness. However, when we struggle to live consciously and see things as they really are, our experiences begin to take on a new meaning. Instead of being worthless, a hindrance, and full of pain and sorrow, our experiences become a source of knowledge, guidance, maturity, hope and accomplishment. So, instead of avoiding our experiences and excusing them as something which is out of our control, we will accept them as a part of who we are and begin to use them to responsibly direct our lives. Our experiences will begin to take on a more realistic and personal quality as we learn to see them as being caused by our own thoughts and actions.

In time, the upward spiral of increasing consciousness and understanding through experience will lead to paradigm shifts—ah-ha experiences, where we will finally see things more realistically and make sense of things in a more responsible and complete way. All of a sudden, we will begin to conceptually recognize our errors in thinking and perception as they occur in our behavior, and enable ourselves to learn from our mistakes so that we can avoid them in the future. A responsible way of life will begin to make sense as we learn to control ourselves and truly direct our lives in a purposeful, productive and meaningful way.

I believe that these paradigm shifts are at the foundation of our change process. As I said before, simply struggling to change our

---

6   Branden, Nathaniel, Ph.D., "TAKING RESPONSIBILITY - SELF RELIANCE AND THE ACCOUNTABLE LIFE" (New York: Simon & Schuster, 1996) pp.65

outward behavior and overcome our criminal thoughts and desires through willpower alone will not result in a lasting change. Only when we begin to see things differently - more realistically, responsibly, and meaningfully - will a responsible way of life begin to make sense and our changes become a permanent part of who we are. Only when our perceptions are properly interpreted through realistic paradigms, fortified by realistic thoughts, guided by good habits and verified by experience, will we truly be able to understand what a responsible way of life entails, and consistently be able to purposefully direct our lives in a meaningful way.

Self-Image

As changing criminals, one of our first objectives in learning to live consciously is to seek, and consistently maintain, a more realistic perception of ourselves...a realistic self-image. In order to sustain the proper focus and personal awareness necessary to change our lives, our perceptions of ourselves must be grounded in reality, not fantasy or self-delusion. We should learn to see ourselves conceptually and objectively as we really are and not simply in terms of concrete events, fragmented sentimentality, or subjective self-image boosting achievements (or self-image deflating failures and imperfections in the case of put-downs). In order to stabilize our self-image, we should learn to recognize, and stay consciously aware of, the faults and imperfections in ourselves along with our good traits and sentimentality. We must learn to see ourselves holistically as the sum of all our experiences, traits and behaviors.

In order to be realistic, our self-image cannot be just a façade, or a face that we wear solely to impress and fool others. A self-image which is based on our perception of how others (with their limited knowledge of the real us) view us, is not realistic. Not to mention the fact that this type of self-image empowers others to control how we feel about ourselves, and is skewed from the outset by our errors in thinking and perception. Sure, our self-image must take into account what others think about us, but in order to be realistic, our self-image must also (and more importantly) be founded on what we know and honestly think about ourselves.

In order to see ourselves realistically, we should first learn to view ourselves as any other responsible individual would view us if they knew the whole truth about our inner thoughts, desires, intentions and secret actions. Realistically, if a responsible person knew that we had just finished robbing a store or assaulting someone right before we volunteered to help them with their yard work, or smiled and said "hi" as we passed by, they wouldn't view us as being helpful or friendly, but instead as a thief, an assailant, and a criminal. In their judgment of us, our criminal behaviors would far outweigh any good we may have done. So, in order to be realistic, our own perception of ourselves must be comparably harsh when it comes to evaluating the significance of our irresponsible and criminal thoughts, motives and behavior.

If we secretly steal money from someone one minute and then help an old lady across the street the next minute, others are likely to only see our good deed and thus may view us as a kind, caring, helpful person. But our own self-image should be that of a thief, a criminal, and a liar. Similarly, if we cheat in order to win, then we must learn to realistically view ourselves not as winners but as cheaters, and if we lie in order to impress others, we should view ourselves not as impressive but as liars. We should never allow ourselves to focus solely on the outcomes of our thoughts, choices, and behaviors, because it is the means by which we obtain these ends which truly defines who we are.

We should also eliminate our past patterns of unrealistically boosting our self-image by doing things solely on the basis of proving ourselves, wanting to be liked and accepted, or impressing others. Good actions don't count for much when they are defiled by ulterior motives, hidden agendas, and evil intentions. And, kindness really doesn't mean much if it is negated by secret crimes, irresponsible behaviors, and unethical means. It is important to understand we can actually undermine our own change process if our effort is solely intended to impress others. Change for the sake of another is just a criminal equivalent, and is destined for failure. We simply cannot succeed in changing a lifetime's worth of habits and criminal tendencies solely to impress other people. True change can only happen when it is recognized as beneficial for the self. At some level, we must desire to change for our own well being and happiness, and because it is the right thing to do.

Again, we must always be on guard against the criminal equivalents that are intended to boost our self-image by enhancing the image we portray to others. Our self-image is only realistic when the image we portray to others is confirmed by the actions and intent of our private self. We cannot ever allow ourselves to be fake to people or to revert back to living a life of lies. If we are ever to overcome our criminal habits and tendencies, our self-image must come more from the true perception of who we are inside than from the distorted reflection we portray to others.

Furthermore, although it is fine to take pride in honestly deserved praise and recognition when our thoughts and behaviors have been consistently pure, praise and recognition should not be the sole motivator behind our choices and behavior. There is a big difference between studying hard for an upcoming test because we want to do our best and studying hard because we want to prove ourselves as better than everyone else. And, there is also a big difference between volunteering to help someone because we would like someone to help us if we were ever in a needful situation, and volunteering to help someone in order to get praise and recognition. Even a desire to change becomes a criminal equivalent if it is solely intended to impress others, to unrealistically prove ourselves, or to build ourselves up as good people without any consideration of our past atrocities.

We must also be wary of boosting our self-image during the change process to the point where we begin to neglect the more important aspects of identifying and struggling to overcome our criminal errors in thinking and perception. There will be a desire to tell our responsible guide, and others, about all the good things we are doing and thinking, yet fail to acknowledge all of those errors which are still a part of our thinking, perception and behavior. However, in order for us to be the most effective in our change, we must not do this. Because our tendency is to do the opposite, we should focus less on our improvements and more on what still needs to be improved.

Being Fake

In order to help us gain a more realistic self-image, it is essential that we recognize the irony of building ourselves up through concrete acts of kindness and generosity. In the past, our charm and kindness wasn't an enduring feature. If it was, we wouldn't have committed crimes. Yet our kind and generous moments provided the foundation for our unrealistic self-image. In our own twisted way, we were able to convince ourselves that because we were kind and generous some of the time, to a chosen few, that we were basically good people, even though we were hurting countless others through our crime and irresponsible behavior. Our self-image was founded on these good features of our personality while we neglected to adequately consider all of our predominantly hurtful, irresponsible and criminal features.

However, in order to maintain a realistic self-image we must acknowledge the consequences of irresponsible and criminal behavior. As long as we continue to view ourselves as basically decent people while simultaneously living irresponsibly and committing crimes, we program our subconscious minds to assume that this thinking and behavior is acceptable. But it isn't. Realistically, however, none of the good we have ever done can make up for even one irresponsible or criminal act. No matter how much good we do, we can never completely erase the damage done through our evil behavior. And in order to be realistic our perception of ourselves, our self-image, must take this fact into account.

I believe that because of our fragmentation and past pattern of unrealistically building up our self-image, we should temporarily avoid volunteering for any image boosting activities - at least until we have begun to recognize and change our errors in thinking and perception, and gained some experience in maintaining a realistic self-image. I am not saying that we shouldn't always be nice, respectful, fulfill obligations and be responsibly helpful, but that we should avoid volunteering to doing favors, because these actions are the most prone to be criminal equivalents. We must never allow ourselves to seek praise, compliments, or recognition for the sake of recognition. This is because our past pattern has been to thrive on these things and allow them to unrealistically boost our self-image. As St. Francis de Sales writes, "...worldly honors are acceptable to him who receives them indifferently without resting in them or seeking them eagerly, but they become very dangerous and hurtful to him who clings to and takes delight in them."[7] And under no circumstances should we ever do any favors for other criminals until we are well advanced in our change and have a lot of experience in living responsibly, because these favors can only lead to implied or perceived debt and exploitation on the part of everyone involved.

The danger of good deeds and praise at the beginning of our struggle to change is that they can unrealistically build us up and lead to complacency. Praise and recognition can cause us to take our focus off of who we are and who we are capable of becoming. To move forward, we must stay completely focused on our purpose, our criminal habits and tendencies, and our desire to change. As lifelong criminals, it will be difficult to live without praise and recognition. But in time, as we gain experience in responsible living, we will begin to realize that our good deeds and many of the things that we sought praise and recognition for in the past, were basically just things that we should have been doing anyway. Thus, the praise and recognition was unwarranted.

We should become self-critical of kind and generous acts and learn to question ourselves as to whether they are sincere, or whether they are fake and simply being done to exploit someone or boost our self-image. It is important to understand that if we are being nice or kind to someone because we know that if we are nice they will give us something we want (even something as seemingly unimportant as some extra food or a piece of art paper), our kindness is exploitive - we want something for it. And if we are being generous in order to help us feel like basically good people after

---

7   St. Francis De Sales, "PHILOTHEA, OR AN INTRODUCTION TO THE DEVOUT LIFE" (Rockford: Tan Books, 1994) pp.122

doing something that we shouldn't have done, then it is a lie. Our kindness itself isn't the issue. Being kind, nice, and generous in order to create the consequences we want in life is an important part of responsible, interdependent living. The problem is that our kindness is not enduring and is frequently exploitive in one way or another. In the past, we usually didn't just do things out of the kindness of our hearts. Yet in order to spiritually progress and develop a realistically good self-image, we must overcome these tendencies.

Ultimately, as we grow and develop in responsible living, we must learn to love and serve others unconditionally. We can't continue to put a price on our kindness. And, if our change is to be lasting, our kindness and goodness must become an enduring feature. If our kindness, gentleness, generosity and concern for others are to be of any value in our lives, they must be more than exploitive facades that transiently boost our self-image - they must be a lasting part of who we are inside.

Unique, Special, and Superior

In the past, our unrealistic self-image was founded on the egocentric idea that we were unique, special, and better than others. From our distorted perspective, the world revolved around us. In fact, a large part of our personal pride and power was derived from these misconceptions.

If someone did something well, we believed that we could do it better - if we wanted to. We were sure that somehow, in some way, we were above the common herd. Even when things weren't going well at the moment, we were almost certain that the future held something special for an individual as rare and talented as we were.

When things didn't go our way or go as planned, we got angry and wanted to get even. We thought bad things should never happen to us and things should never go wrong because we were special. And when we did have problems, even these problems were unique to us. We usually felt like we were the only ones who had ever experienced problems like ours, and that there was no way anyone could ever truly understand everything we had been through.

Realistically, however, it is important that we accept the fact that we are not unique and special, and we are definitely not superior to anyone. As I have maintained throughout this book, from the standpoint of our thinking patterns and perceptions, we are all basically alike. So this book itself should eliminate the idea that we are unique. And, from a prison cell it is pretty obvious that the world doesn't revolve around us. We are just one being among billions each with their own lives and with much the same desire to survive, succeed, and be happy.

It should also be easy to recognize the fact that we are not better than anyone else. In fact, as criminals, we aren't even doing as well with our lives as everyone else is. Most of us are not even good criminals - we keep getting caught. And if we are realistic about our lives, we will realize that many people have overcome much greater problems and hardships, and done much more with their lives than we have.

For years I felt that all of the problems and agonizing experiences I had as an overweight child were unique to me and somehow condoned my irresponsible and criminal behavior. Even after I lost all of my excess weight, my irresponsible behaviors continued. In fact, they got worse. From my distorted perspective, I guess that I was just getting back at all those people who used to pick on me and make fun of me. Yet, while selfishly feeling sorry for myself, I failed to recognize the fact that while many overweight children are confronted with the same type of problems, they responsibly overcome them, and then go on to lead purposeful, productive and meaningful lives. And realistically, being overweight is nothing compared with the awesome hardships and problems which other children must deal with. There are many children who are confronted with life-threatening diseases, and others who can't even see, hear, walk, or feed themselves. Yet they don't revert to getting even or feeling sorry for themselves. On the contrary, they heroically make the most out of their lives, struggle to move forward, and add joy and meaning to their own lives and the lives of others.

If anything, we should be ashamed of who we are and of all the promise and potential we have forsaken. Having all the talent and potential in the world is worthless unless it is used in a responsible, purposeful, and productive manner. In fact, I believe it is far better to have no talent and potential, and still struggle to responsibly succeed in life than to have a lot of potential and never reach it because we are unwilling to make the effort - what a waste.

Through practice, effort, sacrifice, and the proper focusing of our consciousness, we must develop humility - something which has been very foreign to us. Instead of only thinking about ourselves, we must begin to accept responsibility for others' happiness and always treat them as we would like to be treated. Instead of seeking to be viewed as superior by everyone around us, and constantly trying to prove ourselves, we should anonymously pursue excellence. Instead of fancying ourselves as unique, we should struggle to simply be ordinary. As Richard Carlson writes, "Humility and inner peace go hand in hand. The less compelled you are to try to prove yourself to others, the easier it is to feel peaceful inside."[8]

To paraphrase the Bible, there is no lasting reward in doing things solely to impress others (see Matthew 6:2-6), and the irony of life is that when we openly seek to be first, we often end up being last. (see Luke 13:30) "Because everyone that exalteth himself, shall be humbled; and he that humbleth himself shall be exalted."[9]

By consciously altering our point of view, we must begin to see ourselves as but one of the many - one piece of the whole puzzle. Realistically, we are not superior or better than anyone. And we are not entitled to anything special in this life. Our rights, desires, wants, and goals do not preempt those of others. We do not own anyone, or anyone else's right to freedom and happiness. We should recognize that in order to happily co-exist, one person's liberties and freedoms must end where the next begins. And it is important that we learn to identify and respect these social boundaries. We cannot continue to allow ourselves to step on other

---

8   Carlson, Richard, Ph.D., "DON'T SWEAT THE SMALL STUFF....AND IT'S ALL SMALL STUFF" (New York: Hyperion, 1997) pp.101
9   St. Luke 14:11

people's rights simply because we think that we are special or better than them. We must begin to see others as we see ourselves - as individuals who have the capacity to direct their own lives through their choices. And we should recognize that everyone has their own emotions, needs, thoughts, perspectives, and ways of doing things.

In order to help us fully overcome this criminal sense of uniqueness and superiority, we must always remember what we have done and the suffering that we have caused. Just like a recovering alcoholic must always remind himself that he is an alcoholic, we should be aware of our potential for irresponsible behavior and crime. We can never allow ourselves to forget the evil we have done or the pain and suffering we have caused. We should develop and sustain a self-disgust of our past way of life by continually reminding ourselves of who we were and the atrocious consequences we have caused in so many lives. And then we should allow this self-disgust to feed our humility.

Actually, I believe that because of our fragmentation there can be no lasting commitment to change without a total self-disgust based on the honest realization that all of our good and special features have been totally eclipsed by our past criminality. Personally, I have found that it is relatively easy to maintain this self-disgust when I wake up each morning and am forced to think about my past way of life and all the people, including myself and my family, who I have hurt. And, this self-disgust is only heightened when I think of all those people who still love me regardless of the pain I have caused, because they see me not as I am but as, by God's grace, who I may become. I have found that this self-disgust has become more intense as I have moved forward in my life, because it has enabled me to contrast the peace, joy, and happiness of a responsible way of life with the pain, sorrow, and shame of my past way of life.

Pride and Perfection

In the past, the unique posturing of my unrealistic self-image caused me to develop an unrealistic sense of criminal pride - a pride based on arrogance, conceit, and a meaningless sense of quasi-perfectionism, instead of an honest sense of meaningful accomplishment, dignity, self-respect, and integrity.

I was proud of the false image I portrayed to others, of my conquests, and of the clothes I wore and the money I had. Yet, realistically, these things are not worthy of our pride because, for the most part, they are not even of our own making. As St. Frances de Sales writes:

Noble birth, the favor of the great, popular esteem, are not in ourselves, they come either from our forefathers or from the opinion of others. Some are proud and conceited because they have a fine horse, a plume in their hat, or are magnificently attired, but who cannot perceive the absurdity of this, since if anyone has reason to be proud it surely is the horse, the ostrich, or the tailor! And how very contemptible it is to rest our hope of esteem in a horse, a feather, or a garment! Another thinks of his well-trimmed beard and mustachios, or his well-curled hair, his delicate hands, or of his accomplishment in dancing, music, and so on, but is it not very contemptible to try to enhance his worth or his reputation through such foolish and frivolous things? Others, who have acquired a little science, demand the respect and honor of the world on that account, as if all must need come to learn of them and bow before them. Such men we call pedants (a show-off). Others pride themselves on their personal beauty, and think that everyone is admiring them: all of them in their turn are utterly silly, foolish, and impertinent, and their glory in such empty things we call vain, absurd, and frivolous.[10]

In order to develop a realistic self-image and create a healthy self-esteem, we must replace our arrogance, conceit and air of superiority with a pride based on the little every day successes and accomplishments of responsible living. Successes such as:

---

10 St. Francis De Sales, "PHILOTHEA, OR AN INTRODUCTION TO THE DEVOUT LIFE" (Rockford: Tan Books, 1994) pp.120

- enduring to the end and reaching a goal
- overcoming problems and hardships
- being productive
- living righteously
- making others happy
- creating a meaningful life

Realistically, true pride cannot be bought, taught, or derived from frivolous things. It can only result from living righteously and making responsible gains through effort and sacrifice. True pride doesn't come from being intelligent, talented or beautiful. Instead, it is a result of what we choose to do with this intelligence, talent and beauty. True pride, then, is something that we have seldom experienced.

In the past, I often gained an unrealistic sense of pride in striving for perfection in trivial, often meaningless, things. Yet because of my fragmentation, even these struggles for quasi-perfectionism weren't enduring. As I have said before, we are all perfectionists. The problem is, however, that we are usually only selfishly concerned with perfection as far as it serves to boost our own self-image. Much of the time our perfectionism is transient - we only struggle for perfection when we want to impress others or prove ourselves. Our desire for perfection isn't for our own improvement, and it isn't enduring, so it doesn't promote any personal growth or development.

Often, our tendency is to avoid the awareness of our own imperfections by struggling to be perfect in meaningless areas of our lives. So, it is easy to lose focus on the areas we really need to improve. Yet, in order to change, we must learn to recognize and accept our own imperfections, and the imperfections of others. We can't continue to allow ourselves to hide from our imperfections through a facade of meaningless perfectionism. And we shouldn't continue to get angry when others, and the world around us, don't live up to our standards of perfection.

We should realize that, except for God, no one is perfect. Even the great men of history had their shortcomings and imperfections.

Nobody's life ever goes exactly as planned. "No one that ever lived has ever had enough power, prestige, or knowledge to overcome the basic condition of all life - you win some and you lose some."[11]

As changing criminals, we should always strive for perfection in responsible living. In fact, perfectionism is required in regards to our struggle to think, choose, and behave responsibly if we truly want to change ourselves. We can never again allow ourselves to consciously behave irresponsibly or commit another crime. However, perfectionism is not required for each and every individual task. In responsible living there is also merit in simply doing a competent job and not giving up when things don't go as planned. We should always strive for excellence, but we shouldn't make a production out of everything. We do not need to prove ourselves as a unique, superior, and perfect person in every situation. And when things don't go just the way we would like them to, instead of getting angry and only seeing difficulties and obstacles, we must learn to recognize the opportunities for growth which overcoming these obstacles can provide.

One of the steps to living responsibly is learning to determine what aspects of our lives are worth the struggle for perfection. For example, I believe that it is much more important to strive to be a perfect father or a perfect husband than to be a perfect dresser; to have a perfectly clean conscience than to have a perfectly clean home; to live with perfect integrity than to cheat and always win the game; or, to live a perfectly righteous and responsible life than to be praised as a perfect musician or a perfect student. The struggle for perfection can be honorable and heroic, but it can also be frivolous and asinine.

"Mistakes"

We will undoubtedly make mistakes and misjudgments as we struggle to turn our lives around and live responsibly. However, we

---

11 Keyes, Ken, Jr., "HANDBOOK TO HIGHER CONSCIOUSNESS: FIFTH EDITION" (?: The Living Love Center, 1975) pp.20

must not ever allow ourselves to confuse honest mistakes, misjudgments, and imperfections with irresponsible choices. Mistakes happen without intent, knowledge, or choice - they are accidental. However, there is nothing accidental about irresponsible or criminal choices which are the result of our errors in thinking and perception. Now that we are aware of them, even maintaining or sustaining these errors is a matter of choice.

For example, if we unknowingly break a rule because we fail to fact-find or properly conceptualize our behavior, this is not simply a "mistake" - it is our fault for not seeking reality before we acted on our choice. And when we have to pay the consequences, it will be our own fault. Realistically, what we don't know can hurt us, and often will. If we get a hot U.A., we can't just blow it off as some mistake or little slip-up - it is the consequence of a choice we made. And, if because of our prejudices, misconceptions, and misjudgments we allow ourselves to get angry and then vengefully do or say something to hurtful, this is also not a mistake. We may even feel bad that it happened afterwards, but realistically it could have, and should have, been prevented. And even on those occasions where we truly do make a mistake, we must also realize that we are responsible for our mistakes - even accidents have consequences.

As we move forward, we must learn to be imaginative when dealing with mistakes and imperfection. By simply altering our point of view, we can responsibly overcome any disappointment or inconvenience that may result from imperfection and enable ourselves to grow. If it rains on our picnic, we can move everything inside and have just as much fun. Getting angry or frustrated won't change the fact that it is raining or make anything better. But these feelings can be very dangerous and may even have grave consequences for us as changing criminals. If we are stuck in traffic or have to ride the bus to work, instead of impatiently viewing the experience as a major injustice or put-down, we can view it as a minor inconvenience and an opportunity for growth. For example, instead of being a problem, riding the bus or being stuck in a traffic jam can be responsibly viewed and utilized as an opportunity to have extra time alone in order to contemplate:

- our life
- our progress in change
- our growth in responsible living
- the potential consequences of allowing ourselves to get mad at the world's, or our own, imperfections

With every disappointment and imperfection we face in life, we give ourselves the opportunity to transform tragedy into triumph, and add deeper meaning and purpose to our lives. We simply need to maintain the proper attitude and perspective. Realistically, we can learn far more from our setbacks and mistakes than we can from our achievements and success in this life.

Next, not only should we strive to recognize and accept imperfection, but we should also learn to anticipate it. Our past pattern of false pride and perfectionism will be difficult to overcome. Yet, if we want to be successful, we definitely can't allow ourselves to get angry, frustrated, depressed, or feel put down when things don't go our way. We must always remember and anticipate "Murphy's Law" - if anything can go wrong, it will. But rather than inciting pessimism in our lives, this realistic awareness of imperfection in the world should lead to a state of preparedness. As the Boy Scout motto says, we must always "Be Prepared".

Ultimately, we should struggle to keep as many things from going wrong as possible. We cannot ever be careless in responsible living. We should always strive to be perfect in all the responsible aspects of our lives, those parts of our lives over which we truly do have control. However, we must also be realistic. The most important thing is that we consistently struggle for perfection, and then take pride in all our responsible effort and sacrifice.

Put-Downs

Much of the tension in our lives and feelings of self-doubt and worthlessness are the result of our unrealistic perceptions of ourselves and the world around us. Instead of being proactive and actively seeking to responsibly control our circumstances, we are

197

often reactive and allow ourselves to be influenced and controlled by external forces. If people treat us good, or things go the way we want them to, then we feel good and we are happy. However, if things don't go our way, or if others don't treat us with the respect we feel we deserve, we usually get angry, feel put down, and want to prove ourselves. We allow external forces to control our perceptions of ourselves and influence how we respond in any given situation.

Because of our pretentious, egocentric nature, we are abnormally sensitive people. We often perceive put-downs and disrespect where it isn't even intended. Due to the way we have learned to make sense of the world, we often take things the wrong way. And because we think that the world revolves around us, we often think that everything people do or say somehow concerns us. Throughout my life I have seen criminals assaulting others in prison or on the streets for simply looking at them wrong, bumping into them, or sitting in their seat. Even I have gotten into fights and arguments for things as trivial as a basketball game and because someone was using "my weights" in the prison gym.

At times, we may believe that others can see through us; that everyone is aware of our shortcomings, faults, or mistakes, and thus everyone perceives us as a loser. And regardless of whether this is true or not, we tend to allow this perception to dramatically influence our own self-image. This usually causes us to feel like we must respond in some way that proves we are not a loser. For example, we may miss a couple of shots while playing basketball, get dumped by our girlfriend, or even slip on some ice, and if others are aware of these things, we tend to believe that they view us as inept idiots and losers. Even though these things may be frivolous or not even our fault, we allow our misconceptions of what others think to influence how we perceive ourselves.

Realistically, however, many of the things we think others perceive as inept, weak and failures, are things that they don't even notice or care about. Most people are simply too busy responsibly dealing with their own problems to notice. And if they are so shallow and immature that this is truly the way they feel, then it is they who have the problem, not us. Only people who have a poor relationship with themselves augment and make fun of other people's shortcomings, mistakes, and failures in an effort to feel better about themselves.

Ultimately, we must learn to transfer our source of approval and criticism, and the evaluation of our self-image, from others to ourselves. If we continue to allow others to influence our perception of ourselves and dictate how we are going to respond, then it is our own fault, not theirs. Realistically, we can never become what other people think of us unless we allow them to dictate what we think of ourselves. The only way that the thoughtless and immature words and behaviors of others can hurt us is if, through our response to these words and behaviors, we empower them to.

When we value belonging, being accepted, and being perceived as special above our own integrity and self-esteem, then we lose control, and we diminish our ability to grow and change. We also tend to distort reality. However, if we simply refuse to allow others to unrealistically influence how we perceive ourselves, regardless of what they do or say, then we give ourselves the freedom to dictate our own responses and control our own lives. We empower ourselves to grow and change.

Just as we shouldn't falsely boost our self-image by proving ourselves to others through irresponsible behavior, we must not allow others' words and actions, or events beyond our control, to unrealistically deflate our perceptions of ourselves. Instead of feeling put down and getting angry every time things don't go our way, we must learn to realistically assess our perceptions of others, struggle to overcome disappointments, and accept those things we cannot change or control. When we do this, our problems can become opportunities for growth.

To grow, we should focus our energy on those things that we are realistically responsible for, those things that are under our control. If we waste our energy fighting against those things we have no control over, then we defeat ourselves by allowing them to have control over us (by dictating our responses). Struggling to control the things we can't control is like pounding our heads against a brick wall, so all we usually end up with is a headache.

One of the keys to our success is learning to maintain a realistic self-image in the face of discouragement and criticism. Even at the most difficult times, we should struggle to maintain a self-image based on the facts of reality and not on what others think, or what we pretend the facts to be. An individual with a realistic view of himself and perspective on life is very difficult to put down.

Dealing with Criticism

On the other hand, we must also be weary of simply disregarding criticism and shutting off perceived put-downs. Ideally, in order to grow, we must learn to analyze and question all perceived put-downs, without getting angry or feeling like a nothing, in order to evaluate whether we, in some way, influenced or augmented the put-down itself, or the situation which led to the perceived put-down. If the put-down has no basis in reality, then we should simply disregard it. However, often the real issue for us shouldn't even be trying to overcome unrealistic put-downs, but rather learning to responsibly deal with criticism. Instead of feeling put down and getting angry when we are criticized, we should learn to realistically assess this criticism and responsibly utilize it, if applicable, to improve ourselves.

Much of the time, hearing the truth about ourselves isn't easy. Like any medicine intended to cure, criticism can be hard to swallow. But despite its undesirable taste, criticism can help to cure us and set us straight. However, in order to be of any use to us, criticism from others must first be transformed into self-criticism and then followed by an active effort to correct whatever was criticized. Realistically, self-criticism is required to generate the inner drive and desire necessary to initiate and sustain the effort and sacrifice required to change and grow.

A willingness to accept, evaluate and, if necessary, internalize criticism is an important component of maintaining an open channel of communication. As changing criminals, we actually need this criticism in order to grow, because we are unfamiliar with living a consistently responsible way of life. It is this criticism that will help us to recognize our errors in thinking and perception, and any mistakes we may make - a necessary awareness if we ever hope to truly change and learn to live responsibly.

Criticism doesn't always have to be viewed as a put-down. If we simply make the conscious effort necessary to maintain a self-critical attitude, then criticism can become a precious insight. It can enhance our perspective of the world around us and even provide an opportunity for growth. As Stephen R. Covey writes:

> You can be synergistic within yourself even in the midst of a very adversarial environment. You don't have to take insults personally. You can sidestep negative energy; you can look for the good in others and utilize that good, as different as it may be, to improve your point of view and to enlarge your perspective.[12]

It is all in our attitude and perspective. Everyone, at some point in their lives, is confronted with criticism, disrespect, imperfection, discrimination, and all of the other things which we often perceive as put-downs. The real issue is how we choose to respond to these things. We can become angry, feel like a nothing, allow our emotions to overrule our intellect, and focus solely on trying to get even and prove ourselves. Or, we can try to see things from another perspective. We can give others the benefit of the doubt, accept the fact that things aren't always going to go our way, and learn from criticism if necessary. We can rise above discouragement and difficulties, and look for opportunities to grow. We can do whatever we put our mind to.

The Victim Perspective and Other Excuses

Another aspect of our unrealistic self-image is the perception that we are the victims of life's circumstances whenever things don't go our way. As I discussed at the beginning of this book, it is imperative that we eliminate all of the excuses for our behavior. We must begin to realistically see ourselves as the creators of our

---

12 Covey, Stephen R., "THE 7 HABITS OF HIGHLY EFFECTIVE PEOPLE - POWERFUL LESSONS IN PERSONAL CHANGE" (New York: Simon & Schuster, 1989) pp.284

own circumstances and masters of our own destiny. It is impossible to choose to change and live differently until we first accept the fact that it was our choices in the past that led us to where we are now. We simply cannot take responsibility for our future until we hold ourselves completely responsible for our past. In fact, as I have said before, it is impossible to simultaneously view ourselves as the victim of life's circumstance, and still responsibly take control over our lives.

At some point in all our lives, this victim perspective has surfaced in order to excuse and justify our irresponsible and criminal behavior - especially after we have been caught. Many of us contend that we committed our crimes because of:

- drugs
- a drug addiction
- the people we hung around with
- race
- socioeconomic standing
- a lack of education
- our family life
- society's
- the victim

And most of us have complained at some point that we are in prison because someone snitched on us, we were set up, or the system screwed us. Indeed, we have used almost every form of self-deceit and deception to maintain our unrealistic self-image and hide from the reality of the fact that we are who we are, and where we are, because of choices we have made.

In essence, what we are telling ourselves when we maintain a victim perspective is that we don't have total control over our own lives. Therefore, when we fail or get caught, we don't have to personally accept the full responsibility for our own choices or the consequences which are simply the result of these choices. With a victim perspective, our self-image doesn't suffer when we fail or are not perfect. In reality, however, this unrealistic perspective and the excuses it provokes are simply cop-outs that we use to justify a lack of effort and an unwillingness to follow the rules or take responsibility for our own lives.

Yet, even though these excuses and the victim perspective serve to diminish the control we have over our own lives, they in no way absolve us of responsibility for the consequences of our choices and behavior. Sadly, by convincing ourselves that we are the victims, we actually perpetuate our criminality, because we excuse and justify our criminal behavior. We erroneously convince ourselves that we are exonerated of responsibility for our behavior. So, we are able to forego the feelings of guilt, remorse, and sorrow that would force us to recognize and confront our criminal behavior and compel us to change.

Realistically, if we are honest with ourselves, we will recognize and accept the fact that, as criminals, we are more victimizers than victims. We have hurt others far more than they have ever hurt us and we have discriminated against others far more than we have ever been discriminated against. And, on those rare occasions where we have truly been victimized in our lives by things such as discrimination, abuse, and crime, the issue we must learn to focus on is how to responsibly deal with adversity, not how to get back or get even. Being victimized in the past can never give us a right to victimize others in the future. In fact, being victimized and discriminated against should serve to make us more empathetic to the plight of other people and cause us to try even harder not to victimize others.

Even as we make the effort to change, there will be a continued desire to justify and excuse our choices and behaviors, and to view ourselves as the victim. Especially when things don't go our way, when we make mistakes, or when we don't live up to our perfectionist image of ourselves. In prison, I often felt like I was a victim and being picked on when my cell was searched or when I was stopped in the hallway to be patted down. I didn't consider that I put myself in prison and that these things were just a part of being incarcerated. Throughout my life, I have also felt a need to excuse sub-par performance in everything from sports to school by claiming to be a victim of circumstances beyond my control. If it wasn't poor calls by the referee or a bad teacher, then it was something else. I just couldn't accept the fact that it was me.

These excuses, and the victim stance, are just automatic criminal responses that have become habituated throughout our lifetime. So in order to overcome these tendencies, we must consciously fight the urge to make excuses or view ourselves as the victims of life's circumstances. We should struggle to get to the point where our attitude and perspective on life simply won't allow us to make, or accept, excuses for our choices and behavior.

We can eliminate our excuses and victim perspective in much the same way we eliminate other errors in thinking and perception - by actively seeking the thoughts and perceptions which contradict these excuses and justifications. Instead of viewing ourselves as the victim when our cell is searched or when we are patted down, we can choose to focus on the fact that we are in prison, which is meant to be an inconvenience, and then focus on all the reasons why we ended up in prison. And instead of excusing a lack of effort and unwillingness to make the sacrifices necessary to do well at school by saying that the teacher doesn't like us, or for any other reason, we can focus on the fact that as human beings we have the capacity to overcome these obstacles if we really want to. We can create the consequences we want in our lives through the choices we make.

Quite simply, excuses and justifications can be found for almost any irresponsible or criminal act if we look hard enough. Even good intentions can become excuses if we allow them to. In fact, to modify an old adage, for us "the road to prison is paved with good intentions." Even those dubious excuses "I didn't know" and "I wasn't sure" cannot justify or condone irresponsible or criminal behavior. As responsible individuals it is our duty to find out. Again, it is up to each one of us to personally seek to discover and understand exactly what we must do in order to live a purposeful, productive, and responsible life. No one is going to lead us through life like a child. As adults, we must ask questions, seek the proper answers, and make sure that we are doing the right things. And although those foolish excuses "but other people do it" and "I wasn't the only one" can make us feel better by diluting our sense of responsibility, they do not negate the fact that we are personally responsible for all of our own choices, and that they will have consequences which we will have to suffer by ourselves. As my parents used to say, we must ask ourselves the question, "If everyone was jumping off of a bridge would we jump off of the bridge, too?" Just because everyone else did it wouldn't make us any less dead!

"If we stay aware of the fact that we are responsible for our choices, decisions and actions, we are far more likely to choose, decide, and act in ways that will not later become causes of embarrassment, shame, or regret. We are not disassociated from our behavior; we are anchored in reality; we see more clearly and tend to function more wisely."[13] I truly believe that it is much more difficult to behave irresponsibly and purposely lead ourselves in the wrong direction if instead of using excuses we focus on the reality of personal responsibility and the potential consequences of our behavior.

In order to further help us to overcome this victim perspective, we should trace the pattern of our irresponsible and criminal choices, and their consequences, in our lives. This can help us to recognize that it was these choices that played the biggest role in our present situation, and the circumstances of our lives. In the end, we should recognize and accept the fact that our failures and successes in this life have been more a result of the choices we have made than of the circumstances in our lives. In life it's not so much where you are, who you know, or what your circumstances are that counts. Instead what counts is who you are inside, whether or not you make the right choices, how much effort you put forth, and whether this effort is focused in the right direction. We create the circumstances of our lives far more than they shape us. And, even when we are confronted with things over which we have no control, our chosen response to these things is what inevitably dictates our future success or failure. As Victor E. Frankle writes, "when we are no longer able to change a situation…we are

13 Branden, Nathaniel, Ph.D., "TAKING RESPONSIBILITY - SELF RELIANCE AND THE ACCOUNTABLE LIFE" (New York: Simon & Schuster, 1996) pp.97

challenged to change ourselves."[14]

We should also ponder, and learn to focus on, the sad reality that many other people on this earth have been subject to similar, and even worse, environments, circumstances and experiences, and yet have not allowed these to become excuses to behave irresponsibly or criminally. In a highly moving book entitled *Man's Search for Meaning*, Dr. Victor E. Frankle gives an account of his personal experiences in some Nazi concentration camps. The suffering, discrimination, pain, and humiliation which these people endured in these camps was incomprehensible - they were truly victims. Yet, instead of allowing their experiences to become excuses to give up or live irresponsibly, most of the people who survived the camps overcame their tragic experiences and went on to live responsible, productive and purposeful lives. It is true-life stories of human courage and potential like these that, if contemplated and consciously used properly, can put our own difficulties and problems into perspective. They can give us a more realistic point of view and help us to eliminate all the excuses from our lives.

As criminals, we often talk of having "heart" or courage. Now we must learn what having true courage is all about. We must have enough "heart" to overcome any excuses we may have and begin to hold ourselves completely accountable for all of our own choices. We must face the consequences like a man, and quit excusing our actions and pretending we are the victims. If we truly want to take control of our lives, then there can be no excuses!

In fact, I believe that in order to truly overcome our past patterns of avoiding responsibility, we must be willing to go a little overboard and personally accept responsibility for everything that happens in our lives. Even if we think that we are not responsible for something that has happened, we must recognize the fact that our past pattern has been to avoid responsibility for our actions. So we should make sure that our present situation isn't just another part of this habitual pattern. Now, I am not talking about admitting to things we didn't do - that would be lying. Instead, we should

14   Frankl, Viktor E., "MAN'S SEARCH FOR MEANING - AN INTRODUCTION TO LOGOTHERAPY, THIRD EDITION" (New York: Simon & Schuster, 1984) pp.116

maintain a personal accountability. Not only should we eliminate all the excuses from our thinking, but also accept the fact that through our choices and actions we are at least partially responsible for everything that happens in our lives. Most importantly, we should accept full responsibility for coming up with a solution for the problem regardless of whether we are fully at fault or not.

For example, if something goes wrong at work, even if it is seemingly not our fault, we must humbly accept the responsibility, at least partially, for what happened and then take it upon ourselves to come up with a solution to the problem. Instead of thinking "it's not my fault", "it's not my problem", or self-righteously asking "who's to blame?" or "why did this happen?", we must learn to simply take responsibility and ask ourselves "what needs to be done to fix the problem?". Instead of perpetuating the problem through excuses, we must become a part of the solution. And if we are having problems in one of our relationships, we must accept the fact that these types of problems always have two sides. Even if we think it is the other person's fault, we should try to see the problem from the other person's point of view, focus on what we are doing that may be contributing to the problem, and then take responsibility for coming up with a solution. Asking "why?" or "who's to blame?" only causes us to think in terms of those self-serving rationalizations and excuses that have been our criminal pattern in the past. And, they can only lead to further problems. So, we should do much more than simply eliminate the excuses and alter our victim perspective. We should take full responsibility for all aspects of our lives, regardless of whether we think it is our fault or not.

Power and Control

When struggling to recognize and overcome our unrealistic self-image, we must be ever vigilant for our past patterns of irresponsibly seeking power and control. In order to see ourselves and the world around us more realistically, we must quit trying to control everyone, and everything, and concentrate more on simply controlling ourselves.

To grow and change, we must take control of our own

thoughts, choices and behavior, and responsibly direct them to cause the consequences we want in life. In fact, a responsible way of life requires us to assert the proper control over everything that is open to our choice. However, we must never try to control others or seek power without a legitimate purpose in any attempt to boost our self-image.

As criminals, our thirst for power and control is never-ending. Yet we seldom, if ever, truly want to use this power responsibly for a legitimate purpose. Seeking power and control is a defensive phenomenon in that it helps us to conceal our unhealthy relationship with ourselves by serving to create an unrealistic self-image. For us, the purpose of obtaining power is basically a way to prove that we are something, somebody who is in control, rather than a nothing who is controlled by everyone else. Therefore, our thirst for power and control is usually a way for us to selfishly aggrandize ourselves and boost our self-image, rather than being productive, purposeful, and beneficial to those around us.

To help us overcome our past patterns of irresponsibly seeking power and control, we should recognize that these patterns can permeate all aspects of our lives and be manifested in many different ways. We seek power and control at work, at play, in our relationships with others, during sex, while we are driving, when we go shopping, and even in our relationship with God (in that we always want him to do what we want, yet we never fully consider what he wants us to do). And not only is our desire for power and control expressed directly through deception, manipulation, coercion and intimidation, but it is also expressed subtly in the way we charm others through kindness, generosity, and feigned concern. Realistically, any action that is intended to achieve an exploitive purpose or to get others to fall in line with what we want is simply a form of irresponsibly exerting power and control.

In order to change, we must learn to conceptually recognize when we are irresponsibly seeking power and control, and then fully eliminate these tendencies from our lives. We can't simply quit asserting our power and control in our relationship with our girlfriend, or our mother, and yet continue in our attempts to assert our power and control over others when we are at work or playing sports. And we must realize that, for us, there isn't much difference in boosting our self-image by forcing someone to do what we want through physical coercion, and boosting our self-image by getting them to do the same thing by way of our charm or lies.

Our unrealistic sense of ownership is also simply an extension of our desire to obtain power and be in control. We often get angry because someone sits in our seat, talks to our girlfriend, or uses our weights in the weight room because, from our perspective, these actions undermine our sense of power and control. Furthermore, when we believe we own something, this belief fundamentally implies that we have power and control over that thing.

However, it is essential that we recognize and accept the fact that the ownership of material goods must be responsibly earned through effort, and that we can never own people. No one is required to do anything for us and no one owes us anything. In fact, if most of us are honest with ourselves, we will realize that we actually owe the world far more than it could ever owe us for all the harm we have done and all the crimes we have committed.

While reading the A.A. bluebook, I found an interesting section which described what usually happens when we try to control others, or the things around us over which we have no control. Personally, I believe that it applies to anyone, but that it is especially important for us to understand and remain aware of.

The first requirement is that we be convinced that any life run on self-will can hardly be a success. On that basis we are almost always in collision with something or somebody, even though our motives are good. Most people try to live by self-propulsion. Each person is like an actor who wants to run the whole show; is forever trying to arrange the lights, the ballet, the scenery and the rest of the players in his own way. If his arrangements would only stay put, if only people would do as he wished, the show would be great. Everybody, including himself, would be pleased. Life would be wonderful. In trying to make these arrangements our actor may sometimes be quite virtuous. He may be kind, considerate, patient, generous; even modest and self-sacrificing. On the other hand, he may be mean, egotistical, selfish and dishonest. But, as with most humans, he is more likely to have varied traits.

What usually happens? The show doesn't come off very well. He begins to think life doesn't treat him right. He decides to exert himself more. He becomes, on the next occasion, still more demanding or gracious, as the case may be. Still the play does not suit him. Admitting he may be somewhat at fault, he is sure that other people are more to blame. He becomes angry, indignant, <and> self-pitying.[15]

I believe that the word "criminal" could be substituted for "alcoholic" in most of the A.A bluebook. Many of the descriptions and principles apply as much to us as they do to the alcoholic – not to mention the fact that many criminals are also alcoholics and drug addicts. However, for us this pattern of attempted control, anger, and self-pity doesn't simply result in a desire to get drunk or high. Instead, it can lead to a dangerous thirst to prove ourselves and "assert our control" through irresponsible behavior and crime.

The thirst for power and control is at the very foundation of our criminality. It defines as well as helps to create who we are. Therefore it must be overcome through effort and the proper focus. Truthfully, I have found that because it is such an ingrained part of who we are, it is very difficult to fully eliminate this control aspect of our personality. In fact, I believe that it is one of the hardest things we must do, because it involves confronting our inner selves - the part we have hidden from for so long. Personally, it has been relatively easy for me to deter and eliminate irresponsible and criminal thoughts, follow all the rules, quit telling lies, and overcome other forms of irresponsible behavior (such as quitting smoking and doing drugs) when compared to fully eliminating my thirst for power and control.

At times, giving up power and control will cause us to feel like we are being used, controlled and walked over by everyone around

---

15 "A.A. BLUEBOOK", THIRD EDITION (New York: Alcoholics Anonymous World Services, Inc., 1976) pp.61

us. As is our pattern, we will sway from one extreme to the other and create an unrealistic perception of events in order to convince ourselves that if we aren't in control of others, then they are in control of us. Yet, in order to progress in a responsible way of life, we must overcome this perception. We should continually remind ourselves of our criminal tendencies and remember that it doesn't really matter what others may think about us, only what we know about ourselves.

To alter our past pattern of irresponsibly and unproductively asserting power and control, we must quit being selfish and egocentric, and begin to be more self-giving. We should abdicate power and control, and actively seek to humble ourselves. An irony of life is that the less we try to control others, the more control we gain over ourselves and our own lives. When we quit trying so hard to make the world fit in line with what we want, instead of wasting our energy in a futile attempt to control everyone around us, we grow stronger and more centered in reality. And we enable ourselves to spend our energy in more productive, purposeful and responsible ways. We empower ourselves to grow and succeed in life. As Jesus taught "Blessed are the meek for they shall inherit the earth."[16]

As changing criminals, we must be extremely vigilant, and struggle to eliminate our desire to prove ourselves through power and control as soon as it surfaces. We should remember where these tendencies have gotten us in the past and where this type of thinking, and its resultant behaviors, could get us in the future. We should constantly remind ourselves of our desire to change and productively use what we know about ourselves to guide our thinking and perceptions. Realistically, we can't control everything. And it is not right for us to try to control others any more than it is right for them to try to control us.

I believe that at the beginning of our change process we should give up all efforts to control others or gain power, and focus solely on controlling ourselves. This means no being the captain in sports, no being in charge in our relationships, no asserting control over

---

16 Matthew 5:4

our seat or our table in the chow hall, no power words (such as swear words) in our conversations with others (especially other criminals), and no being kind and generous simply to get someone to do what we want. We must learn to be responsibly submissive and give up all attempts to control others - our wife, our sister, the guys on the basketball court, our co-workers, our girlfriend, and even our dog.

I have found that if you truly struggle to responsibly overcome your criminal thirst for power and control, this thirst gives way to a thirst for productivity, purpose, meaning, satisfaction, accomplishment, self-improvement, and success in life. And in the future, any power or control we responsibly gain will more likely be productively used in order to achieve these ends.

In time, when we do begin to responsibly earn positions of power and control, we should always remember who we are. We must never allow ourselves to corrupt this power by using it to control others or to unrealistically boost our self-image. We can't let it become a criminal equivalent. In order to change and live responsibly, we should learn to differentiate between legitimate power and power solely for the means of aggrandizement. We need to be aware that legitimate power comes with burdens, problems and obstacles to overcome; not simply praise, admiration and the envy of others. Legitimate power has a purpose and direction toward meaningful objectives. Legitimate power promotes productivity, accomplishment, and satisfaction in everyone involved. True leadership is service to others.

We must also change our misconception that if we don't control then we will be controlled. Power and control are not the be all and end all in life. We should never pursue power for power's sake. Power and control can be good and mean something if they are responsibly earned and then used selflessly in order to achieve a meaningful objective. But they become contemptible and even evil when they are sought after, demanded or coerced from others to simply impress ourselves and those around us.

As I said before, maintaining a realistic self-image has been one of the most difficult things I've had to do in my own struggle to change. In fact, I still catch myself slipping from time to time and reverting back to my old patterns of wanting to be in control, and feeling like I need to maintain a good image, impress others, and prove myself. For example, I have caught myself arguing about the best team in football (as if it really matters), and allowing this argument to incite very dangerous feelings and emotions. The fact that I am a Denver Bronco's fan and I was arguing with a Raiders fan doesn't justify it either!! And, there have been times when I didn't get my way when playing sports, or didn't live up to my self-image of quasi-perfection, that I felt put down and caught myself getting angry and attempting to assert my control and power through words and intimidation. I also still catch myself talking to, and about, other people as though they were somehow beneath me. And I still allow myself to get angry and defensive whenever someone disrespects me, talks bad about me, or makes me look bad. I still feel somewhat put down when I am corrected, criticized, or things don't go my way. I even catch myself feeling like a nothing and unrealistically believe that everyone else perceives me that way. Yet at other times I still feel like I am better than others. In fact, at the beginning of my struggle to change, I wanted so much to continue to be viewed as cool and not as a punk or scared, that I kept my efforts at change as low key as possible. I often even felt like I had to come up with excuses for my responsible behavior. I felt like I had to explain why I was trying to humble myself instead of arguing or fighting, and why I was choosing to follow all the rules, just so that all the other criminals around me didn't think that I was weak or scared.

Even now, more than a decade after my decision to change, I still have problems humbling myself at times. And it is still difficult to maintain a realistic perspective of myself and others when I am confronted with disappointments and disrespect. However, the important thing is that I am continuing in my struggle to grow and maintain the proper focus and attitude. I truly believe that as long as I continue to make the effort and sacrifice necessary to move forward in my life, and never give up, I will be able to fulfill my purpose and provide meaning to my life. **The key to our success is not perfection, but perseverance.** Although we must be perfect in regards to never committing a crime again, our struggle for personal and spiritual growth must simply be enduring.

This unrealistic perspective of others and ourselves has been with us for a lifetime, so it will take time to overcome. From the outset, our challenge is to simply learn to recognize the situations in which our errors in thinking and perception are evident, and then correct these errors so they don't perpetuate themselves and lead to more irresponsible behavior. To do this, we should discuss and analyze these situations with our responsible guide to identify the root of our behavior, decide how we could have more responsibly dealt with the situation, and imagine how we can deal with, or avoid, it in the future.

When we catch ourselves acting as though we are unique and superior to others, we should immediately remind ourselves that we are not. We should recall our past criminal way of life and imagine the potential consequences of thinking that we are better than others. We should eliminate all pretensions of ourselves and others so that when things don't go our way we don't get angry or feel frustrated and put-down. When we do catch ourselves becoming angry or frustrated, we should replace these emotions by creating a more realistic perception of ourselves and the situation, reminding ourselves of the consequences of being angry, and focusing on the opportunity for growth which could be had by simply overcoming this obstacle in a responsible way.

If we find ourselves feeling put-down, we should identify and assess what is causing us to feel that way. We need to ask ourselves why we are allowing ourselves to feel this way and remind ourselves of the potential consequences of continuing to allow ourselves to feel put-down. We should then struggle to create a more realistic perception of ourselves and the situation by talking to those who may be involved, and discussing it with our responsible guide. If something we did contributed to the perceived put-down, then we must have the courage to criticize ourselves, accept responsibility, and grow. And if we find that we honestly did nothing to provoke the situation, or had no control over it, we should simply let it go. We should disregard the situation as beyond our control, accept it for what it is, and not allow it to control us by making us feel put-down. In our struggle to develop and maintain a realistic perspective of ourselves and the world around us, we can derive focus and guidance from the beautiful prayer composed by clergyman Reinhold Niebuhr, which was made famous when it was adapted by Alcoholics Anonymous. "O God, give us serenity to accept what cannot be changed, courage to change what should be changed, and wisdom to distinguish the one from the other."[17]

Finally, we should learn to view ourselves and the world around us based on our responsible purpose. Are we doing what we committed to do? Are we living responsibly? And, for our change to be true and lasting, we must not be afraid to be viewed as a punk or scared for living responsibly and following the rules. Although as criminals we often viewed other responsible people this way, we will undoubtedly discover how unrealistic and wrong this perception is. It takes true courage and "heart" to face life and take responsibility for ourselves. As criminals, we were cowards who didn't even have enough confidence in ourselves to believe that we could be responsibly successful in life. Our gains were always at the expense of others. We never contributed to the world – we were parasites who only took.

Again, I truly believe that if we consistently struggle to recognize, examine, correct, and eliminate our errors in thinking, we can develop a more realistic point of view and the foundation for a responsible way of life. In time, we will learn to face and overcome our obstacles in life and prepare ourselves to be responsibly successful.

Perspective of Others

Throughout our lives we have developed contempt for the ordinary and mundane. Thus, we tend to view ourselves, and the world around us, in extremes. When it comes to our self-image, we have to be perfect and superior to others or else we are a nothing. And from our distorted perspective, the world is either black or white, good or bad, and others are either for us or against us - there

---

17 "A.A. BLUEBOOK", THIRD EDITION (New York: Alcoholics Anonymous World Services, Inc., 1976)

is no middle ground.

However, if we are going to develop the attitude and perspective necessary to live responsibly, this "polarized thinking" must change. No matter what we may perceive, the real world simply isn't full of extremes. Everything isn't just black and white. Life isn't that predictable, or that easy. To be successful we must:

- learn to weigh perspectives
- temper expectations
- conceptually judge between right and wrong in a variety of contexts
- determine the best way to fulfill our purpose, reach our goals, and provide meaning in our lives

As I have said before, in order to develop a realistic perspective, we must first eliminate our egocentric view of the world and accept the fact that the way we see things is not always the right way, or the only way, to see them. This is especially true when it comes to developing a realistic perspective of others. Our tendency is to form a general conclusion of who others are based on our prejudices, their external appearance, and even just things we have heard about them. We then allow this small amount of information to unrealistically distort our perceptions of them as a person. To change, we must understand that others are more than just the sum of their appearance or a few behaviors and experiences, and that our perspective of a certain individual is ultimately just one of millions. Thus, the individual we see as a geek or nerd because he is short, bald, dresses funny and wears glasses may be seen by others as an honorable, intelligent, and handsome man. Remember, to some "bald is beautiful" and "beauty is always in the eye of the beholder." Similarly, the person we may view as weak or scared for following the rules and obeying the law will undoubtedly be viewed by others as strong and fearless. And, many people in society view us criminals as the cowards. Even the people we perceive as enemies, or impossible to get along with, have friends and loved ones who focus more on their good qualities. Our perceptions of others, then, are limited at best. Thus, we must always try to keep an open mind in our relationships with others and try not to label them on the basis of our own limited perceptions.

In order to gain a more realistic perception of others, we should first eliminate all of our personal prejudices and generalizations. Often we have a variety of different prejudices, generalizations, and categories that we place certain people into. We have the tendency to prejudge people and then to allow these prejudgments to distort our perceptions of them. We may judge people by the color of their skin, their external appearance, the size of their arms, the color of their clothes, the amount of money they have, the way they look at us, the career they choose, or their status and position of power. The specific prejudice or generalization doesn't matter much, because in the end <u>all</u> labels and prejudgments lead to unrealistic perceptions. And while I only discuss some of the more common prejudices we have, in order to fully change we must struggle to eliminate <u>all</u> of our prejudices and take responsibility for developing a realistic perspective of others. We should strive to view and treat all others the same, regardless of what they look like or what they believe.

One of the first unrealistic generalizations we must eliminate is that everyone is basically a criminal, just like us. The popular criminal saying, "the only difference between us and them is that they haven't been caught," is a fallacy. It is an error in thinking that leads to errors in perspective. It must be corrected by actively seeking the realities which contradict this point of view. Although people, in general, are not perfect and many even act very irresponsibly at times, most are not criminals like us. Most people wouldn't think of doing the atrocious things that we have done. And if they did, they wouldn't just keep doing them until they were caught. Personally, I know for a fact that my mother, father, grandparents and siblings wouldn't think of doing many of the things I've done. And reminding myself of this is a good way start correcting this unrealistic generalization. I have discovered that while this world has many examples of irresponsible and evil people, it is basically full of honest, hardworking, ordinary people who are all trying to responsibly make it in this life. And most people, unlike us, would much rather help others than hurt them.

As criminals, we also tend to hold the view that if people aren't for us they are against us. This misconception stems from our victim perspective and often becomes an excuse when things don't go our way. If someone won't do what we want, then we automatically believe that it is personal instead of considering other possibilities. We are likely to think that the other person doesn't like us, is out to get us, or is holding a grudge for something we did in the past. For example, if a girl tells us that she doesn't want to go out with us one night because she has to study, we are likely to believe that the real reason she doesn't want to go out with us is because she doesn't like us, or that she thinks she is better than us. Based on this unrealistic conclusion, we are unlikely to ever ask her out again. And, because for most of us being turned down will be seen as a put-down, we are likely to end up feeling like a nothing and be driven to prove ourselves somehow (usually through crime or criminal equivalents). Similarly, if someone we know doesn't acknowledge us as they pass by us in the hall, instead of thinking that they just didn't see us or were preoccupied with something important, we are likely to convince ourselves that they are mad at us for some reason or that they think they are better than us. Personally, there have been many occasions when I have felt that someone was against me or didn't like me simply because they said or did something I didn't like, or because they looked at me the wrong way, only to end up discovering that they weren't against me after all. I am lucky that I overcame this, though, because I had to ask my wife to go out with me several times before she actually agreed.

For the most part, these perceptions are unrealistic and can be overcome by simply being honest about our own thoughts and feelings, and then asking questions. When someone isn't for us instead of automatically thinking that this person is personally against us, we must be open about how we feel and ask them why they are choosing to behave in such a way. Often, we will find that instead of being against us, they have a very good reason for not doing what we want or conforming with our pretentious expectations of how we should be treated. And even when people are truly against us for one reason or another, we must not allow them to have control over us by dictating how we feel and how we choose to respond to them.

The other extreme from our perspective that others are against us is our unrealistic perspective that others are automatically for us. This misconception is especially evident when someone does us a favor, or in our relationships with the opposite sex. This is dangerous for us, because it can set us up to be put down; to get angry and feel like a nothing. Sure, I believe that there are some people who will almost always be for us. Our family and other true friends are usually always rooting for us. But these are not the people I am talking about. Instead, it is those people we barely know. The ones who we think are on our side based on a single act or a couple of words. And also the other criminals we hang around with. Often, for example, when someone takes our side on some issue, we pretentiously believe that they will always take our side. And then when they don't, we feel angry and put down. This unrealistic perspective of others stems from our own narcissistic self-image, our thirst for control, and our unrealistic sense of ownership. To overcome it, we must learn to see others and ourselves more realistically and accept who we are. We should also develop the understanding that just because someone does what we want or is nice to us, doesn't mean that they are personally for us, and it sure doesn't mean that we can expect them to do what we want in the future. They could just happen to agree with us, want to be friendly, or even want to take advantage of us. So, we should learn to temper our expectations and perceptions of others, and eliminate the unrealistic idea that everyone should automatically be on our side because we are special.

Another pessimistic perspective of others is created by the idea that by placing stumbling blocks in front of us, others can set us up and cause us to fail. Many of us complain that as we progress through the system and are released back into society, we are given just enough rope to hang ourselves. And ultimately, many of us do hang ourselves. However, this isn't because others set us up and cause us to fail, but simply because we were unable, and unwilling, to follow the rules or accept the increased responsibility which comes with increased freedom. It is a fact of life that with more freedom comes greater responsibility simply because there are more areas open to our choice. If we are given the freedom to stay out all night long, then we automatically incur the added responsibility to choose to go home at an appropriate time so that we can get enough rest to fulfill our obligations the next day. Similarly, if we earn the freedom to drive, we incur the responsibility to follow all the traffic laws and drive safely. Thus, the rope that we are given as we are released is simply the added choice that comes with freedom. We have "more rope to hang ourselves" because we have more <u>choices</u> to hang ourselves with.

Our pattern in sexual relationships, like in many other areas of our life, is to use and exploit our partner for our own benefit, and then, once we have sexually conquered them, move on to our next conquest. Sex, like other things, is a way for us to prove ourselves. If we can get a woman to have sex with us, then it proves that she cares about us and loves us. And if she won't have sex, we automatically think she doesn't like us. Again, if she isn't for us, she is against us.

Although we expect our partner to be totally faithful, we often feel that we are free to roam and continue to prove our virility through further sexual conquests. Therefore, not only must we struggle to develop a more realistic perspective of the opposite sex, but we must also develop a more responsible perspective of sexual relationships and temper the importance of sex in our lives. We must learn to deal with these sexual patterns in the same responsible manner as we deal with the rest of our criminal tendencies - by becoming more aware of them and then eliminating them through the active implementation of the appropriate correctives.

For us, all sexual relationships should be responsible, monogamous, and mutually beneficial. Not only must we consider the feelings and spiritual needs of others, but we must also keep mindful of all the destructive consequences of irresponsible sex. Realistically, responsible relationships are not simply about sex. In fact, sex can never be an early consideration in the formation of a truly responsible relationship, because it interferes with the development of trust, compassion, loyalty, and an open channel of communication. Responsible relationships take work. They involve the mutual effort and sacrifice of both partners, and considerations which go far beyond self. Without these things a relationship is not a mutually beneficial relationship, but instead it is a sort of hostage situation in which one person always gives, the other always takes, and neither is ever happy or satisfied.

Following the Rules

To be successful, it is very important that we struggle to develop a more realistic and responsible perspective of rules and the law. We must learn to be obedient and, as I have said before, follow all the rules out of a sense of duty to our purpose and our desire to change, regardless of whether we like them or not.

In order to live harmoniously and be productive in a free society, we must learn to abide by the rules. Contrary to the opinion of many criminals, rules are not made to be broken. Although we may not personally agree with, or even understand all the rules which are set forth by representatives of society, the majority of them have a good reason and purpose behind them. While most rules are intended to inhibit individuals from infringing on the rights of others and to prevent them from hurting themselves, the rest are usually a consequence of someone else's actions - one person messes it up for everyone else. For example, because some teenagers have chosen to be irresponsible and become involved in delinquent activities when they are allowed to stay out late at night, there are now curfew laws which are imposed on all teenagers in many major cities and towns. And, because someone decided to blow up a Federal building, no one can now park next to a Federal building—you have to park blocks away and walk.

If we don't like a rule, then we have the option to go through the necessary steps to responsibly get it changed. We can circulate petitions, plan lawful protests, and argue our case in front of those who are responsible for making and imposing the rules and laws. However, we must never allow ourselves to view rules as optional or intended for other people. We must follow all the rules no matter how petty, meaningless, stupid, or obscure they may be. If we

221

choose to follow our past patterns of complaining about, arguing about, bending, and just plain disregarding the rules we don't like or understand, we will assuredly fail in our attempt to change, and we'll suffer the consequences. And realistically, if we can't follow the rules set forth by a free society, if we can't accept the responsibilities which are our intrinsic part of freedom, then we don't deserve to be free.

In the end, I believe that our obedience to the rules and laws of society must be the result of an understanding, acceptance, and respect for these rules and laws. Obedience must become a fundamental part of our character and consistently define how we are going to act in any given situation. If we are having problems understanding, accepting or abiding by a rule, then it is our own responsibility to actively seek and find a reasonable explanation for the rule, which can satisfy our doubts, fortify our commitment and realistically correct our thoughts, perceptions and behavior. If we cannot find a reasonable explanation, then we should endeavor to responsibly get the rule changed. We must not, however, view rules as burdens which are set up to make life difficult. As long as we continue to view the rules and responsibilities of freedom as a burden or something we have to put up with in order to please or impress others, our struggle to change is destined for failure. We simply will not put up with these burdens for long.

Perspective of Time

As we work towards developing a more realistic view of ourselves and the world around us, we must also struggle to develop a more realistic and responsible perspective of time. Through effort, practice, and by properly focusing our conscious awareness, we should strive to enhance our abilities to:

- learn from the past
- set and work towards goals
- anticipate the potential consequences of our choices
- imagine a responsible and productive future.

We must learn to allow our perspective of time to work for us, not against us.

From the beginning, we will need to eradicate the erroneous belief that all of our troubles are simply the result of one or two bad choices. As criminals, we often complain that "life is so cruel - one mistake and you end up paying for it your whole life!" We recognize the one choice that resulted in our being caught, prosecuted, and imprisoned, but we fail to remember the series of other choices that propelled us down an irresponsible path of criminality and finally resulted in our arrest. As criminals, we chose to lie, cheat, break the rules, and disobey our parents as children; steal, do drugs, and subvert authority as we got older; and then we progressed to even greater crimes and atrocities as adults. Our downfall was gradual and not simply the result of one or two bad choices or actions. We just happened to only get caught for one or two.

We need to learn to recognize how our thoughts, choices, and actions flow over time to create the circumstances and momentum of our lives. Step by step as we proceed through life, our choices actually compound themselves by bringing about the situations and circumstances which require the next choice. Then, with each successive choice, we create the conditions surrounding further choices. So with each choice, we initiate or sustain a momentum in our lives, a momentum going forward or in reverse. And once we get the momentum going in either direction, it becomes more and more difficult to stop. Thus, one irresponsible choice can cause us to be faced with another, even more difficult choice that we may not have confronted had we simply made the proper choice in the first place. Personally, I have discovered that it is much easier to make a responsible choice if we make it from the very beginning. For example, if we choose to go to a bar or party with our coworkers after work, then we will undoubtedly be faced with the choice of whether or not to drink alcohol or do drugs. And then, perhaps, to drive home drunk. I believe it is much easier to make the responsible choice from the beginning (not going to the party) than to put ourselves in the situation of overcoming the temptations once they are there. Similarly, if we choose to hang

223

around with irresponsible and criminal acquaintances, then sooner or later we are going to be faced with the choice of whether or not to participate in their irresponsible and criminal activities. It is much easier to simply choose not to hang around with these types of people than to make the responsible choice when we are being pressured by them to compromise ourselves and behave irresponsibly.

Once we have begun to recognize and accept the lifelong regression that has led us to where we are now in life, then we can begin to imagine the responsible step-by-step progression it is going to take to get us where we want to be. As criminals, we often dreamed of instant success and betrayed our future potential for instant gratification. Yet, in order to reach our responsible goals, we must overcome this distorted perspective of success and develop a more realistic perspective of time, effort and sacrifice.

It is important to understand that success is not an achievement, but a way of life. True success comes from within. It is the result of who we are, not what we do. "Real success is success with self. It's not in having things but in having mastery, having victory over self."[18] Success is actually the fruit of our abilities to imagine what we want in life, properly direct our efforts in a purposeful way towards what we want, and then sacrifice what we want now for what we want in the future. **Our success should be measured by effort.** If we hit the jackpot in the lottery, marry a rich person, or make that one big score in crime, we are not successful - we are lucky! That is why these things don't provide the inner sense of satisfaction, self-worth, happiness and accomplishment that true success does. If we achieve or accomplish things through underhanded or deceitful means, then our success cannot be called true success, because our achievements are based on lies. And even if we graduate from high school, earn a promotion at work due to our hard work, or accomplish something spectacular and then allow ourselves to become complacent or regress in our lives, I don't believe that we can truly be called successful. It is not

---

18 Chaffee, John, "THINKING CRITICALLY: 4TH EDITION" (Boston: Houghton Mifflin Company, 1994) pp.104

the individual achievements that lead to true success, happiness and satisfaction in this life, instead it is the process by which we continually achieve.

In order for us to truly be successful in life, we must take responsibility for our future, consistently set realistic and responsible goals, and then actively work to achieve them. Developing and working towards responsible goals can help us develop self-discipline and enhance our self-esteem. It can also give us something concrete by which we can gauge our progress in life. Our achievements will then be like milestones on the road to creating a meaningful life. However, we must not get so blinded by our goals that we fail to pay attention to the process by which we achieve them. As far as responsible living is concerned, it is this process which is of utmost importance. We should always focus on the little steps that are necessary to achieve our goals and struggle to build a successful life like we would a house - one brick at a time. I have found that the process by which we succeed often provides even more satisfaction than the success itself. And, responsible goals are much easier to meet when they are broken into smaller, more easily-handled pieces.

While struggling towards our responsible goals and objectives, we should also practice anticipating the consequences of our choices and behavior. Then, once our choice has been made, we should evaluate whether it led us in the right direction. By becoming more aware of these consequences and assessing their impact on our lives, we can develop a more realistic understanding of the cause and effect relationships that serve to create our circumstances. In this way, we can enhance our ability to responsibly direct our lives.

If we can learn to realistically anticipate the consequences of our behavior and imagine our future, then we will gain a much better perspective on life. We can enable ourselves to use a sort of 20/20 hindsight (through our imagination) and "Live as if (we) were living already for the second time and as if (we) had acted the first time as wrongly as (we) are about to act now."[19] We can make our choices as if we were getting a second chance to make them right!! With this powerful perspective, we can actually eliminate regret and sorrow from our lives.

Finally, we must develop a concept of old age and start preparing for this time. As it teaches in the Bible, we should learn to number our days and thus responsibly make the most out of each one. We don't have a whole lot of time here on earth to reach our potential, accomplish what we have set out to do, and provide meaning to our lives. And, the older I get, the more I realize this fact.

Our life is transitory. Eventually, the day will come when it is no longer full of possibilities and potential, but only memories. Thus, we must learn to view the present, the here and now, as the time to make the most of our opportunities, strive towards our potential, and build a meaningful life. Today is the day that we create our memories and shape the legacy we will eventually leave behind. The legacy which, for good or bad, will be our eternal mark on posterity and will determine how we will be remembered, and how we will spend the rest of eternity.

In order to gain a more realistic perspective of our own life and the meaning of a lifetime, it can help to talk to others who have already lived much of their lives. As humans, although our circumstances and choices differ, we all go through much the same progression in life as we mature. Everyone is, at some point, a child, a teenager, and a 25-year-old on their journey through life. So, we can be sure that all older people have already been at the same point in their lives as we are now at in our own lives. They have already experienced life. So, not only can we gauge our own progress in life by comparing ourselves with them when they were our age, but their experiences, insight and advice can help us to better define our own purpose and recognize our possibilities. This, in turn, can enable us to set goals that are more realistic and help us to responsibly prepare for the inevitable time when we reach their age.

---

19 Frankl, Viktor E., "MAN'S SEARCH FOR MEANING - AN INTRODUCTION TO LOGOTHERAPY, THIRD EDITION" (New York: Simon & Schuster, 1984) pp.114

Once we have learned to envision ourselves as we would like to become and gained a more realistic perspective of a lifetime, we should then practice imagining ourselves at the end of our lives looking back on our accomplishments (or failures and regrets) and ask ourselves questions such as:

- Did I realize my potential?
- Was my life meaningful?
- Was my life complete?
- Did I leave a positive impact on the world?
- Did I accomplish my purpose?
- What were my regrets?

Realistically, if we continue to live as criminals, we can be pretty sure what the answers will be. And, they aren't very promising. But if we decide to change and begin building a meaningful future today, if we make it our purpose to live responsibly and productively right now, then our potential possibilities are limitless. We will go as far as our desire, talents, and personal effort will take us. And in the end, we will be able to truly call our lives a success.

CHAPTER 10

Seeking the Realities of Our Inner World

T hroughout my life I often hid from my emotions and avoided the moral lessons that I was taught by my parents and society. And because my pattern was to shut off undesirable or painful emotions such as guilt and fear, I did not develop the strong internal conscience that could have helped me consistently deter criminal behavior and overcome my fragmentation. Nor did I gain the self-awareness and emotional intelligence required for the development of such important traits and abilities as self-control, self-motivation, delaying gratification, and empathy for others. I became so good at hiding from myself that I undermined the internal characteristics that could have helped me live responsibly.

In order to learn to live responsibly, I had to first learn to maintain a realistic self-awareness, an awareness of who I was inside. However, this wasn't easy. As difficult as it was to become, and remain, consciously aware of the realities of my outer world, becoming consistently conscious of the realities of my inner world was just as difficult, if not more so. It took much strength and courage to do things such as responsibly live with fear, be guided by guilt, overcome anger and frustration, and responsibly deal with disappointments. But, with the proper focus and effort, I was able to overcome my past tendencies and improve my self awareness.

Strengthening Our Inner Guide

I believe that as human beings we are innately moral creatures. Most of us have the internal ability to judge between right and wrong, good and bad. And, we have the capacity to be emotionally guided by this judgment. We have a conscience. However, listening to our conscience requires effort and sacrifice. It requires choosing to pay attention.

In order to develop our ability to make the right choices, we must actively seek to strengthen our conscience and increase our moral abilities. Through practice, effort, and the proper focus, our conscience needs to become a consistent guide to our lives. Without fully developing this inner guide, we can never hope to overcome our fragmentation, live responsibly, or change.

From the beginning, it is very important that we begin with a clear conscience. This is the reason why I have stressed the importance of confessing and making amends for all of our past faults, crimes and transgressions, and forsaking our past criminal way of life. A clear conscience is stronger because it is not polluted with the distorted reality of past irresponsible behavior and crimes. Instead of burdening ourselves with the weight of lies and secrets, we can free ourselves by recognizing and accepting responsibility for them.

Our conscience is like a mirror in which our soul reflects upon itself and weighs what it sees against the highest standard of reality we perceive. And, much like any mirror, this reflection will become more realistic and clearer when we clean it. When we eliminate the blemishes caused by our past atrocities (along with their excuses and justifications) we enable ourselves to recognize reality and see things more clearly. Not only do we increase our ability to realistically judge between wrong and right, but we also augment our human capacity to be emotionally guided by this judgment.

Once we have totally cleared our conscience, it can be further strengthened as a deterrent to irresponsible and criminal behavior by simply using our moral abilities to judge between wrong and right. Because it is a uniquely personalized characteristic, our conscience can only judge our actions and choices against our own beliefs, values, experiences, thoughts and perceptions. We can only judge ourselves against the highest moral standard of reality we know. Our conscience derives much of its guiding power from our moral abilities to discern between wrong and right. If our beliefs, values, thoughts, and perceptions have not been morally judged and are unrealistic, then our conscience can only guide us unrealistically.

Thus, in order to enable our own conscience to guide us more realistically, we must actively use our moral abilities to judge our current beliefs, values, standards, thoughts and perceptions. In essence, we must educate our conscience by teaching ourselves to habitually recognize, and focus on, the fundamental truths of right and wrong; the realities of good and bad. As author John F. MacArthur Jr. writes, "All spiritual growth is based on <the> knowledge of truth."[1] It is simply impossible to consistently make the proper choices or to live responsibly until we first understand what the proper choices should be.

The lessons we learn throughout life can play an important role in developing the beliefs, values, and standards which direct our thoughts and perceptions, and thus impact our assessment of good and bad, right and wrong. But, the fundamental moral truths and principles based on reality remain unquestionable. Even if we are not properly taught the difference between wrong and right in every situation, this does not alter the external reality of the elemental goodness or badness of a certain act, or the fact that we will ultimately be personally responsible for the consequences of this act. In fact, as human beings, it is our responsibility to utilize our moral abilities to judge between right and wrong and assess every situation as completely and realistically as possible. Our moral responsibility, then, is to utilize everything at our disposal to realistically judge between right and wrong, and then to guide our lives by this judgment.

In the past many of us convinced ourselves, or were even outright taught, that for one reason or another it was alright to lie, cheat, steal, disregard the feelings of others, and drink alcohol or do drugs. Yet these criminal values and beliefs cannot change the reality of the fact that these things are wrong and come with many negative consequences. In fact, if we actively seek to morally judge these things, the reality of their wrongness is unavoidable.

---

1   MacArthur, John F., Jr., "THE VANISHING CONSCIENCE - DRAWING THE LINE IN A NO FAULT, GUILT FREE WORLD" (Dallas: World Publishing, 1995) pp.86

The problem is, however, that we can also choose to forego this moral analysis and simply continue to hold onto our old unrealistic beliefs, values and standards.

There are many times that individuals, and even societies as a whole, may choose not to accept or recognize these moral truths based on reality. Yet even this mass misconception cannot confound the ultimate reality of good and bad, wrong and right. For example, many people in society today believe that it is not that big of a deal, or actually even alright, to commit adultery, have premarital sex, cheat, lie, hate others, or use drugs and alcohol. Yet, even the global extent of these values and beliefs cannot alter the fact that, realistically, these things all carry with them the fundamental possibility of too many negative consequences - both internal and external in nature, momentary and eternal in time – to be right. Fatherless children, unwed mothers, venereal diseases, AIDS, loss of life, loss of possibilities and potential, hurt feelings, unanswered questions, pain, suffering, humiliation, spiritual destruction, and emotional disintegration. No matter what beliefs, standards, or values we hold, any choice or behavior which contains the possibility of these types of consequences simply cannot be right - that is just unrealistic.

The challenge is to actually use our innate ability to realistically judge between wrong and right, and this takes work. We need to become more consciously discerning about our values and beliefs, and actively seek to discover their correctness and appropriateness in reality. We should struggle to gain an awareness of the correct principles by which we must guide our lives. And, we are also responsible for educating ourselves about all the rules and laws which we must follow in order to live responsibly and productively in society and on earth.

Ultimately, this moral search can help us to develop:

- inner control
- a healthy self-concept
- goal directedness

- a realistic level of aspiration
- an increased ability to tolerate frustration
- an identification with lawful purposes

The more we actively search for the truth in responsible living, when it becomes our fundamental objective to judge between wrong and right, the more we will find the truth. And the stronger and more realistic our thoughts, our perceptions, and our conscience will become.

The easiest way to judge between right and wrong is to assess the potential consequences of our choices and behavior. We should also examine whether our values, standards, and beliefs are causing the consequences we want in our lives. If a certain choice or behavior could have hurtful, painful, or undesirable consequences, then we should view this choice as wrong and refrain from doing it. And if a particular belief or value we hold continually gets us in trouble, then there is most likely a problem and it needs to be re-examined.

Much of the time the potential consequences of particular beliefs or behaviors are predetermined by laws and rules. So, all we need to do in order to judge between their fundamental rightness and wrongness is to recognize these potential consequences, and then utilize a critical thinking process to evaluate our choices, beliefs, and behavior based on these consequences. However, if the consequences are less certain, or more complex and conceptual, then we must learn to ask questions and seek the appropriate realities. We must learn to ask ourselves questions such as:

- If everyone knew exactly what I was doing, or thinking of doing, is there any way that I could get in trouble?
- Would I be ashamed or embarrassed if I were caught?
- Could I possibly hurt myself or anyone else through this choice or behavior?
- Will this belief, value, choice, or behavior cause the consequences I want in my life, or could it lead to some undesirable consequences?

However, in order to be effective, this type of moral thinking must be used to deter irresponsible and criminal thinking at the moment of its inception, because once our minds have become flooded with irresponsible thoughts, the battle will have already been lost. It won't be long until we shut off the awareness of these consequences and behave irresponsibly.

In order to become an effective part of responsible living, this most basic moral thinking must also be consistently practiced and consciously applied until it becomes an automatic deterrent to any type of irresponsible or criminal thought. By reprogramming our subconscious mind, we must learn to habitually replace the thoughts of irresponsible or criminal behavior with the thoughts of their worst consequences. We should also remind ourselves such things as:

- Even the thoughts of crime or irresponsible behavior mean a return to prison.
- Telling one small lie can lead to my past patterns of crime and irresponsible behavior.
- Cheating just this once can mean the loss of everything I am working for.
- Building myself up at the expense of others means a return to my old hurtful and selfish way of life.
- Even thinking about letting up just a little bit in my struggle to change and live responsibly, could result in my returning to my past way of life. And it could lead to more innocent victims, including all those people who love and believe in me.

The Next Step

A basic moral judgment is necessary for the total development of our moral abilities. It can also be an effective first line defense against irresponsible and criminal thoughts and behavior. However, it is not adequate enough to sustain long-term change.

Moral judgments based solely on the potential consequences of certain behaviors are, at best, incomplete and inaccurate. Realistically, many wrong choices can have beneficial consequences while good and righteous choices can potentially have undesirable results. For example, we may get away with robbing a bank and potentially make a lot of money. Or, ironically, by telling the truth we could potentially hurt someone we care a lot about. And, our moral judgment could be unrealistically swayed by what potential consequences we choose to focus on. If we focused on the potential for getting rich instead of the potential for getting caught, then even selling drugs could be made to seem right.

Our unrealistic self-image and extreme optimism can also lead us to shut off the awareness of the consequences of our choices and behavior by leading us to believe that we won't get caught. Therefore, because we convince ourselves that we really don't need to worry about the potential undesirable consequences to our behavior, this moral thinking becomes inoperative and thus ineffective.

Due to our tendency to think concretely, we are often unable to conceptualize the relationships between our present circumstances and the moral lessons we have already learned, so we are left to continuously analyze the potential consequences of every little situation in order to determine whether it is right or wrong. This agonizingly repetitive process cannot last for long, because it requires too much energy and leaves little time left for growth.

Thus, in order to sustain a responsible way of life and totally overcome our moral fragmentation, we must develop more complex and conceptual moral abilities. When judging our choices and behaviors, we must learn to think about more than just the potential consequences of these choices and behaviors or if we will get into trouble if we are caught.

To grow, we must also learn to deter wrong thoughts and choices based on a moral inventory of where these choices got us, or others, in the past. We should learn to conceptually apply the lessons and experiences of our past to future thoughts and choices. A deterrent moral inventory along these lines involves thinking about all we have lost and everyone we have hurt in the past in order to develop the sense of guilt, sorrow, and self-disgust that can then help us to make the proper decisions the second time around.

In fact, I have found that once this moral inventory has become fully operative, we will begin to develop a sense of guilt for even thinking about behaving irresponsibly or criminally.

However, as a total deterrent to irresponsible and criminal behavior, this moral inventory also has its drawbacks. The biggest problem is that when we are already to the point where we are actively pursuing criminal excitement or a proof of power, we are unlikely to use this inventory properly to invoke a sense of guilt, because we subconsciously won't want to talk ourselves out of what we really want to do. Again, in order to be effective, we must use this moral inventory habitually in order to eliminate irresponsible and criminal thoughts from their inception.

We can further improve our moral abilities by learning to form a connection between what we regard as wrong for others and what we believe is wrong for us. In order to become more realistic we should eliminate our sense of superiority and uniqueness, especially when it comes to making moral judgments, and learn to treat others as we would like them to treat us. We simply can't continue to imagine that we are allowed to do certain things that others aren't allowed to do just because we are who we are. What's wrong for others can never be right for us. In fact, as changing criminals, we must actually learn to avoid all of the wrong things that others may unrealistically think are alright for them. We can't speed, litter, "borrow" office supplies from work for our personal use, drink alcohol, cheat on our girlfriend or wife, lie, or even take 12 items through the "10 items or less" line at the supermarket. For us, these things can lead to further problems and moral regression.

We can further improve our moral ability to see ourselves as we see others through the consistent practice of imagining ourselves as the victims of our own, and others' crimes. By exploring what we would think, how we would feel, and how we would view the person who victimized us, we can enable ourselves to gain a more realistic moral perspective of our own irresponsible and criminal choices and behavior. And we can develop an increased awareness of the mutual benefits of treating others as ourselves.

Also, because it is often easier to see faults, weaknesses, and wrong-doing in others than it is to see these things in ourselves, we should learn to stand apart from ourselves and view ourselves from the same perspective as we view others. We must recognize that, as human beings, others are often blind to their own flaws and shortcomings, then learn to honestly ask ourselves whether we are also blind to our own faults and wrong-doings. In fact, whenever we see bad in others, instead of worrying so much about criticizing, we must learn to focus on ourselves and determine whether we have the same, or similar, faults or weaknesses. By watching others in a self-critical way, we can become better at seeing our own shortcomings and weaknesses.

The next step we should take in developing our moral abilities is to actively practice weighing our thoughts, choices and beliefs against our goals, objectives and purpose in life. In essence, we should begin to view each choice in terms of the direction which it takes us in life. If part of our purpose is to live a healthy life, then we shouldn't smoke. If part of our purpose is to live a productive life, then instead of choosing to party all day, or filling our days with trivial pursuits, we should struggle to be productive. And, if one of our goals is to graduate from college and we are faced with the choice of either going out with our friends to party or staying home to study for a big test we have the next day, we should make the choice that will best help us reach our goal of graduating - and stay home to study.

If a choice ever leads us away from one of our goals or our responsible purpose in life, we can be reasonably sure that it is the wrong choice. And, we should avoid it at all costs. Even choices that lead us to become stagnant in our lives can be dangerous because, as I have said before, we must always continuously struggle to move forward in our lives or else we risk the chance of regression. For us, there is no standing still in life. **We must either move forward or we will move backward.**

Finally, in order to truly develop an uncompromising morality, we must develop and maintain a strong self-concept - one that is founded on fundamental truths and principles. Through sincere thought, meditation and soul searching, we must define who we are, what we want out of life, our purpose, our goals and values, and what things are truly important to us. And then we must rely on this self-concept to help us make all the tough moral choices before they arise and become moral debates.

By continuously reminding ourselves of who we want to be, we must learn to consciously view the act of making responsible and proper choices as if we have no other option. Eventually, we should get to the point where, when we're faced with a moral decision, we habitually have righteously directed thoughts such as:

- I have no other option but to tell the whole truth.
- I simply do not lie, cheat, steal, or break the rules, because that is not who I am or who I want to become.
- I have no other option but to humble myself and try to see things from others' points of view, because that is the only way I can fulfill my purpose and change my life.
- I live responsibly, productively and with integrity in order to give my life meaning and purpose, and to create the consequences I want in my life.
- I don't hurt or victimize others, because I wouldn't want to be treated that way myself

Another part of this preemptive morality involves learning to recognize and avoid those difficult moral situations which could cause us to be tempted to think or act irresponsibly. For example, if we can reasonably anticipate that if we choose to hang around with old irresponsible acquaintances or visit our old hangouts that criminal or irresponsible thinking will inevitably ensue, we must avoid these situations at all costs. If we don't then we will have problems. Putting ourselves in these situations can only serve to create negative self-fulfilling prophecies and have disastrous consequences. And, if we know that by allowing ourselves to think about committing a crime or behaving irresponsibly we diminish our resolve to live responsibly, then we must habitually learn to avoid this type of thinking at all costs.

As changing criminals, we must work hard to develop a strong self-concept and overcome the temptations we are confronted with, but we must also make no provisions for irresponsible thoughts, choices or behavior. As the saying goes, "if we don't want to slip, then we should always try to avoid walking where the floor is wet." We should prepare ourselves to responsibly and righteously meet all of the challenges and temptations of responsible living, but for us to unnecessarily put ourselves in questionable situations in a misguided effort to strengthen ourselves, is not heroic. It is foolish and just plain stupid, and may even lead to our demise.

Eventually, even more advanced moral values will develop after we have responsibly plugged away in life for an extended period of time and honestly made some internal and external gains. Gains such as:

- developing self-respect
- building our self-esteem
- earning the respect of others
- saving money
- starting a family
- responsibly building our future

These are gains which we will come to prize and value, and which we will be sorely afraid to lose through irresponsible or criminal behavior. And as our moral abilities develop and become habitual, we will begin to automatically direct our thoughts, choices and actions in a righteous manner. Our whole point of view will change. The irresponsible and criminal thoughts that were once savored and acted upon will no longer permeate our mind.

Ultimately, our objective is to develop a consistent personal integrity which is based on our responsible purpose and guided by an uncompromising morality. We must start making the right choices in all situations, not simply to avoid punishment, but because we recognize that this type of behavior is the most beneficial for ourselves and those around us. And, because we truly believe that it is the right thing to do. In the end, if we can get to the point where our moral abilities have become habitual, then we will become more productive and successful in life. Instead of continuously struggling to simply deter irresponsible and criminal thoughts and behavior, we will be able to concentrate more on our spiritual, physical and mental growth. But this will take time.

As with all human abilities, our moral abilities must be consistently practiced in order for us to effectively develop them. We should make it our daily goal to properly prepare ourselves and exercise a realistic judgment of right and wrong in all areas of our lives. But this is not all that is required to strengthen ourselves and develop our inner guide or conscience. We must also actively follow this righteous judgment to the best of our ability. Improving our ability to morally judge between wrong and right can only serve to strengthen our conscience as an inner guide to living responsibly when this knowledge is actively used to guide our lives. Again, once we know the truth, we must struggle to live in line with this knowledge or else it becomes worthless. In order to enable ourselves to grow, we must live with integrity. And we can't live with integrity if we talk and behave differently than we think and perceive.

Integrity

In his book *The Six Pillars of Self-Esteem*, Nathaniel Branden defines integrity as the "integration of ideals, convictions, standards, beliefs - and behavior. When our behavior is congruent with our professed values, when ideals and practice match, we have integrity."[2] I agree with this definition, but only to the extent that our ideals, convictions, standards, and beliefs have already been morally judged against the realities of right and wrong. I believe that true integrity must also be based on the fundamental moral truths which are found in reality. Without this truth, integrity would be worthless. An unquestioning adherence to unrealistic and immoral beliefs, values and standards is psychopathic behavior - NOT integrity.

If we begin to live with integrity, we will become at peace with

---

2   Branden, Nathaniel, "THE SIX PILLARS OF SELF-ESTEEM" (New York: Bantam Books, 1994) pp.143

ourselves. We will no longer feel a need to prove ourselves, or always be in control, because we won't be at war with who we are inside. Our behavior will be congruent with the moral judgments of our conscience. And the longer we live with integrity, the stronger our conscience will become, because our behavior will serve to validate it instead of contradict and confuse it.

If we learn to be consistent in our integrity and keep our conscience clear, our conscience will become more sensitive. We will begin to feel a sense of peace and wholeness that is the result of living in harmony with the fundamental truths which we have personally discovered through our moral evaluations. Conversely, we will begin to experience dishonesty, immorality and irresponsibility as uncommon, emotionally disturbing, and even frightening. If we do something wrong, it will agitate this inner peace, and we will feel a strong emotional desire to resolve this dissonance in order to regain our inner sense of moral cleanliness and purity. In essence, our conscience will begin to emotionally guide us to live with integrity.

However, if we continue to betray our conscience and live without integrity, then we will eventually lose this inner guide. "Sin defies and deceives the human conscience, and thereby hardens the human heart."[3] If we continue to respond to our conscience by suppressing or silencing it through shut-off and erosion, or overrule it with excuses and justifications, we defile it through confusion and deceit. And, by betraying our conscience, we will desensitize ourselves to the point where it no longer continues to guide us.

When the violation of integrity damages and weakens our conscience, only the consistent practice of integrity can repair it. So, in order to strengthen our own conscience, we must live with complete honesty, morality, responsibility and openness in all aspects of our lives. We should never allow ourselves to lie, cheat, steal, break the rules, advance ourselves at the expense of others, or sway at all from a total integrity. And, because our conscience

---

3   MacArthur, John F., Jr., "THE VANISHING CONSCIENCE - DRAWING THE LINE IN A NO FAULT, GUILT FREE WORLD" (Dallas: World Publishing, 1995) pp.57

knows all of our true thoughts, inner motives, and intentions, we shouldn't even allow ourselves to do the right things for the wrong reasons, or the wrong things for the right reasons. For example, we can't be nice or generous to someone else simply to get something in return, or tell the truth simply to build up our opinion of ourselves, and for no reason can we allow ourselves to lie or cheat - even if by doing so we would make someone else happy, help them, or save them from the painful truth.

It is very difficult to live with total integrity, especially at the beginning of the change process, but it is possible. There will undoubtedly be times when we catch ourselves stretching the truth, breaking a rule, withholding information from our responsible guide (which is in itself a form of lying), degrading others in order to build ourselves up, or in some other way swaying from our goal of total integrity. However, even in these moments of weakness it is possible to repair the damage and morally advance ourselves in a responsible way. Although I have found that, in the end, it is much easier to simply live with integrity from the beginning. When we do live without integrity, we can repair this breach in sense of our wholeness and regain our integrity by:

- recognizing and admitting our lack of integrity
- accepting the consequences
- seeking to understand why we behaved without integrity
- sincerely vowing never to allow these things to happen again

We must never just shut off or forget about a breach of integrity, or convince ourselves that it isn't that big of a deal. And, we need to do much more than just try better next time - we must do everything in our power to fully regain our sense of wholeness and peace. When we lie, we should not only repair this lie by telling the truth, but also by explaining why we felt like we needed to lie in the first place. We must honestly search our inner selves in order to fully understand this breach of integrity so that we can do whatever it takes to keep it from happening again.

Similarly, if we withhold important information we must not only make amends by divulging this information, but we should also struggle to honestly understand and explain why we failed to divulge this information in the first place. If we cheat or break a rule, we should immediately humble ourselves, report the violation to those in authority, take full responsibility for our actions, accept the consequences, and then struggle to understand our motivation behind this cheating or disobedience.

Yes, we must tell on ourselves and invite the consequences to our behavior, no matter how harsh they may be. We can never allow ourselves to feel that it is alright to break a rule as long as we don't get caught. In fact, if we know that in the end we are likely to tell on ourselves for a breach of integrity, then we will be more inclined not to allow this violation to happen in the first place. Finally, if in any way we degrade or disrespect another person, we must immediately make amends for this action by humbling ourselves, sincerely asking for forgiveness, explaining why we felt we needed to disrespect them in the first place (no excuses, just an honest explanation), and then promising to never let it happen again.

When seeking to understand and explain our breaches in integrity, we will often find that they are directly, or indirectly, the result of a selfish desire to sustain our unrealistic self-image. For example, we are likely to catch ourselves stretching the truth in order to impress others or to avoid any undesirable consequences; putting others down in a futile attempt to build ourselves up; or, withholding information when we think it would show weakness, cause others to lower their opinion of us, or in any way serve to deflate our own self-image as being unique, superior, and special. And at times, if there is anything that we are doing or thinking about doing that we don't want to be deterred from, we are unlikely to reveal this until it is too late. However, we must understand, and constantly remind ourselves, that we hurt no one more than ourselves when we hide the truth and live without integrity for any reason. And, we desensitize our conscience even more when we don't immediately repair a breach of integrity through honesty and understanding.

This one concept has helped me immensely in my own progression in life. In everything from overcoming bad habits to improving my decision-making abilities, it has helped me remain true to my convictions. I have had to tell on myself many times. And now I know that if I do something wrong that I will eventually feel bad enough and tell on myself. I may not tell on myself right away, but I know that I will eventually talk to somebody about my problems. So I don't do anything that I wouldn't want anyone else to know about.

I will never forget the look in my case manager's eyes when I went in and told her that I had been stealing from the commissary where I worked and then offered to pay for it. Or, how difficult it was tell my mother that I had lied to her. But, I will also never forget the sense of peace and relief that I felt once I did these things. It wasn't easy, but it was worth it.

Ultimately, as we progress and change, our violations of integrity will become less and less frequent, our moral abilities will develop, and our conscience will become stronger. In turn, a strong conscience will work as an emotional guide to living with increased integrity, because, when we damage a potent conscience by violating our integrity, it punishes us by triggering unpleasant emotions such as guilt, shame, disgust, regret and fear. Its judgment is inescapable. However, when we live with integrity, our conscience rewards us by bringing about feelings of cleanliness, peace, joy, and self-respect. "An educated, sensitive conscience is God's monitor. It alerts us to the moral quality of what we do or plan to do, forbids lawlessness and irresponsibility, and makes us feel guilt, shame, and fear of the future retribution that it tells us we deserve, when we have allowed ourselves to defy its restraints."[4]

"Emotional Intelligence"

A strong conscience rallies our emotions in an attempt to morally direct our lives. The problem is, however, that our past pattern

---

4   MacArthur, John F., Jr., "THE VANISHING CONSCIENCE - DRAWING THE LINE IN A NO FAULT, GUILT FREE WORLD" (Dallas: World Publishing, 1995) pp.35

has been to simply shut off those painful emotions, such as guilt, shame and fear, that our conscience is using in an effort to guide us. Thus, in order for us to be able to fully utilize our conscience as an inner guide to righteousness, we must develop emotional intelligence. Instead of hiding from our emotions, we must learn to recognize, accept and responsibly use them to guide our lives.

Feelings and emotions are an important part of being human. Not only do they morally guide us through our lives, but they also provide meaningful insight into who we truly are. Additionally, they can reflect perceptual nuances taking place outside of our conscious awareness which can manifest themselves in the form of human intuition and hunches. However, emotions such as anger, resentment, hate and depression can be very dangerous if they are not properly recognized, confronted and responsibly eliminated or controlled. In order to truly live responsibly, we must learn to feel the right emotion at the right time, to the right degree, for all the right reasons. And, we should begin to responsibly control our own emotions, and not continue to allow them to control us.

The awareness of our own emotions is the cornerstone of emotional intelligence. Before we can ever learn to control our emotions, use them to morally guide our lives, or properly recognize these emotions in others (develop empathy), we must first learn to consistently pay attention to the realities of our inner self and accept our emotions as being a part of who we are. Not only must we struggle to consistently stay aware of our emotions, but we must also examine our thoughts about these emotions, assess how we feel about these emotions, and understand how these emotions can serve to distort our perceptions, and influence our thoughts and behavior. Our emotions must not simply be ignored, dismissed, or allowed to surge out of control. They should be acknowledged, examined, and then questioned in order to uncover their root, and to identify whether they offer a pathway to valuable information - or are simply a product of some misinterpretation or distortion of reality.

Again, the practice of keeping a detailed journal can help us to gain the habitual self-awareness and emotional insight which is necessary to develop emotional intelligence. Keeping a good journal can help us stay consciously aware of the relationships between our inner states and external realities.

In order to begin developing emotional intelligence, we must first learn to properly focus on our emotions by asking ourselves such penetrating questions as:

- What am I feeling?
- Why am I feeling this way?
- What, if anything, are these emotions trying to tell me?
- What are the potential consequences of these emotions?
- How are these emotions affecting my thoughts, perceptions and behavior?
- How should they be influencing my thoughts and behavior?
- Are these emotions in line with my purpose and goals of change and responsible living?

And with each question we ask, we should look inside and struggle to gain a more realistic understanding of ourselves, and the realities of the world around us. By asking the right questions and actively seeking both the cause and consequences of our own emotions, we must learn to form a connection between the realities of our inner world and the realities of the external world. This can help us develop an understanding of the reciprocal relationship between our thoughts, our emotions, and our environment (our circumstances).

When writing in our journal, we should spend a large amount of time and effort focusing on this relationship in all those situations where we are having the most difficulty responsibly causing the consequences we want in our lives. For example, if we are having problems controlling our anger, then we should focus on all the anger-provoking incidents we encounter and how we reacted to them, how we felt, what we thought, what the consequences were, and what the potential consequences could have been. Once we have learned to recognize and understand our emotions, then we can begin to develop our ability to responsibly control them. And, by taking control over our emotions, we will enable ourselves to direct them in ways that are beneficial, purposeful, and productive instead of allowing them to become irresponsible and self-destructive.

Research has shown that certain emotions (such as fear and surprise in fight or flight responses) can be triggered automatically by certain areas of the brain before we even have time to think. This can be seen if someone claps their hands as the killer is about to slay his victim in a horror movie, and scares everyone else into a heightened awareness of fear before they have the time to realistically assess the situation as not being dangerous. And, emotional responses can become a habitual part of certain thoughts and external stimuli so that when we are confronted with this thought or stimulus, our mind responds by automatically triggering the emotions that have been habitually associated with this stimulus. This is evident in that we automatically feel love when we see or talk to our mother or our child, or fear when we see a police officer, especially if we have done something wrong.

However, for the most part, we do have control over our own emotions. Circumstances don't sustain our emotions. Our interpretation or perception of these circumstances is what sustains our emotions. When we get angry at someone, it isn't because they are forcing us to become angry, it is because we are consciously focusing on all the things that make us angry. And when we feel depressed or put–down, it isn't the situation itself which makes us feel that way. Instead, it is the things we say to ourselves and the way we choose to focus our perceptions which makes us feel depressed and put-down. Most of the time, our feelings and emotions are the direct result of our thoughts and perceptions.

So, in order for us to gain control over our emotions, we must develop the proper balance between our emotions and our intellect. We must learn to subordinate our impulses, feelings, and desires to higher principles and values. It is important to understand that because the way we feel is not always based on reality, feelings do not necessitate action or mandate certain choices or behaviors. In fact, responsible living often requires us to do things, or not do them, regardless of how we feel.

As changing criminals who desire to live responsibly, we must learn to habitually think before we act. Reason, reality testing (our moral judgment), and our purpose must become the ultimate deciders of action in decision-making. Even though our feelings and emotions can serve to lead us to sounder decision-making when they are properly used, they can also serve to obscure the real issues, distort the reality of the situation, and lead to disastrous consequences if we allow them to overrule our intellect. Prison is full of young men and women who allowed their emotions (anger, jealousy, envy, and depression) to grow to the point where they overrode reason and reality, and led to such atrocious crimes as assault, rape, robbery, burglary, theft, and even murder.

If we allow our emotions to become self-confirming and self-justifying by distorting our thoughts and perceptions of reality; if we fail to look beyond our feelings and emotions to the future consequences of our choices and behavior; if we fail to test our emotions against reality by examining the emotion itself and the circumstances which gave rise to the emotion; and, if we continue to disown or avoid the awareness of our emotions through shut-off and erosion, we will lose control of not only our emotions but also of ourselves. We will diminish our ability to live responsibly. However, if we simply struggle to overcome these errors in thinking and perception and change our point of view, we will gain more control over our feelings and emotions. And eventually, they will help us to better control our lives. No longer will we feel put down or angry when things don't go our way, or bored when confronted with things we don't really want to do. Fear and guilt will become more realistic and consistent moral guides to our lives. And, our thirst for power and excitement will be replaced by a thirst for accomplishment, integrity, satisfaction and self-worth. As our thoughts, attitudes and perceptions change, our feelings and emotions will change correspondingly. By learning to take control of ourselves and our emotions, we will improve our ability to control our lives.

Fear and Guilt

Throughout our lives, we have had a habitual tendency to avoid painful feelings such as fear and guilt, because they had the ability to deflate our unrealistic self-image and didn't fit in line with our desired way of life. However, in order for us to live responsibly, we must learn to confront and properly use emotions such as fear and guilt in order to guide our lives. "Fear and pain should be treated as signals not to close our eyes but to open them wider, not to look away but to look more attentively."[5] Just as physical pain can tell us that there is a physical problem which must be dealt with, guilt and fear are often signals that there are spiritual or moral problems that need to be confronted.

In order for guilt and fear to be effective, they must be directed in line with our responsible purpose in order to make it harder to live irresponsibly. If they are properly used, fear and guilt are powerful enough emotions to help us abort our quest for power and excitement, and pre-empt irresponsible behavior. In fact, Arthur Fay Sueltz writes, "Intelligent fear often proves to be the best way to conquer powerful evil."[6]

We cannot allow ourselves to simply live in a world of fear and guilt, or else we will be unable to move forward and reach our goals. However, as changing criminals, it is better for us to live with excessive fear and guilt than not enough. For us to overcome our fragmentation and fortify our choice to change, we must sustain some guilt over our past way of life, and always live with the fear of returning to our old irresponsible patterns and crime. We should also learn to develop a sense of fear and guilt if we even think about behaving irresponsibly or criminally, so that these emotions can help us to abort these thoughts before they grow into action. Some fears we should eliminate, however, are the fear of being put down, the fear of imperfection, the fear of failure, the fear of criticism, and any other unrealistic or unfounded fear. To live responsibly we must learn to feel afraid and guilty about the right things, at the right time, for all the right reasons.

---

5   Branden, Nathaniel, "THE SIX PILLARS OF SELF-ESTEEM" (New York: Bantam Books, 1994) pp.74
6   Sueltz, Arthur Fay, "IF I SHOULD DIE BEFORE I LIVE" (Waco: Word Books, 1979) pp.17

Anger

While learning to responsibly use fear and guilt in order to guide our lives, we must struggle to pre-empt and overcome emotions such as anger, hate, resentment, frustration, jealousy, boredom and depression. If we don't, these emotions have the potential to build on themselves, distort our thoughts and perceptions, and take control of our choices and behavior. While these emotions can be harmful and even somewhat dangerous for normal men, for us they can only lead to tragic consequences.

Anger and its core emotions (such as hate, resentment, frustration, irritability, annoyance, etc.) are dangerous because they are powerful enough to momentarily override rational thought and eliminate the deterrents to behaving irresponsibly. Similarly, boredom and depression can lead us to seek excitement and prove ourselves through irresponsible and criminal behavior.

Much of the time, anger results when the world around us doesn't fit in line with our pretensions of how things are supposed to be. Our errors in thinking and perception set us up so that when things don't go our way, even if it is a misperception, we get angry. When we think someone has disrespected us, we get angry because no one is ever supposed to disrespect us. When we have to wait at the doctor's office, we get angry because, although it's alright for us to make others wait, we are special and shouldn't have to wait for anyone. And, if we run into any difficulty fixing our car or doing work around the house, we often get frustrated and angry to the point where we beat on the car with a hammer or just quit because we believe that everything is supposed to go perfectly.

Throughout our lives, anger has often been a way in which we have attempted to avoid feeling like we are a nothing after a perceived put-down. Instead of simply falling into a state of severe depression every time things didn't go our way, our anger allowed us to take the focus off of ourselves and our own imperfections. Our anger allowed us to focus on excuses and justifications while emotionally creating scapegoats for all the problems and difficulties in our lives. In essence, we hid behind these emotions in an attempt to avoid the awareness of our own imperfections, and our inability to force the world to fit in line with our egocentric expectations of how things ought to be.

Since emotions are basically just chemically-induced responses to our thoughts and perceptions, anger cannot be dealt with as an emotion. However, we can learn to deal with it as a way of thinking. In fact, the emotion of anger is actually triggered by thoughts and perceptions that encourage an anger reaction, and then this emotion is perpetuated by our thinking processes during and after the anger-provoking incident. In essence, by focusing our thinking and perceptions on the things that make us angry, we actually fuel the flames of our own anger. So, because we create and perpetuate our own anger, we can also overcome and eliminate it. It is totally under our control. Much of the time anger reactions themselves can actually be pre-empted if we eliminate the pretentious errors in thinking and perception that lead to anger. We can also prepare ourselves to responsibly deal with any potential anger-provoking situations by anticipating their occurrence. This way we can think rationally about our actions and emotional reactions before these situations arise.

As changing criminals, our ultimate goal should be to totally eliminate anger from our lives through choice, preparation, and a total change in our unrealistic thoughts and perceptions. Each time we allow ourselves to become angry, we produce a mental state in which we are vulnerable to unrealistic thoughts and perceptions, and more likely to behave irresponsibly and return to a criminal way of life. Contrary to popular belief, anger is not a naturally inherent part of life. Anger as an emotion is actually unnecessary and can only impede performance. There are no positive effects to being angry. And any objective that can be accomplished through anger can be accomplished much easier, and better, through other means.

However, because the total elimination of anger from our lives will take much time and effort, we must start by learning how to responsibly control our anger and deter its expression. From the beginning, it is important to understand that anger builds on anger. When we hang onto our anger, it begins to perpetuate itself. Our perceptions and thinking actually become more and more distorted the longer we are angry - to the point where we actually begin to seek out those things which feed our anger, and discount or ignore facts that would serve to undermine it. Instead of seeking reality, we react to the world out of self-pity and focus solely on the grievances that have built up in our mind (many of which have no merit), thus feeding the flames of our anger until it has the potential to surge out of control.

However, it is possible to short-circuit or dilute our anger before this happens. The key, though, is not to vent or displace our anger, as some people would suggest, but instead to defuse it in our thinking by focusing on things that can serve to contradict and calm our anger as soon as possible after the original anger-provoking incident. Studies have shown that venting or displacing anger does not serve to diminish our anger, but actually increases it. Outbursts of rage usually provoke an increased emotional response from our brain that calls for the release of even more emotive chemicals and leaves us feeling even angrier.

It is important that from the outset we prepare ourselves to overcome our anger by deciding beforehand that we are not going to allow our anger to build on itself, and that we are willing to do anything in order to keep this from happening. Controlling our anger in the heat of the moment when we are angry isn't easy, but it is possible. To strengthen our resolve, we should review the consequences of our anger in the past and consider the potential consequences in the future. Some of the consequences include:

- bad decisions
- injury to ourselves and others
- illogical thinking
- insane excuses
- irresponsible and criminal thoughts and behavior
- distorted perceptions
- lost relationships

And in the future, anger has the potential to return us to our past irresponsible and criminal way of thinking and viewing the world, and eventually to our old criminal way of life. Anger is so potent that if we allow it to grow uninterrupted, it can serve to undermine everything that we have responsibly gained - no matter how far we have progressed.

On those occasions when we do find ourselves in anger-provoking situations, we should learn to habitually consider the past (and potential future) consequences of our anger in an effort to dilute our anger. We must convince ourselves that the situation isn't worth the risk. We should also learn to habitually seek out any mitigating information that may challenge the thoughts and perceptions that provoked our anger in the first place. If we strike out in softball or miss a shot at basketball, we should focus on the fact that it really is not that big of a deal and no one is going to remember anyway. If someone makes fun of us, then we should focus on all the times we have made fun of others, and then try to find the humor in it. And, if we get stuck in traffic or in a long line at the grocery store, we should remind ourselves that at least we are not in prison. We should focus our perceptions on those things that can calm our anger and always stay consciously aware of the reciprocal relationship between our emotions, our thoughts, and our perceptions. We simply cannot allow ourselves to distort our thinking and perceptions to the point where we are focusing solely on those things that serve to fuel our anger and ignore those things which could help us control it.

Often, if we simply make a calmer and more realistic appraisal of the situation, we will often find that our anger is unwarranted and simply the result of a misperception, misinterpretation or error in thinking. As Benjamin Franklin is quoted as saying, "Anger is never without a reason, but seldom a good one."[7] It isn't uncommon to get frustrated and angry at some toy or new piece of office equipment, such as a calculator, for not working, only to open up the back and find that the batteries have been put in backwards or that it hasn't been put together correctly. Or, to get angry at someone for saying something we believe is disrespectful only to discover that they truly didn't mean what they said to be disrespectful

---

7   Goleman, Daniel, "EMOTIONAL INTELLIGENCE" (New York: Bantam Books, 1995) pp.59

(we only perceived it that way). I remember once getting so angry at an electronic game I was trying to play that I threw it against the wall, only to discover that I had not put any batteries in it. The worst part was that the game shattered into a hundred pieces when it hit the wall, so I never got to play with it.

When struggling to control our anger, it can be very helpful to imagine that the people we are interacting with are actually trying to teach us something and giving us the opportunity to grow. The man who criticizes us is teaching us to responsibly deal with criticism and to overcome potential put-downs. The woman who makes us wait is trying to teach us patience. The person who is standing in the way of responsibly reaching our goals is trying to teach us the art of negotiation and compromise. And, the guy who always seems to be pushing our buttons is trying to teach us to humble ourselves and control our anger. With a perspective like this, anger-provoking incidents and potential put-downs can become learning experiences and opportunities for growth.

Our anger is often the result of one, or many, of our errors in thinking and perception such as:

- superiority over others
- perfectionism
- uniqueness
- unrealistic pretensions
- failure to fact-find

So, it can also be very helpful to consciously focus on the correctives to our errors in thinking as we struggle to overcome our anger. Nothing serves to deflate frustrating encounters and anger-provoking incidents more than realistic expectations and having empathy for others. And, by maintaining a realistic self-image and perspective of the world around us, and making it our purpose to overcome our anger and live responsibly, we will undoubtedly learn to control ourselves and eliminate anger from our lives.

Finally, to fully eliminate anger from our lives, we should learn to pre-empt its occurrence by using our past experience and imagination to anticipate future anger-provoking incidents. Through role playing with our responsible guide and talking about the things that could possibly make us angry, we can prepare ourselves by deciding beforehand how we are going to think and behave in potential anger-provoking situations. Then, when confronted with these situations, or ones like them, we will be better equipped to think responsibly and reasonably without the distorting effects of anger. We will be able to see things more clearly. In turn, we will enhance our ability to solve our problems and overcome the imperfections of life, and actively cause the consequences we want in our lives.

Depression and Despair

During the change process we are bound to experience discouragement, depression and despair, especially if we let ourselves become overwhelmed with the strict requirements of change and living responsibly. However, as changing criminals, we must understand that these emotions are also very dangerous. We will not endure them for long before we are driven to seek excitement and revert back to our past patterns of proving ourselves through irresponsible behavior and crime (or criminal equivalents).

We are likely to perpetuate these feelings of depression, despair, and worthlessness in our thinking by asking ourselves questions like:

- Why even try?
- Is this all really worth it?
- How long am I going to allow the world to walk all over me before I do something (prove myself)?

And we are likely to begin thinking things like:

- I will never change.
- I am alone in this world, so why even care about anyone else.
- To hell with it all - I am tired of living a boring, worthless,

255

meaningless life. I may as well not be living at all.

Worst of all, we are likely to shut off all of the things that made us want to change in the first place and forget about all the joy, happiness, and wonderful feelings that a responsible way of life has to offer.

However, if we learn to view these moments of depression and despair simply as obstacles to overcome, instead of a never-ending gloom, then we will be better equipped to overcome them. These feelings, like all emotions, stem from our thinking and perceptions. So, in order to overcome them, we must struggle to identify, dissect and correct their thought components. We can't allow ourselves to simply focus on the feelings themselves, because this can serve to exacerbate them by causing us to get even more depressed about being depressed. Instead, once we have properly identified our feelings and accepted them as a part of us, we should focus on understanding what is causing these emotions and then try to identify any errors in thinking or perception that could be contributing to our feelings of depression.

In order to overcome feelings of depression, we should focus our awareness on the realities of the present situation, try to mentally recreate what made us feel the way we feel, and examine whether our interpretation of the events that provoked these feelings is based on reality. Next, we should try to uncover and examine any personal insecurities that may be underlying these emotions, and try to identify exactly what it is that is bothering us. Are we depressed for a good reason, or is it simply because we, or the world around us, didn't live up to our standard of perfection. Or maybe it is because we feel fat, stupid, ugly or unpopular. If we can simply identify the true problem at the core of our thinking, we will better enable ourselves to accept, confront and responsibly overcome this problem. We will also usually find that what we thought was a disaster or a disgrace isn't that big of a deal after all, at least not a big enough deal to risk returning to a criminal way of life and forsaking our purpose and potential.

Once we have uncovered the root of these emotions, we should explore our options, decide what we want to do about these feelings, and examine all the possible consequences of these actions. We should ask ourselves questions such as:

- What did I do because of these emotions in the past?
- Were my past reactions to these emotions effective?
- What response to these emotions would be most in line with my purpose and cause the most beneficial consequences?
- Is my response to these emotions simply my past pattern of irresponsibly covering or avoiding my feelings of depression, or will my chosen response help me to eliminate the thoughts and insecurities that are the underlying cause of my depression?

If we find that we are depressed because we didn't live up to our standard of perfection or because things didn't go our way, then instead of seeking to prove ourselves and unrealistically build ourselves up, we may need to reexamine our thinking and struggle to develop more realistic expectations and reasonable quotas for failure in an imperfect world. If we simply prove ourselves, seek excitement, or get high, like we have in the past, then most likely we are just going to feel depressed again the next time things don't go as planned. But, if we can eliminate our unrealistic expectations along with any other errors in thinking and perception, then we will be eliminating the very basis for our depression and despair. Instead of simply covering the symptoms, we will be curing the disease. Similarly, if we feel fat, stupid, ugly, poor, or unpopular, then instead of simply covering or avoiding these insecurities through irresponsible means, we should confront them, accept what we cannot change (and thus refuse to be miserable), and then work to change those things we can control. This may mean making the sacrifice and effort necessary to work out, go on a diet, work overtime, get another job, return to school, read more, study more, or even seek counseling. But somehow, we must eliminate the reasons for our depression and despair. We must cause the consequences that we want in our lives.

When we are confronted with feelings of depression and despair, it can also be helpful to remind ourselves that these feelings are not going to last forever. They will only last as long as we allow them to. Like the darkness of night, feelings are not permanent. Personally, I have found that there is much truth in the age-old saying "it is often darkest before dawn". If we just persevere and live responsibly, our depression will eventually disappear and be replaced by the warmth and brightness of the son.

We should learn to focus on our purpose and desired future course in life, and actively seek out all those positive things in our lives which may help us to overcome our depression and convince us that we are not worthless or losers. Whatever it takes, we must never allow a misconception of ourselves as a loser to become a self-fulfilling prophecy in that it causes us to revert back to our old irresponsible and criminal ways, and leads us back to prison where we really are a loser.

There are times when our depression may be appropriate and justified. If a loved one dies, if we lose our freedom, and when we finally truly realize the potential and possibilities we have forsaken because of our criminal way of life, we are likely to become depressed. However, appropriate depression does have its benefits. It enables us to recognize that something is missing from our lives. It saps our energy and diminishes our interests in other diversions in order to allow us to focus our attention on what has been lost so that we can analyze the loss, come to terms with it, and ultimately make the necessary psychological and emotional adjustments necessary to move on in our lives. In essence, healthy depression allows us to grieve, to confront, to accept, and then to continue our lives in the right direction.

If, after assessing the root of our depression, we find that it is justified, then as responsible individuals we must find some way to accept and overcome the situation, turn tragedy into triumph, and move forward in our lives. We must not, however, allow our depression, or anything else, to become an excuse to give up or quit struggling to live responsibly.

Our past pattern has been to allow our depression and feelings of being a "nothing" to perpetuate themselves through our thinking to the point where they overwhelm reason, and provide excuses and justifications for irresponsible behavior. So, at those times when we feel depressed, discouraged, and feel like giving up, it can help if we find someone to talk to. We must find someone who can help us to short-circuit our depression and regain our responsible focus on life.

It can also help to:

- Realistically evaluate our assets and all the rewards which change and responsible living can bring.
- Consider how those people who really love and care about us regard us and our desire to change and live responsibly.
- Consider how we would hurt the people who love us, ourselves, and all the potential victims of our future crimes if we allow our depression or feelings of nothingness to become an excuse to behave irresponsibly.
- Think about all the reasons why we wanted to change in the first place, and remind ourselves that we were in the process of creating a better life.
- Remind ourselves that, "When the going gets tough, the tough get going!"

In the end, we must simply struggle to be more realistic about ourselves and the world around us. We are inevitably going to meet adversity, disappointment, imperfection and even tragedy - that is just a fact of life. The real issue, however, is whether or not we are going to allow ourselves to drop into a state of depression and despair, and then remain there knowing all the potential consequences of this choice. Or, are we going to do everything in our power to responsibly overcome our depression by properly dealing with all the issues at its root. It is all a matter of choice.

Boredom

Because of our makeup, we will also have to struggle to overcome feelings of boredom and apathy. These emotions can be very dangerous, because they can cause us to seek the high octane excitement which in the past we derived from irresponsible and criminal behavior. Boredom can also lead to drugs and alcohol, and their disastrous consequences.

Realistically, boredom is rarely, if ever, truly a result of having nothing to do. Although we may tell ourselves that there is nothing to do, we can usually find many things that need to be done if we simply take a closer look. This is especially true for us. As changing criminals, we can productively use every free moment in order to practice:

- focusing our conscious awareness
- controlling our thinking
- examining the consequences of our past way of life
- learning to live and think responsibly
- struggling to reach our responsible goals
- working in an effort to build a responsible future

Usually, the problem is simply that we don't feel like exerting the effort necessary to do what needs to be done, so we feel bored. In the past, our pattern has been to feel bored and exhausted whenever we were faced with a responsible task or obligation which required effort or wasn't exciting enough for us. However, if something exciting enough came up, the energy and enthusiasm would suddenly be there. To overcome our boredom, we must simply change our attitude and learn to redistribute our energy for effort in responsible living. Usually, if we can just get started, our focused effort will actually generate energy and help us to overcome our boredom. And if it doesn't, then we don't have the proper focus or the right attitude and perspective to begin with.

By simply changing our thoughts, attitudes and perceptions, we can make the most boring tasks seem agreeable, and even enjoyable. It can help to view what may seem like boring tasks (such as mowing our lawn, going to work, studying, or paying our bills) as things which we must do in order to responsibly cause the consequences we want in our lives. If we learn to consider our long-range objectives, we can maintain a perspective that extends beyond the mundane and repetitious details of responsible living, and find meaning and a purpose in even the most tedious and boring tasks. This purpose can then help provide us with the energy and conviction we need to overcome our boredom. Conversely, if we choose to focus on how much we hate doing what we are doing and how boring the task seems to be, we will make it seem even more boring and detestable.

I have found that if I simply focus on responsibly fulfilling the task to the best of my ability, no matter how much I would rather not do it, I find all of the energy I need. Time also seems to fly by while I'm busy and before I know it, I am finished with the task or obligation. And not only do I feel a sense of personal pride and satisfaction once I have completed the task, but I even find a certain sense of purpose, meaning and enjoyment while doing what needs to be done.

Ultimately, our goal must be to make a habit out of keeping ourselves busy, and exerting effort in order to overcome our boredom. We should accept the fact that life isn't just one excitement after another. Mundane and repetitious tasks are an essential part of a responsible, purposeful and productive way of life. And they must be completed regardless of our feelings or a lack of desire. If we truly want to change and live responsibly, we have no choice but to overcome our boredom and fulfill all of our responsible tasks and obligations. However, we do have a choice as to our attitude and perspective.

Emotional Self-Direction

Another important aspect of learning to manage and control our emotions is developing the ability to channel or direct our emotions in the service of some goal or objective. Self-motivation, self-discipline, self-denial, delaying gratification, and stifling impulsiveness are all emotional related qualities that we must actively seek to develop in order to live responsibly. As with all other types of emotional self-control, we develop these abilities through practice. And, the key to emotionally directing ourselves is, once again, in our thinking.

For us, true change necessitates the development of emotional self-direction. We must motivate and discipline ourselves to take responsible initiatives, fulfill obligations, overcome boredom, and do all the responsible things we may not really want to do. We must also develop self-denial and refrain from doing many things we may want to do, or which may have even become habitual. No more seeking irresponsible or criminal excitement, no drugs or alcohol, no proof of power, no secrecy, no lying, no cheating, no anger, no irresponsible or criminal fantasies, thoughts or behavior. And finally, we must learn to delay gratification and control our impulsiveness if we ever hope to responsibly achieve any worthwhile goals or learn to purposefully direct our lives. Responsible living requires emotional self-direction. Ironically, however, the true development of these emotional virtues can only happen as a result of living responsibly.

<u>Self-Motivation</u>

In order for change to occur, it is imperative that we learn to responsibly motivate ourselves. As I have said before, change cannot occur by osmosis, only through properly directed, effortful action.

To live responsibly we must learn to generate and sustain responsible initiatives, much like we generated and sustained irresponsible and criminal initiatives in the past. If we don't take initiative in responsible living, just like a boat that isn't propelled is at the mercy of the wind and tide, we are left at the mercy of life's circumstances. And even though we can still choose to live correctly, our choices themselves are severely limited by our circumstances. However, if we take initiative, we direct and propel ourselves. We go where we want to go in our lives and not simply where our circumstances take us. So, by taking responsible initiatives, and choosing to act and not simply be acted upon, we can personally cause the consequences we want in our lives, and create our own circumstances and possibilities.

Taking responsible initiative means not only exerting the effort necessary to take action, but also exerting our effort in the right direction. We can't just do something; we have got to do what is right. So, we should properly prepare ourselves to take action and then ask questions, fact-find and assess what consequences we want to cause in our lives. Then we must see our objective or obligation through to the end. Although true responsible initiatives will usually cause the consequences we want in our lives, they often do not result in immediate payoffs. So, it is very important that once we have taken the beginning initiative and started something, that we see it through to completion. Realistically, doing something like going out looking for a job for a week or two and then quitting because we can't find one that suits us is not taking initiative, but simply our past pattern of starting off strong and then giving up.

Again, responsible living requires stamina, patience and conviction. We aren't going to be successful overnight. True responsible initiatives will often require us to become long-distance runners instead of sprinters. Responsible initiatives which are not sustained and completed are worthless. We may as well not have taken the initiative in the first place.

Ironically, the motivation for sustaining our initiatives often develops only after we have already taken the initiative in the first place. In other words, taking initiative can actually feed our desire to sustain our actions and responsibly direct our lives. And it can even lead to other responsible initiatives. For example, while in prison I lived with an inmate who, although he wanted to improve himself, wouldn't take advantage of any of the educational programs that were offered. Not only did he have the unrealistic idea that school was too difficult, but he had also convinced himself that he didn't want to make the effort necessary to go to school and learn something new. However, once he took the initiative to enroll in a basic computer class, he discovered, to his amazement, that he not only understood what he was learning, but that he actually enjoyed working with computers. Because he had taken the initiative to enroll in the computer course, he found the motivation necessary to complete it. And he even went on to take further responsible initiatives by enrolling in, and completing, other more advanced computer courses.

The interest and motivation to do something can only come from experience. In fact, there is no way to know what we are going to like or be motivated to do until we have already started to do it. And even on those occasions where our interest fails to develop, we must always remember that as responsible individuals there are things that we must do in the name of a responsible future, regardless of how we feel.

In the past, we never had a problem taking initiative in irresponsible or criminal activities, and we were very active and self-sufficient when it came to pursuing what we wanted. However, when it came to taking responsible initiatives, we were not quite the same eager beavers. In fact, we rarely, if ever, had a desire to even try doing the responsible things we thought would offer no excitement or immediate gain. Thus, our past pattern has always been to try to get others to do the things we would rather not do.

In order to overcome this criminal tendency, we must learn to do things for ourselves. We must avoid our exploitive pattern of having others do what we don't want to do or don't think we can do ourselves. We must wash our own clothes, clean our own rooms, do our own work, pay our own bills, find our own jobs, mow our own lawn, budget our own time and money, and do anything else which is necessary for us to responsibly direct our lives. We should take responsible initiative for everything that we are responsible for. But, we must also be aware that responsible initiatives taken solely to impress others or to enhance our opinion of ourselves are simply criminal equivalents.

If we are having problems with any initiative we can ask questions and ask for advice, but for a while we should avoid asking for help. We need to first become self-sufficient and self-reliant (independent) before we can truly understand what responsible interdependence is all about. Ultimately, in responsible life we are going to need others help in order to reach our goals and accomplish our objectives. We are going to need to learn how to responsibly live interdependently. However, we must not ever demand this help as our due. Nobody owes us anything. Instead, we should learn to sincerely appreciate it as an act of generosity and pray for the day when we can somehow return this kindness to the same person or someone else.

For some time after our decision to change, we will undoubtedly continue to rely on others and not take initiatives that are in our responsible self-interest for many different reasons. We may fear being put down. We might not want to offend anyone, or look weak and scared in front of our old partners and criminal associates. However, if we are sincere about our desire to change, then any person who would be offended by our decision to take a responsible initiative isn't someone we should care about offending in the first place. We also might not take initiatives because we lack the basic knowledge necessary to take the initiative. We may not know how to enroll in a college course, find a job, or even properly wash our clothes. But even this cannot be an excuse because, as responsible individuals, we should ask questions, fact-find, and do whatever it takes to learn how to do these things. Finally, in line with our perfectionism and fear of failure, we may not take responsible initiatives because we have no guarantee that they will result in success (or not lead to failure). Realistically, however, even though taking a responsible initiative dramatically increases our chances for success, there are no such guarantees in life. One thing that can be guaranteed, however, is that if we don't take the initiative, then we fail from the very outset. We simply can't succeed if we don't even try.

As responsible individuals we must overcome our excuses, struggle to consistently motivate ourselves, and learn to take responsible initiatives. And, as with any human ability, it becomes easier to motivate ourselves the more we do it. We should make a habit of motivating ourselves and occasionally try doing something for no other reason than we would rather not do it. Doing things that we would rather not do, such as fasting (not eating for a specific period of time), can help us gain control over our emotions, and ourselves. Through practice, preparation, and the proper conscious focus, we must learn to proactively take control of our lives. As a recent automobile commercial advertises, "On the road of life there are passengers and there are drivers." In order to truly change and live responsibly, we can't simply be passengers in life, we must become the drivers.

265

Self-Discipline, Self-Denial, and Delaying Gratification

Self-discipline is required in order to consistently focus our efforts, or motivate ourselves, in the right direction. We must struggle to eliminate our errors in thinking and perception, practice thinking and living responsibly, and attend to all the little details of a responsible life. Our every thought and action must be carefully scrutinized and directed towards our purpose and goal of living responsibly. As changing criminals, we are not allowed to have "bad days" when it comes to living responsibly and maintaining a crime-free life. Regardless of how we feel or how many things don't go the way we would like them to, we must be persistent in our change. We can't allow disappointments to become excuses to give up or quit. Even on the bleakest of days, we are required to continue in our struggle to think and live responsibly.

Throughout our change, it is important that we develop and adhere to a strict routine. Not only can following a routine help us to practice and develop self-discipline, but as writer Flannery O'Connor once observed, "Time is very dangerous without a rigid routine...Routine is a condition of survival."[8] With a properly formulated routine, we can schedule ourselves so that we have no idle time. We can keep ourselves busy and our minds occupied with our responsible goals and objectives. In this way we can pre-empt and avoid irresponsible thoughts and behavior, not to mention the fact that following a carefully planned routine is also the best way to reach any worthwhile long-term goal or objective. True change and responsible living also requires the development and continued practice of self-denial. In order to live responsibly, we must refrain from lying, cheating, breaking the rules, seeking criminal or irresponsible excitements, or even thinking about irresponsible behavior and crime. There can be no secrecy, no irresponsible fantasies, no irresponsible sex, and no proving ourselves. And, in order to be successful and reach our responsible goals, we must delay gratification and control our impulses - two key components of responsible

---

8   Bennett, William J., (Editor) "THE MORAL COMPASS" (New York: Simon & Schuster, 1995) pp.239

self-denial and a productive life.

Delaying gratification and denying ourselves the high-octane excitement of an irresponsible and criminal way of life will be very difficult at first. The sudden loss of our high-octane excitement will likely make us feel angry, bored and depressed. We may also despair about life, or even experience psychosomatic withdrawal symptoms (headaches, stomach problems, fever). However, if we simply endure, we will overcome these feelings and emotions, and get to the point where we don't miss our old criminal excitement at all. This high-octane excitement will be replaced with the more fulfilling and meaningful excitement of responsible living.

Again, in order to strengthen ourselves we should continually remind ourselves of our choice to change and improve our lives. We have made the choice to change and now we must endure the consequences of that choice. We can feel sorry for ourselves, slacken in our struggle, and possibly revert back to our old patterns in life, or we can face the fact that everyone must struggle to live responsibly. Everyone must learn to delay gratification, control their impulses, and deny themselves things for their own benefit or for the common good. We should remember that no matter what we choose, we are always saying "no" to something. If we don't say "no" to drugs, then we say "no" to the higher level of consciousness which is required to be successful in a responsible way of life. If we don't say "no" to crime, then not only do we say "no" to the inner sense of integrity, peace, goodness, self-worth and self-esteem that is the consequence of living righteously, we also say "no" to our freedom - internal as well as external (when we are eventually caught).

Self denial and delaying gratification are both an essential part of success and happiness in this life. As Stephen R. Covey writes, "Happiness can be defined, in part at least, as the fruit of the desire and ability to sacrifice what we want now for what we want eventually."[9] Not only is it impossible to achieve worthwhile goals and objectives without delaying gratification or denying ourselves

9   Covey, Stephen R., "THE 7 HABITS OF HIGHLY EFFECTIVE PEOPLE - POWERFUL LESSONS IN PERSONAL CHANGE" (New York: Simon & Schuster, 1989) pp.48

something, but we simply cannot say yes to happiness and success unless we first say no to all the things which could cause us to be unhappy and unsuccessful.

<u>Empathy for Others</u>

The next emotional ability which is essential to true change is the ability to realistically recognize emotions in others - to have empathy. In fact, a truly responsible way of life is impossible without empathy. Empathy is required to enable us to shift our perceptions so that we can fully understand the consequences of our actions on others. And having empathy for others not only helps us to cause the consequences we want in life, but it can also strengthen our desire to live righteously.

Empathy for others builds off of self-awareness. We must first be attuned to our own feelings before we can become skilled at reading feelings in others. As criminals, however, we also have another barrier to developing true empathy. We have very little experience at living, thinking, and viewing the world responsibly, so we have no way to truly understand how responsible people think or feel.

Thus, in order to develop true empathy we must also work to form an accurate concept of how responsible people think and feel. Realistically, this can only be done through the very act of consistently struggling to live responsibly. It is impossible to know how it feels to live responsibly until we actually do it ourselves. However, with the right attitude and perspective we can start to develop a more realistic empathy for others from the very beginning of our change process.

First, as I discussed in the last chapter, we must struggle to overcome our tendency to form extreme and unrealistic perceptions of people based solely on concrete events. We should learn to develop a more holistic view of others and recognize that people are much more complex than single actions portray. Many different internal and external variables influence how an individual will act or behave in a particular situation. And people often function differently in different roles. An overbearing, seemingly unmerciful boss may be a kind, compassionate and loving father. A difficult or obstinate client or employee may, on the other hand, be a very easy person to get along with as a friend. And, our very best friends may be easy to get along with as friends but be very difficult to work for or have as clients. Not all people think, act or feel the same in similar situations either. Some people are good as bosses, clients or friends while others aren't. Some people feel more comfortable leading while others would rather follow. And, some of us think the cup is half full even though others would swear it is half empty. Ultimately, in order to truly develop empathy for others we must seek to recognize and understand these differences in people, learn to accept and value them, and then use our awareness to create a more realistic perspective of others.

Next, we must quit being so judgmental. We must always be careful of criticizing others for making errors similar to the ones we are trying to correct. Nobody is perfect, and wasting our time and energy by judging others can only serve to hinder the development of empathy. And it can even blind us to our own weaknesses. Real empathy only comes when we can temper our perceptions of others and learn to be more compassionate of their thoughts, feelings and behavior. Instead of only focusing on the worst, we should look for the best in others, and give them the benefit of the doubt whenever their behavior doesn't seem appropriate. We must not, however, use this as an excuse to hang around, or associate with, other irresponsible people or criminals. We shouldn't judge others, but we shouldn't be foolish either.

Through consistent practice, role playing with our responsible guide, and actively seeking reality, we must also learn to recognize every consequence our actions may have on others - tangible and intangible, concrete and conceptual. Every action we take, whether it is sitting at home watching a movie, or going out for milk and gas in the middle of the night, will somehow affect another person. Even by not having an effect on other people we have an effect on them, because things would undoubtedly be different if we were around. And, only by learning to realistically conceptualize how our actions influence others can we truly be empathetic to them. Because, without knowing the full extent of the harm (or good) that has been done, it is impossible to realistically put ourselves in another's place.

To develop better empathy, we must also radically alter our perspective of responsible people. Rather than viewing responsible individuals as suckers who are inferior and scared to have fun, or who simply want to stand in our way of having fun, we must learn to respect and admire them. We can immediately begin to alter our perspective of responsible people by actively seeking the realities which will cause us to respect and admire them. For example, they work hard to fulfill their potential, struggle to overcome obstacles, save for the future, create loving families, are trusted and respected, and so on. However, true respect and admiration will only develop as we struggle to live responsibly ourselves and begin to recognize the true inner strength, focus, effort, and personal sacrifice which is necessary to live a responsible way of life. In fact, only by first correcting all of our errors in thinking and perception can we ever hope to gain a true and lasting empathy for others. Only by living responsibly and developing a responsible perspective of life can we learn to truly understand how a responsible individual thinks and feels.

In time, as we learn to live responsibly and develop empathy for others, we will gain an understanding of how responsible individuals viewed us as active criminals in the past. We will begin to truly understand the far-reaching ramifications of even one single irresponsible or criminal act. And we will learn to appreciate the fact that we don't have any right to use, exploit, or victimize others any more than they have the right to do these things to us. We will also begin to recognize the sad fact that our perceptions have been wrong. They weren't the ones who were weak and scared; it was us.

The best way to identify how another person thinks and feels is to simply ask them. But, because this isn't always possible, and because even when we do ask we often don't get a completely truthful answer, it is important that we learn to examine situations from as many different perspectives as possible. In fact, I believe that the more perspectives we take into consideration, the closer we come to truly identifying the way things really are. Although there are often many different perspectives of reality, there is only one true reality. Things are the way they are regardless of how we or others perceive them. Individually, our perceptions are almost always incomplete, but if we examine things from as many different perspectives as possible, we will undoubtedly become more realistic ourselves.

There are a few different methods we can use in order to enhance our own perspective and develop a more realistic empathy for others. First, as I said before, we can simply ask a person how they think or feel. Second, we can ask others (especially our responsible guide) how they would feel in a certain situation or under a given set of circumstances. Often others can provide a personal insight into situations which can be invaluable to our emotional progress. Next, we can ask someone who is close to the situation how they think the other person feels - we can ask someone who knows what is going on from their perspective. Finally, we can learn to analyze our own thoughts and perceptions, alter our point of view, and thus create our own unique perspectives.

When we find ourselves in a difficult situation or faced with a problem, we can mentally put ourselves in the other person's place and put them in our place. We can question ourselves as to how we would like to be treated in the same situation or how we may responsibly feel under a given set of circumstances. When we judge others, we can pretend that we are the ones who are being judged. Only then will we be able to judge fairly. When we buy we can imagine that we are the seller, and when we sell we can perceive ourselves as the buyer. Then we can buy and sell with integrity. When we are offended, we can imagine that we are the offender and when we hurt someone, we can envision ourselves as the ones being hurt. Only then can we show true mercy and sincere sorrow. And, we can also use our human abilities to stand apart from ourselves and envision the people we are dealing with as being someone we love and care about, such as a wife, mother, grandmother, father or brother, and then ask ourselves how we would view the interaction if it involved a person who we care about. How do we think our loved one would feel in the same situation? How would we like our loved one to be treated? It is much easier to have empathy for others when we are disconnected from the situation and not emotionally caught up in it ourselves. And it is usually easier to have empathy for another person if we remember that they, too, are a mother, brother, father or friend to someone in some other aspect of their lives. Thus, they have much the same thoughts and feelings as our loved ones do.

When learning to have empathy for others, it is also important to realize that while the mode of communications for the rational mind is verbal, the mode of communications for our emotions is non-verbal. Often, the emotional truth can only be uncovered by focusing on how an individual says or does something rather than focusing solely on what he says or does. And, because people's moods and feelings can change from day to day, moment to moment, we must learn how to accurately read these non-verbal cues to develop a more realistic empathy and enable ourselves to effectively interact with them.

Things such as the tone of a person's voice, facial expressions, eye contact, gestures, dress, and even the way they walk can give us valuable information into how they feel if we can learn to read these cues correctly. And, as responsible individuals who sincerely want to change our past way of life, it is our own responsibility to actively seek the knowledge which is necessary to accurately read these cues. (hint: Try reading a book on non-verbal communications. You should be able to find one at your local library or bookstore.)

Once we begin to understand what non-verbal cues to look for, we should practice reading them in others. We can do this by observing those who are closest to us and then questioning them as to the correctness of our interpretation of these cues. In this way we can discover if we really know how they feel and use their responses to help us fine tune our empathetic abilities. We can also practice reading the non-verbal emotional cues of strangers at the mall, work, or even at a party with our responsible guide, and then compare our interpretation of these cues with theirs. Not only can this help us to develop our empathetic abilities, but it can also serve to strengthen our responsible perspective on life, because it will allow us to see things the way that our responsible guide sees them.

Ultimately, only through the consistent practice of consciously putting ourselves in other's shoes at the right time and for the right reasons can we give our empathy a responsible purpose and meaning. It is not enough to simply practice having empathy for strangers who we aren't even involved with, or to simply have empathy for others when we "feel like it" or when we are in a good mood. Our empathy must become operative at the times we need it the most - when we feel like fighting because we think someone has just put us down; when we are angry because others won't fall in line with our idea of how things are supposed to be; and especially when we think about behaving irresponsibly or committing a crime. Although having empathy for others after we behave irresponsibly or criminally can help us to increase our self-disgust and our commitment to change, it does no good for our victim. And this empathy is worthless if our self-disgust and commitment to change is simply shut off when we want to behave the same way again. So, for our empathy to truly be of value, it must be used as a deterrent to irresponsible behavior and crime. We must learn to put ourselves in our victim's place, and strive to understand how they will feel before we follow through on our irresponsible or criminal thinking.

Responsible Relationships

Responsible relationships build off of empathy for others. "The art of relationships is, in large part, skill in managing emotions in others."[10] So, in order to develop a responsible relationship not only must we work to cause the consequences we want, but we must also take responsibility for helping the other person cause the consequences they want within the bounds of the relationship itself. The relationship must be mutually beneficial or it isn't a responsible relationship. Thus, in order to develop a responsible relationship we must not only pay attention to our own thoughts, feelings, needs and desires, but, just as importantly, the thoughts, feelings, needs and desires of the other person as well.

---

10   Goleman, Daniel, "EMOTIONAL INTELLIGENCE" (New York: Bantam Books, 1995) pp.43

In order to be handled responsibly, every relationship, no matter how intimate or casual it may be, requires the ability to see things from another's point of view. We must be able to feel what the other person feels and then take this knowledge into consideration when interrelating with the individual. For example, we must be able to recognize when a stranger with whom we interact is in a bad mood in order for us to avoid unnecessary confrontations and potential put-downs. Then we must understand how to use this knowledge in order to responsibly handle this situation. Because of our past we must always work do defuse volatile situations. And the only way to do this is by having empathy for others. At work it is important that we stay aware of the thoughts and feelings of our coworkers and bosses in order to help create productive and effective working relationships. Without empathy we can't effectively work together to achieve the mutually beneficial consequences that everyone wants. Even lovemaking should be an act of mutual empathy and not an act of conquering women as a way to build ourselves up. Responsible romantic relationships must be unselfish - not exploitive. Women are not ever to be viewed as conquests to be had, but rather as mutual partners who have needs, feelings, and desire for happiness just the same as us and everyone else. If we choose to have a relationship, it is our responsibility to recognize and fulfill these needs and desires in our partner. If we can't do that, then we simply shouldn't have a relationship in the first place.

Responsible relationships also require the development of a certain degree of interdependence and mutual trust. Our old way of life mandated that we trust and depend on very few people. As changing criminals, however, we must not only learn to be dependable, trustworthy, and full of integrity, but we must also learn to responsibly depend on and trust others.

As we struggle to change ourselves, we must learn to recognize and accept the fact that interdependence is just a natural part of life. As human beings, we are all dependent on one another to some degree. In fact, it is this dependence which, when properly used, can foster increased freedom and productivity. Together, we can be greater than the sum of our individual potential. We make more of our own existence when we just simply learn to responsibly work together.

Interdependence can be seen in all aspects of life. Employers depend on employees for production while employees depend on their employers in order to help them make a living. Anyone who drives a car on one of the nation's highways depends on all the other drivers for their safety and comfort, as well as on the car manufacturer and the company who constructed the highway. Even bees and flowers are interdependent for survival. Bees help to pollinate the flowers while the flowers provide pollen for the production of honey.

As you can see from these examples, responsible interdependence relates to the concept of teamwork. True interdependence is mutually beneficial to all parties involved and is contrary to our old patterns of control, ownership, exploitation, and proof of power. Thus, learning to be interdependent means discovering what true sharing is all about - not only materially, but emotionally and mentally (thoughts and ideas) as well.

To develop responsible relationships we must also learn to gauge the appropriate degree of interdependence and trust. We must learn to depend on and trust the right person, at the right time, for the right reasons. We must always be dependable and trustworthy, and we should always value openness and seek to build trust in all our relationships. However, not everyone we encounter will be so dependable and trustworthy. So, in order to eliminate any unwanted negative feelings or potential put-downs which could arise when others fall short of our expectations, we should learn to realistically evaluate all the components of every relationship. We need to consider things such as the intimacy of the relationship, past patterns of dependability and trustworthiness, and the other person's frame of mind. Learning who we can trust and depend on is not a matter of quick judgments or prejudiced thinking. It requires fact-finding, critical thinking, and emotional intelligence. Although we must always assume a certain degree of trust and interdependence, the true development of these qualities in a relationship requires a slow progress of personality identification.

As we begin to develop more responsible relationships, we

must keep in mind that things won't always go our way. We can't ever afford to feel put down or become angry when we are inconvenienced because others are undependable or untrustworthy. Even in the worst of circumstances, we must learn to function calmly, rationally and responsibly, and focus on getting along with, and having compassion for, others. And no matter what others do, we must always keep up our end of the bargain in our relationships. We cannot control what others do and we shouldn't try. We can, however, control ourselves.

As with all aspects of our lives, the only way we can improve our relationships is by working on ourselves. No matter how hard we try, we simply cannot change others directly. But I have discovered that much of the time we can change the way other people relate to us by changing the way we relate to them.

We can lay the foundation for the development of responsible relationships that are mutually beneficial and satisfying by:

- personally working to develop empathy and compassion for others
- abdicating control
- learning to cooperate and compromise
- living a life of integrity that shows we can be trusted and depended upon
- being completely honest and open

Realistically, these qualities have the tendency to flow from one person to another in relationships. If we are respectful and polite, others will usually be respectful and polite back. If we are open and honest, others tend to be open and honest. And, when we abdicate control and show a willingness to cooperate and compromise, others will usually follow suit and begin to treat us in the same way. It is much easier for others to be cooperative, polite, and respectful when we are doing the same thing. And, like enthusiasm and excitement, these personal qualities are often contagious. Thus, the changes we make in ourselves will often produce changes in others.

In order to improve the quality of our relationships, we should also learn to be assertive. We should openly be who we are and accept others as they are. Instead of being passive, manipulative or aggressive, we must learn to be open about our own thoughts and feelings, and receptive to others' thoughts and feelings. As the authors of *Managing Your Mind* write, "Assertiveness is a skill based on the idea that your needs, wants, and feelings are neither more nor less important than those of other people: they are equally important."[11] Being assertive doesn't mean being pushy, it means living with honesty and an open integrity in order to be fair to ourselves and others. It means actively seeking to understand things from another's perspective, and then to communicate in ways in which we are fully understood. It means openly exchanging ideas, feelings, and concepts with others and then struggling to take their thoughts and perspectives into consideration. It means saying "yes" when it is in the responsible best interest of the relationship and not being afraid to say "no" when we are asked to do things against our better judgment. It means learning to form a balance between ourselves and others – one that is founded on empathy and understanding, and directed by our purpose and responsible objectives.

As we develop emotional intelligence in our lives and interdependence in our relationships, we will begin to understand what it means to have a heart. Realistically, this word has nothing to do with proving our manhood or aggressively asserting our power and superiority if anyone has the audacity to disrespect us. Having heart has more to do with having compassion for others, taking others' feelings into consideration before we act, and responsibly facing and dealing with life's problems. An individual has heart when they can avoid a fight and resolve conflicts by negotiating responsible compromises without getting angry or upset instead of instigating confrontations and always trying to gain the upper hand. Realistically, it takes more of a man to avoid a confrontation and strive to find a positive solution to his problems than it does to

---

11 Butler, Gillian, Ph.D., and Hope, Tony, M.D., "MANAGING YOUR MIND - THE MENTAL FITNESS GUIDE" (New York: Oxford University Press, 1995) pp.128

simply uphold one's distorted idea of pride and power through retaliation. An individual who has heart considers the feelings of others above their own. They are helpful and caring when others are in need, not exploitive and demanding when things are getting difficult or when they feel that they are in need. A person who has heart controls their irresponsible impulses because they recognize that if they don't, they are likely to hurt someone else. A person who has heart is guided by their conscience. A person who has heart puts the needs of others above their own. A person who has heart knows what he wants out of life. He has a purpose and direction. And he doesn't ever exploit others, demand his due, or feel a need to prove his supremacy. Instead, he not only gives his fair share, but he gives even more in order to reach his own potential and to help others reach theirs. In essence, a person with heart has emotional intelligence.

Opportunities for Growth

Personal success in our struggle to responsibly control and direct our emotions and the emotions of others begins by becoming aware of all the reasons why we want to control and direct these emotions. Our first barrier to emotional intelligence, then, is our tendency to erode and shut off these reasons. We are very unlikely to delay gratification or humble ourselves in order to overcome perceived put-downs and anger unless we can first give ourselves, and learn to stay consciously focused on, a good enough reason.

This is why it is so important for us to develop a purpose and identify all the reasons why we want to responsibly change from the very beginning. I believe that if we give ourselves a good enough reason we can overcome almost any obstacle, achieve almost any goal, and do almost anything we set our minds to. The important thing is that we stay consistently aware of our purpose, our higher power, our responsible goals, and all the reasons behind our choice to change at all times, regardless of our feelings. And then we should consistently use these responsible reasons to purposefully direct our lives in a meaningful way. Realistically, we are much more likely to motivate ourselves in a meaningful way, delay gratification, and control our emotions, if we have a sound purpose, meaningful goals and objectives, and the spiritual support of a higher power.

Again, learning to direct and control our emotions in a responsible way is a human ability and thus can only be strengthened and developed through practice. So, once we have identified and learned to stay consciously aware of all the reasons to responsibly direct and control our emotions, we must make the sacrifice and effort necessary to direct them in a meaningful way. We can only become better at responsibly motivating ourselves through the actual practice of responsibly motivating ourselves towards our purpose and goals. We can only strengthen and develop responsible self-denial by actively denying ourselves things we really want. We can only develop our ability to control our impulses through the consistent practice of responsible self-control. We can only become more attuned to guilt and fear as a guide to responsible living by actively using them to guide our lives. And, we can only get better at overcoming anger, boredom and depression through the active practice of overcoming them when we are confronted with them.

Thus, the best opportunities for emotional growth and development come when we are emotionally charged. Although we can work to prepare ourselves, it is difficult to practice overcoming our anger, boredom or depression until we are confronted with these emotions. Furthermore, I believe that the more intense these emotions are, the more growth we will experience by overcoming them. Thus, the best time for us to work on developing self-denial is when we are confronted with doing something we would really like to do, but that isn't in line with our responsible goals and purpose. And the more we would like to do it (or the harder it is not to do it) the greater our opportunity is for growth. Similarly, the best opportunity to improve our self-discipline comes when we are confronted with obligations that need to be fulfilled, but we really don't feel like taking the initiative to do them. And again, the more we don't want to do them, the greater the opportunity we have for personal growth by overcoming our feelings and taking the initiative required to fulfill the obligations.

If we really want to change, it is our duty to make the most of every opportunity to develop our "emotional intelligence". It won't always be easy to responsibly control and direct our emotions. In fact, it is often very difficult. However, we can strengthen ourselves and enhance our ability to emotionally succeed if we simply change our attitude and point of view. To do this, we should learn to focus on all the reasons we have for responsibly controlling and directing our emotions, and remind ourselves that the harder it is to responsibly overcome or direct our emotions, the greater an opportunity we have to grow beyond ourselves.

Instead of seeing these situations as problems, we should consider them as challenges, because each time we succeed, we will become emotionally stronger and it will become easier for us to succeed the next time. Each time we responsibly practice self-motivation or self-denial, the easier it becomes for us to responsibly motivate or deny ourselves the next time. And each time we overcome our anger or boredom, the easier it will become to overcome them the next time we are confronted with them. The reason for this is that we become better at these emotional abilities with practice, and we also increase the confidence we have in ourselves. By simply proving to ourselves that we can responsibly overcome, control and direct our emotions, we take much of the uncertainty and fear of failure out of the experience the next time. And thus, we free ourselves to focus solely on our own possibilities and potential instead of being hindered by our fears and self-doubts.

Conversely, however, the more we let these opportunities pass, the easier it becomes to let them pass in the future. Not only do we become emotionally weaker, but we also lose confidence in ourselves. And then we begin to see only problems where all of our opportunities are supposed to be.

Ultimately, the key to true emotional intelligence is consistency. As with all the aspects of a responsible life, emotional intelligence won't develop without practice. And it also becomes worthless if it doesn't consistently guide our lives and become a habitual part of who we are. We must remember that in the past we often went through phases of transient sentimentality where we were sensitive to guilt and fear, controlled our anger, and developed relationships that seemed to involve interdependence and mutual trust. The problem, however, was that these sentiments, like us, were fragmented. They didn't consistently guide our lives. If they had, we wouldn't be where we are right now in life.

Instead of being true virtues, these sentiments were simply criminal equivalents. They were exploitive in nature because they were only transient attempts to get something we wanted either directly (as in a favor from someone) or indirectly (in the sense that they were used to build up our opinion of ourselves as a good person). And, although transient sentimentality and true virtue may have considerable external resemblance, they are easily distinguishable. Transient sentimentality is a selfish hypocrisy and does not endure, except as long as it fulfills its selfish purpose. However, emotional intelligence, as any true virtue, is a selfless part of who we are. It wants nothing in return and thus it abides firm and constant.

CHAPTER 11

Strengthening Our Muscles

A rmed with the awareness of our errors in thinking and perception, and the basic knowledge required to live responsibly, it is now up to each of us to make the consistent effort necessary to turn our lives around. The most important part of change involves doing our part. Only we can eliminate our old habitual patterns of irresponsible thought and behavior and begin to live responsibly. No one else can do it for us.

For us, true success means more than simply never allowing ourselves to lie, cheat, steal, break any rules, or commit any crimes. We must totally eliminate the person we once were in order to make room for the person we want to become. We must correct our errors in thinking and perception, alter our beliefs and adjust our attitudes. I believe that the key to true change lies not in simply eliminating the person that we once were, but instead in shaping who we want to become. And, the way we do this is through the repeated practice and counter-habituation of all the components, or virtues, of a responsible way of life. Virtues such as:

- Honesty
- Integrity
- Trust
- Loyalty
- Humility
- empathy for others
- emotional intelligence
- conceptual thinking
- critical thinking

- prayer and meditation
- responsible decision-making
- fulfilling obligations
- following a responsible routine
- setting and working towards goals
- seeking reality
- properly focusing our conscious awareness

Virtues such as these are both the cause and consequence of choosing to do right and living responsibly. We can only learn to become responsible individuals by actively practicing these virtues towards a meaningful, productive and purposeful end. Not only will the simple act of consistently implementing these virtues help us to overcome who we once were, but it is these virtues which are the very foundation of a responsible and successful life.

Aristotle is quoted as saying, "We are what we repeatedly do. Excellence, then, is not an act, but a habit."[1] We don't become responsible individuals by simply eliminating our errors in thinking and perception, and not behaving irresponsibly. Instead, we must move forward. We must do something. We must struggle to strengthen and habituate all of these responsible virtues by consistently implementing them at every opportunity life affords us. We must be honest. We must have integrity. We must employ critical thinking. Realistically, a truly responsible way of life is simply an amalgamation of all these virtues. And, our success will depend on learning to properly apply all of these virtues towards our responsible goals and objectives.

As we struggle to develop and strengthen these virtues, it can be helpful to understand that they are analogous to our physical muscles in a variety of ways. While our physical muscles provide strength and stability for our physical body, these virtues are the muscles of our soul. They can stabilize our self-concept, enhance the relationship we have with ourselves, and solidify who we are inside. And, just as physical muscles can be strengthened through

---

1   Covey, Stephen R., "THE 7 HABITS OF HIGHLY EFFECTIVE PEOPLE - POWERFUL
    LESSONS IN PERSONAL CHANGE" (New York: Simon & Schuster, 1989) pp.46

repeated use, these virtues can also be strengthened through repeated use. As they become stronger, they can better help us overcome spiritual obstacles and temptations, aid us in our struggle to live responsibly, and allow us to reach our full potential.

Conversely, much like a weak physical muscle is more susceptible to injury and disease, when these virtues are underdeveloped, temptations and life's obstacles are more likely to overwhelm us. Without developing these spiritual muscles, we leave ourselves unprepared to responsibly face the many vicissitudes of life. And, we severely limit our possibilities and potentialities.

It is important to understand that, from a holistic point of view, solely focusing on developing and strengthening only one or two muscles will have little impact on the health, strength, and stability of the body as a whole. Similarly, concentrating on developing only one or two virtues will not adequately prepare or strengthen us enough to truly live responsibly, let alone reach our potential.

In the physical realm, we are only as strong and healthy as our weakest muscle. What good does it do to have strong arms and a strong back if we have weak legs or a sickly heart? Similarly, what good does it do to fulfill our obligations if they are simply going to be criminal equivalents, or even to develop empathy for others if we are just going to shut-off this empathy whenever we want to behave irresponsibly or criminally? Thus, in order for us to truly change and live responsibly, it is not enough to simply exercise and strengthen certain components or aspects of a responsible way of life - we must focus on them all.

It can be real easy to neglect or postpone working on those skills and virtues that are the most difficult for us, and simply focus on developing and exercising those that may come easy. Although this type of counterfeit effort may lead us to believe that we are actually doing enough to change and live responsibly, in reality we are not. Again, if we ever hope to truly change and strengthen ourselves enough to live a consistently responsible way of life, we must struggle to develop all of our muscles. In fact, I believe that we should concentrate more on developing those virtues and responsible skills that are the most difficult for us in order to bring them up to par with the rest of our spiritual muscles. If our biggest problems are humbling ourselves, overcoming put-downs, and eliminating anger, then these are the things that we should spend the majority of our time and effort working on. However, if our biggest problems are eliminating shut-off and erosion, trusting others and overcoming boredom, then these should be the ones that we work hardest on. This isn't to say that we should neglect those virtues and skills that come easier to us, but only that these usually won't require as much effort or practice to develop and maintain.

Each of us is different, so we are likely to have our own strengths and weaknesses. Thus, in order for us to optimally grow and develop, it is up to each one of us to be completely honest with ourselves and realistically assess our own personal strengths and weaknesses. Only we can truly know where our biggest problems lie. And then we must properly focus our efforts not only to sustain our strengths but, more importantly, to strengthen our areas of weaknesses.

Realistically, just as all the muscles in our body must work together in order to produce purposeful, productive and meaningful movement, all of the components or virtues of a responsible way of life are also interrelated. For example, we must first develop self-awareness, a sense of interdependence, trust, and realistic thoughts and perceptions before we can ever truly have empathy for others. And, responsible decision-making skills are ineffective, even useless, in a responsible way of life without the ability to properly focus our conscious awareness and seek reality, or to have empathy for others.

As we move forward, we will recognize that because all of these virtues are co-dependent, the development of one virtue or skill not only encourages, but also necessitates, the development of another. For example, when we overcome our anger, we not only develop and strengthen many of the components of emotional intelligence (having empathy for others, emotional self-control, self-awareness, etc.), but as a by-product we also strengthen our abilities to think critically, to humble ourselves, and to realistically appraise our situation. So, by properly handling one anger-provoking incident, we can actually take advantage of the opportunity to strengthen many different spiritual muscles.

Just Do It!!

Again, in order for us to develop these spiritual muscles at all, we must first properly use and practice them in our life. In the physical realm we simply cannot develop or strengthen our muscles by just reading a book, watching others lift weights, or thinking about starting a weight-lifting routine - no matter how hard we try. Although reading a book or watching others may offer some helpful tips and strategies for best developing our muscles and lead us in the right direction, the muscle itself can only be strengthened through a consistent active effort - no pain, no gain. Similarly, only through the consistent practice of living responsibly and exercising all the muscles of a responsible way of life can we adequately strengthen ourselves to consistently live a responsible, productive and meaningful life. Insight and awareness alone will not strengthen our spiritual muscles or help us to change and live responsibly. Again, true change cannot, and will not, happen by osmosis. Ironically, we can only learn to live responsibly by repetitiously practicing all the skills and virtues of a responsible way of life - only by living responsibly can we learn to live responsibly.

In order to fully strengthen and develop our spiritual muscles, we must struggle at every opportunity to push them to the extreme. In the physical realm our muscles become stronger when we overload them by pushing them past their previous limits. Similarly, when we push our spiritual muscles past their previous limits they will develop and we become stronger. Each time we overcome a new temptation, implement a new virtue, or take the opportunity to actively use a new responsible skill, we grow. We progress in life. And, as these individual muscles develop, we become spiritually stronger and more stable. We fortify our will so that next time we are confronted with the opportunity to flex these spiritual muscles in a responsible way it becomes easier and more natural for us.

As I discussed in the last chapter, I believe that the greatest opportunities for us to strengthen our spiritual muscles come when the obstacles to living responsibly and righteously are the most difficult to overcome - when they are beyond our previous limits.

Thus, we have the best opportunity to develop our ability to overcome anger when we are the angriest. We have the best opportunity to develop openness and honesty when it is the most difficult to tell the truth. And, we have the best opportunity to develop humility when it is the most difficult for us to humble ourselves.

This doesn't, however, demean or decrease the importance and value of repeatedly overcoming all of the smaller, easier obstacles, or implementing and practicing the virtues and skills that come easy to us. As St. Francis de Sales writes:

> Although we must struggle with invincible fortitude against great temptations, and the victories obtained over such are most useful, yet on the whole we gain more by struggling against the lesser temptations which assault us. For although the greater are of a more important nature, the number of lesser temptations is so much more considerable, that the victory over them is worthy to be measured against that over those which are greater but rarer.[2]

Realistically, it is the small steps we take each and every day that will lead to the most growth and provide the most meaning in our lives. In fact, without these small steps true growth and success would be impossible. It is by overcoming smaller temptations that we fortify ourselves and prepare ourselves to overcome greater temptations. And it is by implementing the virtues and skills of a responsible way of life in all our daily endeavors that we prepare ourselves to implement them when the going gets rough. "True greatness...requires regular, consistent, small, and sometimes ordinary and mundane steps over a long period of time."[3]

While working out in the gym I have often seen new guys come in to work out. Usually these guys will throw a bunch of weight on the barbell in an attempt to be impressive and try to do

2   St. Francis De Sales, "PHILOTHEA, OR AN INTRODUCTION TO THE DEVOUT LIFE" (Rockford: Tan Books, 1994) pp.260-61
3   Quote of Pres. Howard W. Hunter in Pearce, Virginia H. "KEEP WALKING AND GIVE TIME A CHANCE" (Ensign, May, 1997): pg. 86

a bench press, only to be crushed under all the weight. They are unable to lift this heavy weight because they have never worked out before. So, they have never developed or strengthened their muscles. They simply haven't prepared themselves enough. On the other hand, I have seen men consistently struggle to become stronger by adding a little weight to the amount they lift each day. In time these men are able to lift incredible amounts of weight that were previously beyond their capacity to lift, simply because they made the consistent effort necessary to strengthen and prepare themselves.

Similarly, this type of consistent day-by-day preparation, or lack of it, can have the same kind of impact on our ability to overcome the spiritual. If we actively make the consistent effort and sacrifice necessary to strengthen and develop our spiritual muscles at every opportunity life affords us, if we consistently struggle to take the little steps, then we will strengthen and prepare ourselves enough to overcome the greater obstacles when we are confronted with them. However, if we don't consistently struggle with the little things, and consistently move forward by taking the small steps in our lives each and every day, then we won't be adequately prepared to take advantage of the greater opportunities in life. Instead, we will be crushed under the weight of our obstacles and we won't be strong enough to implement all the skills and virtues necessary to live a responsibly successful way of life.

The importance of this continual step-by-step preparation in our lives is beautifully illustrated in the quote of Phillip Brooks which warns:

> Some day, in the years to come, you will be wrestling with the great temptation, or trembling under the great sorrow of your life. But the real struggle is here, now....Now it is being decided whether, in the day of your supreme sorrow or temptation, you shall miserably fail or gloriously conquer. Character cannot be made except by a steady, long continued process.[4]

---

4   Covey, Stephen R., "THE 7 HABITS OF HIGHLY EFFECTIVE PEOPLE - POWERFUL LESSONS IN PERSONAL CHANGE" (New York: Simon & Schuster, 1989) pp.297

In the physical realm when we consistently exercise a muscle, it becomes bigger and stronger - it develops. And the longer we exercise it, the stronger and more developed it becomes. The same can be said for all the virtues and skills of a responsible way of life. Each time we successfully implement one of the components of a responsible way of life, the stronger we become and the further we progress in life. We become stronger and take another small step forward in life each time we do things such as:

- overcome a temptation
- tell the truth
- fulfill an obligation
- properly use the responsible decision-making process
- write in our journal
- humble ourselves
- think critically
- learn from our mistakes
- work towards a responsible goal
- keep a promise
- go to work and be productive
- read a spiritually uplifting book
- meditate on our progress in life
- accept responsibility for our shortcomings and mistakes
- pray and thank our higher power

However, no matter how long we have been consistently exercising a muscle, no matter how much it has been strengthened and developed, if we stop exercising this muscle not only does it cease to develop, but it actually atrophies - it becomes weaker and less developed. And, the longer we neglect it, the weaker and unhealthier it becomes. This process may happen slowly or quickly depending on how bad we abuse or neglect this muscle, and how infrequently we use or exercise it.

Similarly, if we are not consistent in the exercise of our responsible skills and virtues, our spiritual muscles, we don't simply cease to develop and move forward in life, but we will inevitably regress.

If we ever become complacent or lose our focus on responsibly progressing in life - in one year, five years, ten years, or even forty years - then we ultimately risk the chance of regressing and returning to our old criminal way of life. Thus, our lives should revolve around change and growth. We should always work to improve ourselves and move forward in our lives. And because the principles of a responsible way of life are eternal, our struggle to follow these principles and implement them in our lives must never end.

Consistency in Responsible Living

In the past, I was fragmented and very inconsistent. When making decisions, instead of acting on reason and being guided by a higher purpose, I listened primarily to my inner feelings and desires - much like an animal. And these were anything but consistent. Instead of actively seeking reality in order to make the appropriate choice, I struggled to make reality fit in line with my feelings through erroneous thoughts and perceptions. For example, if I felt like going out to party with my friends when I knew that I shouldn't, I would simply shut off the awareness of the potential consequences of going out partying, convince myself that it wasn't that big of a deal, and then focus solely on all the reasons why I deserved to go out partying. I allowed my feelings to guide my thoughts and perceptions, so they ultimately played the biggest part in my decision-making.

Also, although I professed to have values and standards (and there were indeed things that I would never think of doing), the problem was that these values and standards only guided my behavior when it was convenient—when it didn't interfere with what I wanted to do at the moment. When these things got in my way they were simply shut off and disregarded only to be reapplied at future dates so that I could once again feel good about myself. For example, I have long held a sentimental value against doing anything to hurt the elderly or my family. However, there have been numerous occasions during my life when, because of my behavior, I have done just that. The pain and suffering that I caused my family and others is undeniable. I did exactly what I had a personal value against doing. So as a criminal, not only was I unwilling to follow the rules set forth by God and society, but I couldn't even consistently follow my own rules.

Throughout our change process we must be consistent. It is essential that we are aware that spontaneous or impulsive shifts in purpose, thought, and desire are not normal. Inconsistency is actually very dangerous. Although it is appropriate to change one's mind and attitude after a more careful review of the facts and an examination of our personal priorities and purpose, it is not appropriate for these priorities, our purpose, or our basic beliefs and standards to change like the wind.

Our change itself will require tremendous repetition and consistency towards our responsible goals and purpose. Again, the only way we can truly learn to live responsibly is by consistently struggling to implement all the components of a responsible way of life. Each and every day we must realize that living a responsible way of life means living consistently. An irresponsible person who acts responsibly for a moment only to return to his old irresponsible ways is still an irresponsible person - one responsible act does not a responsible person make. But sadly, one irresponsible or criminal act can label even the most responsible person as irresponsible, and cause him to suffer many undesirable consequences. For us, a consistently responsible way of life is not only possible, it is required. To truly be responsible individuals, we can only serve one master.

During our change process, it is inevitable that we will go through fragmented shifts of thinking and desire, especially at the beginning. One day we will be enthusiastic about change and consistently focus on implementing a responsible way of life, and the next day we will catch ourselves questioning why we ever wanted to change in the first place, or excusing irresponsible behavior. One moment we will know exactly what we want out of life and what we need to responsibly do to achieve our goals, and the next moment we will be trying to convince ourselves that it is alright for us to start trying to take shortcuts at the expense of our integrity. Even behaviors and thoughts that we know are wrong or irresponsible will somehow become questionable or alright under different circumstances. Excuses and justifications can become so easy.

As criminals we became accustomed to living without any conviction or consistency in life. Our fragmentation became a habit. So, if we don't maintain the proper focus, we are capable of coming up with any number of insane excuses to distort reality, shut off our own moral reasoning, and stray from our responsible course in life. Yet, in order to truly change and grow, we cannot let ourselves succumb to this fragmentation. We must learn to recognize this destructive tendency for what it is. And then we must eliminate this fragmentation by making the conscious effort necessary to consistently behave responsibly and righteously, regardless of how we feel. Again, our fragmentation is totally under our control. We are not mentally ill. We are just not used to living consistently. Regardless of how difficult it may seem, we always have a choice. And with each consistently responsible choice we make, the less fragmented we will become.

In addition to our fragmentation, there are other barriers we must struggle to overcome in order to remain consistent in our lives. They are complacency, super-optimism, and even our own enthusiasm for change. As has been our pattern throughout life, the tendency for us during change is to start strong and then gradually fade back into our old patterns of thought and behavior. When we begin to change and start struggling to live responsibly for the first time in our lives, there will be an initial enthusiasm and sense of excitement. Because responsible living is new to us, the struggle to learn more about ourselves and to responsibly create a more productive, purposeful, and meaningful life will seem fresh and exciting. However, as the newness of responsible living wears off and it begins to truly become a struggle, we will be confronted with competing desires for excitement and proof of power. And, the change process itself will start to become boring and thus more difficult for us to endure.

I believe that it is only at this point that true change can begin to occur. Anyone can transiently live responsibly when it is new, exciting and easy - the true test comes when we really don't feel like struggling to do it any more. That's when it becomes a way of life instead of just being a fragmented phase. So, when our enthusiasm begins to wane and the struggle to change starts to become repetitious, mundane and boring, instead of becoming complacent and allowing ourselves to regress, we must push forward and struggle even harder.

I must warn you, however, that after this initial enthusiasm wears off, the tendency is not to struggle harder. Instead it is to justify complacency and excuse our unwillingness to persevere by convincing ourselves that we have done enough - that we have changed enough - to relax in our struggle. We will begin to think that we don't really have to try so hard any more; that it is alright for us to be like everyone else and do the little irresponsible things that "everyone does". Things like:

- telling little white lies
- borrowing office supplies from work without the intention of returning them
- going out drinking with our buddies
- calling in sick to work when we aren't really sick

We will try to convince ourselves that the true struggle is over when it has only just begun - much like the alcoholic who, after several months of sobriety, feels like he has his drinking problem under control and begins drinking again, only to discover that he still has no control over alcohol.

As changing criminals, we can never allow ourselves to become lazy or complacent in life. Instead, we must always struggle to generate our own momentum towards the fulfillment of our responsible goals and purpose. Other people may be able to become complacent or stagnant in their lives, act irresponsibly, and even avoid the awareness of their own inadequacies. However, for us, any relaxation or regression in our struggle towards perfect morality, integrity, and responsibility has the potential to cause a return to our past irresponsible and criminal way of life. We simply cannot allow ourselves to become complacent for even one day, because this is how our problems begin.

I believe that in life you are either going to be moving forward or moving backwards. Complacency is simply the moment in time when the momentum begins to shift. If we become complacent, then we risk the chance of regressing back to some point where we were before, or even worse. That's the problem with ever letting ourselves become complacent. While others may simply regress back to being a childish spouse, an unproductive worker, or an irresponsible student, we run the risk of regressing back to our old irresponsible thoughts and desires, and eventually back to a criminal way of life. We have much further to regress than the average person. Thus, we have much more to lose if we don't struggle to be consistent in our eternal progression.

So, just as a diabetic must take insulin every day for the rest of their lives and the alcoholic must never touch another drop of alcohol, we must continually struggle to grow and develop in a responsible and righteous way of life. We can never again allow ourselves to act irresponsibly. We must continually move forward. Again, we will make mistakes, encounter setbacks, and even catch ourselves thinking and behaving irresponsibly from time to time. However, the important thing is that we do whatever is necessary to turn these setbacks into growing experiences. And, that we ultimately take more steps forward in life than we take backwards.

Realistically, developing and maintaining consistency in our lives will take a lot of effort, sacrifice and dedication. The temptation to give up on the quest for continual spiritual growth and responsibility is intrinsic to the human condition. We all have an innate disinclination to exert the conscious effort required to perfect ourselves, an impulse to be lazy that we all must confront and conquer if we are ever to responsibly succeed in this life. However, there are several ways in which we can aid ourselves in our struggle to live consistently.

First, we can help ourselves to be consistent by writing down our purpose, our goals, and all the reasons we want to change - and then reviewing this list daily. In fact, no matter how far we progress in a responsible way of life, we should never allow ourselves to shut off or forget all the things that made us want to change in the first place. And, we must always stay focused on our responsible goals and purpose. Personally, I have found that whenever I begin to lose enthusiasm for the struggle to live responsibly and start to become complacent, it simply takes reviewing this list to get me back on track. At these times I am compelled to think about all those people who love and believe in me, and who have endlessly prayed for me to change, live righteously, and just be happy and successful. I am confronted with the pain and suffering that I have caused my family and those around me. I am forced to recognize where my past criminal way of life has ultimately gotten me, and all of the talent and potential I have wasted. And, I am driven to remember how much I want to get out of prison, stay out, and do something meaningful and productive with my life. It was these things that made me want to change in the first place. So, it is these things which help me to maintain the consistency required for a true and lasting change. And, by reminding ourselves of our responsible goals and purpose, we can enable ourselves to better see the whole picture and to look beyond the momentary thoughts and feelings which may lead to inconsistency in a responsible way of life.

We can also help ourselves to consistently maintain the proper perspective and focus on life by always looking for the opportunity to tell our story to others. We should always be prepared to openly talk about the pain and suffering caused by our past way of life as well as the inner joy and happiness we have found as a result of consistently living responsibly. If we have truly begun to change, then we have rekindled the light of goodness inside our soul. So, now we must let this light shine so that it can grow. I believe that a large part of our change involves continually presenting our newfound concepts to others through both word and action. Not only can this help to reinforce these principles and values in our lives, but it also serves to actually verify a responsible way of life in our own thinking. And, by telling others about the things that we have discovered, we will not only strengthen ourselves, but also gain the inner joy and satisfaction which comes from helping others.

Next, we can allow others to help us overcome temptation and complacency by always keeping an open channel of communication. This means that we must not only be totally honest and truthful, but also open and receptive to others' criticism and point of view. I believe that one of the best defenses against the temptations that threaten our consistency is to fully open up and talk to someone about them when they arise. When we are silent about our temptations or our irresponsible thoughts and desires, then we are left to deal with them alone. And because struggling to overcome temptation is new to us, if we don't responsibly confront them, then we are eventually likely to fold under their pressure. Just as small drops of water can, in time, wear through the hardest rock, our temptations can wear through our willpower if we don't eliminate them as soon as possible. If we open up and make our inner thoughts, feelings, and temptations known to our family, friends and responsible guide, then we can be strengthened through their support and encouragement. And, they may also be able to give us some useful advice in order to help guide us in our struggle to live responsibly. Ultimately, the simple act of being totally honest and open about all our thoughts and behaviors will help us to deter irresponsible thoughts, because we simply won't want to think about, or do, anything that we can't be fully open and honest about.

Next, we can help ourselves to live consistently by always maintaining an awareness of who we are and what we have discovered about ourselves. We should always stay consciously aware of all the irresponsible habits, and errors in thought and perception, that have contributed to our irresponsible and criminal behavior in the past. This way, we can better recognize them if they return to threaten our consistency. We can then eliminate them before they have a negative impact on our lives. For example, if we are aware that one of our tendencies is to shut off the deterrents to irresponsible and criminal behavior, then when we are faced with a difficult choice we can actively compensate for this tendency by forcing ourselves to focus more strongly on these deterrents. And, if we know that our tendency is to selectively pay attention to those things that agree with an old criminal point of view and ignore or downplay those things which are in conflict with this habitual perspective, then we can use this knowledge to gain a more realistic perspective. We can remind ourselves that we need to make the effort to expand our point of view and take other perspectives into consideration.

Once we become more consciously aware of ourselves, our

tendencies, and the world around us, we can also actually preempt any potential inconsistency in our lives. We can properly question our every thought, choice, and action to determine whether they are sincerely focused by our responsible purpose - or whether they are simply just our old patterns of unrealistic thought and perception. As changing criminals, we should always be on the lookout for any remnant of our past irresponsible patterns of thought and behavior. And, if we notice any of these patterns or tendencies reappearing, we should struggle to eliminate it from our lives, ask our higher power for help and guidance, and discuss it with our responsible guide.

Developing and maintaining a responsible routine can also help us in our struggle to remain consistent. By developing a responsible routine, we leave no room for question or debate as to what we should be doing, even if our attitude, thoughts or desires happen to momentarily change. When developing a responsible routine, we should take into account things such as:

- our purpose
- our goals
- our problem areas
- our unwanted habits and tendencies
- and our continual need for spiritual, psychological and emotional growth.

A responsible routine should keep us busy and preempt irresponsible thoughts and behavior. It should also encourage psychological, spiritual, and emotional growth through daily study, meditation and prayer. And it should allow time for us to do all the things we need to do each day in order to responsibly grow and be productive. Things such as:

- working a full-time job
- keeping a journal
- fulfilling our obligations
- working towards our goals

- critically reviewing our day's progress
- talking with our responsible guide

When developing our routine, it is also important to remember that "Things which matter the most must never be at the mercy of things which matter the least."[5] Although it is important to schedule time for recreation and relaxation each day, it should never be allowed to interfere with other more important obligations, such as work, keeping our promises, and spending time on our spiritual growth and development. The primary goals of our routine should be to help us develop more responsible habits, deter irresponsible thoughts and behavior, and enable us to consistently grow and move forward in our lives.

Ironically, we can also make it seem easier to live consistently by simply making the effort necessary to implement the individual components of a responsible way of life. Personally, I have found that consistency in desire is directly related to consistency in action. In fact, the desire to consistently live responsibly can only grow from the struggle to live responsibly. Only when we begin to recognize the benefits of living responsibly can we truly develop the desire to live responsibly over an extended period of time. We simply can't feed the desire to do something until we make the effort to do it in the first place. And, when we focus on living responsibly, then our thoughts and perceptions are directed in a way which verifies a responsible way of life and sustains the desire to live responsibly. Remember, success is all a matter of attitude and our choice of perspective.

Finally, we can help ourselves to maintain our consistency by focusing on living responsibly "one day at a time". Realistically, consistency in responsible living is just a matter of putting together a series of responsible days. Often, we can actually psyche ourselves out if we try to imagine a lifelong consistency in responsible living. However, if we simply focus on living responsibly right here and now, and not worry so much about having to

---

5   Covey, Stephen R., "THE 7 HABITS OF HIGHLY EFFECTIVE PEOPLE - POWERFUL LESSONS IN PERSONAL CHANGE" (New York: Simon & Schuster, 1989) pp.146

remain consistent for the rest of our lives, then before we know it, we will have been consistent in our struggle to responsibly grow and develop for a week, then a month, then a year. And in time, consistency in responsible living will simply become a habitual way of life.

If properly used, all of these aids to consistency can help us to remain consistent in our struggle to change and live responsibly. However, as I have said before, it is ultimately up to each one of us to use these aids and to exert the individual effort necessary to maintain a responsible course - no one can do it for us. Again, we do have control over our own thoughts, feelings and behavior. Thus, to a large degree, we have control over the direction of our lives. We must simply choose to exercise this control and add consistency and stability into our lives.

The Never-ending Journey

Consistency in thought and action is not only required for true change, but it is also an essential component of a responsible way of life. Without lifelong consistency in responsible living, our change isn't a true change, but simply from another fragmented part of our criminal lives - another transient phase. Realistically, without struggling to remain consistent in our lives, any responsible choices, productive gains, or meaningful accomplishments we make today have the potential to become worthless and even meaningless tomorrow. All of the good in the world simply cannot erase the pain and suffering caused by even one irresponsible or criminal act.

In the past we often convinced ourselves that because we had been good and done everything we were supposed to, it was alright for us to slip up and make a mistake every once in a while. However, we must understand that being responsible and productive in our lives today doesn't ever give us a license to take a break from responsibility and behave irresponsibly in the future. We don't earn the right to behave irresponsibly by learning how to live responsibly. On the contrary, with this new knowledge and increased ability, we incur even more of an obligation to live responsibly. No matter how many responsible and productive things we have done in the past, these things don't ever diminish the fact that we are also responsible, and held accountable, for all of our future choices and behavior.

True change, then, is not an event but a lifelong process. Our change cannot be viewed in terms of specific accomplishments or achievements, such as receiving a G.E.D., finishing a book, fulfilling an obligation, completing parole or probation, or saving a certain amount of money in the bank. These things are just steps along the way; a requisite part of our eternal progression - not the end of our journey.

A responsible way of life is not some goal which once obtained can be celebrated and then forgotten about. We don't simply become responsible individuals like we may become college graduates, parents, or sergeants in the army. As changing criminals, we will never get to the point where we have it made and be able to take a break from responsibility. By struggling to think and live responsibly each and every day, what we actually earn is a daily reprieve from the consequences of an irresponsible and criminal way of life. However, this reprieve is contingent upon our consistent effort and sacrifice. Ultimately, if we are truly sincere about turning our lives around, our goal shouldn't simply be to see how long we can stay away from crime or refrain from certain irresponsible behaviors. Instead, it should be to permanently live a responsible, productive, meaningful and purposeful life.

It is also important for us to realize that a responsible way of life is the result of a series of daily choices. And with each choice, we will always have the option to behave responsibly or irresponsibly no matter how far we have progressed in our lives. We can choose to do wrong or we can choose to do right.

In time, the desire or urge for irresponsible excitement and proof of power will fade (much like the ex-smoker's urge for a cigarette fades with time), and living responsibly will become more natural or habitual. However, responsible choices don't ever become automatic or perfunctory. Strengthening ourselves by correcting our errors in thought and perception, and habituating new, more responsible and productive patterns of thought and behavior, does not automatically make us responsible individuals. It simply makes it easier to live responsibly and harder to live irresponsibly.

We won't become immune to irresponsible thoughts, desires and temptations. Nobody does. The struggle to overcome these things is ongoing, because it is a necessary part of our eternal progression. Not only does the struggle itself help us to continually grow as human beings, but it also enables us to experience joy, happiness, self-worth, satisfaction and pride. And, it adds meaning to our lives. We simply can't grow beyond ourselves or experience the true joy of victory and success without the underlying potential for failure and defeat.

Strengthening Our "Self"

In the end, our effort to live a consistently responsible way of life will reap many rewards. We will strengthen the relationship we have with ourselves and develop a more responsible perspective on life. We will begin to view, and relate to, ourselves and the world around us from a totally different, more responsible and realistic, perspective. And as this happens, our lives will simply become a reflection of who we are inside.

The relationship we build with ourselves is so critical, because it is our inner conversations, ideas, thoughts, attitudes and motives that define who we truly are. And, it is also impossible to love, respect and trust others if we do not love, respect or trust ourselves.

As Nathaniel Branden writes in his *Little Blue Book of Self-Esteem*, "We all operate out of a self-fulfilling prophecy. How we see ourselves determines what our expectations are. What our expectations are determines how we are likely to act..."[6] And, as I have said before, how we think and act will ultimately determine how we see ourselves. Thus, with every thought and action, we create an ever-increasing spiral of personal growth and enhance the reputation we have with ourselves, or we create a downward spiral of shame, mistrust and regret. The choice is ours.

---

6   Branden, Nathaniel, "NATHANIEL BRANDEN'S LITTLE BLUE BOOK OF SELF-ESTEEM" (New York: Barnes & Noble, 1995) pp.16

The tragedy of our lives is that we have looked for happiness, success, self-esteem, and self-respect every place except within ourselves. However, I have come to realize that true happiness and success isn't found in what we have, who we are with, or where we are. It can only come from inside. Things can't make us happy and successful, only we can make ourselves happy and successful.

Lasting happiness and self-esteem can never be found in material possessions, the praise of others, the number of people who like us, or even the amount of money we have. Realistically, most of these things are external in nature and not even totally under our control. Yet, true happiness and a healthy self-esteem can only be the result of things that are under our control. Thus, only by living a consistently responsible and righteous way of life can we truly be happy and successful. Only by consistently implementing all the principles and virtues which enable us to responsibly cause the consequences we want in our lives can we truly develop trust and confidence in ourselves, and feel the inner sense of happiness, pride and satisfaction that comes from responsibly confronting and overcoming the challenges of life. In turn, it is when these practices become habitual that we make it possible to truly be successful in our lives.

Ultimately, with each responsible act, we move forward in life and improve the relationship we have with ourselves. Not only does our ability to live responsibly develop through practice, but with each subsequent responsible and realistic act we fortify our expectations that we will behave similarly in the future. Thus, we increase the confidence we have in our own abilities to live responsibly and to responsibly confront and overcome the challenges of life.

I have come to believe that living a responsible way of life full of integrity is the most fundamental source of personal worth, satisfaction and self-respect. It shows that we value ourselves enough to openly be who we are inside. And, it also enables us to personally cause the consequences we want in our lives. True happiness and peace of mind can only come when we live our lives in harmony with reality, and the time-tested principles and moral guidelines of a responsible way of life. No other way.

The reason why we can never truly be happy or successful when we achieve, accomplish, or gain something through irresponsible or criminal means is that we don't earn any inner sense of self-worth, pride, self-respect or accomplishment. If we cheat and win, although others may praise us, <u>we</u> know inside that our success is worthless because we cheated. And we actually diminish our self-esteem and self-respect because through our actions we tell ourselves that we don't have enough confidence in ourselves to try winning without cheating. And if we steal from others, we don't earn the sense of accomplishment, pride and self-worth that comes from responsibly being productive and we perpetuate a reputation with ourselves as a thief and a liar. And, again, we also damage our self-esteem by convincing ourselves that we need to steal in the first place. Thus, even though we may win or become wealthy, we remain empty inside because we don't reap any internal rewards, which are much more important than any external reward could ever be. This is why, when we live an irresponsible and criminal way of life, we are never satisfied. We endlessly continue to try to fill this inner void - to make ourselves feel proud, worthy, happy, successful and satisfied. Yet, unless we change and begin to honestly achieve and accomplish things through responsible living, we will never be able to truly feel any of these wonderful emotions, and we will continue to crave excitement and power in a misguided attempt to cover the inner void that this creates.

Doing it for Ourselves

Throughout our lives a big problem for many of us has been that we have valued others' image of us above our reputation with ourselves. We valued a sense of belonging, being praised and being perceived by others as unique and special above our own sense of integrity, self-worth and moral cleanliness. What was important to us was what others thought about us - not what we knew about ourselves. Yet, as many of us have discovered, this perspective on life can only lead to sorrow, frustration, anger, emptiness and pain. We simply cannot please everyone all the time. And in the end, no matter what others may think about us, we can never hide from the truth about ourselves.

Thus, early in our change we must focus on transferring the source of our self-approval and self-worth from external sources that we have no control over to the internal sources we do have control over. This is the only way we can heal ourselves and truly enhance our inner relationship. Instead of searching for our sense of personal affirmation and approval in the words and praise of others, we must learn to generate our own self-approval and affirmation. We can do this by actively living with integrity, setting and working towards responsible goals, and responsibly overcoming the obstacles of life. And, instead of allowing our sense of self-worth to unrealistically hinge on what we have or what others think about us, we should learn to generate an inner sense of self-worth by living productively, reaching our goals, keeping our promises, and responsibly causing the consequences we want in life.

Realistically, when our purpose is to prove ourselves to others through external means, we become like an empty shell. While we are trying to convince others of our worth, we neglect to convince ourselves. Our achievements, no matter how noble or praiseworthy, simply become an outward show of excellence with no inner substance. Because they are done out of vanity and for the praise of others, we reap no inner rewards, or develop any inner depth or strength of character. Thus, we become like a bone without marrow or a pearl without substance, ready to be crushed when the pressure of life's obstacles and temptations becomes too great.

We must realize that it is not our accomplishments or successes that prove our worth. Instead, it is the process of achieving. It is the continual struggle to grow towards our potential and succeed in a responsible way of life that is the means by which we develop our own effectiveness, increase the confidence and trust we have in ourselves, and enable ourselves to reap the true inner rewards of self-worth, pride and satisfaction. And in the end, our achievements and successes will be much more satisfying when instead of being a brief pretentious declaration of our perceived self-worth, or a transient boost to our unrealistic self-image, they are a product of our true self-worth and a fundamental part of who we are inside.

It is also important to remember that having a healthy self-esteem doesn't simply mean that we can uncritically feel good about ourselves, our thoughts, and our actions in all situations. As imperfect beings in an imperfect world, this is an unrealistic self-perception. And a healthy self-esteem is intrinsically reality oriented. Having a healthy self-esteem doesn't imply having an unrealistic self-image or a false confidence that we are perfect and can never make a mistake. No matter how far we progress in life or how healthy our self-esteem is, we will never become infallible. Thus, even the healthiest self-esteem can never preclude feelings such as guilt, shame, sorrow, and fear, or the self-criticism which is necessary for growth. Although some people may say that these feelings and this criticism is bad for our self-esteem, this is not the case. Instead, it is how we choose to deal with these feelings and criticism which will ultimately affect our self-esteem. If we make excuses, hide from reality, and refuse to change despite these feelings and criticism, then our self-esteem will undoubtedly suffer. But if we use these feelings and self-criticism to help us properly focus on the necessity of change, and to sustain the effort necessary for personal growth, then our self-esteem will become healthier in spite of our shortcomings and mistakes.

Sincere Change

Ultimately, if we are sincere in our desire to change and consistently make the effort and sacrifice necessary to implement all the components of a responsible way of life, we will grow and develop both spiritually and emotionally. We will gain confidence and trust in ourselves. We will build a responsible relationship with ourselves and develop a more realistic self-image (a necessity for any personal change and growth). We will develop more responsible expectations of ourselves. And, we will come to value ourselves much more. In essence, our self-esteem will become healthier. In turn, by improving our self-esteem, we will enhance our ability to implement all the other components of a responsible way of life. And because the relationship between our self-esteem and a responsible way of life is reciprocal, we will create a spiral of personal happiness and success in our lives, and learn to value and respect ourselves more.

As we progress, the feelings of worthlessness, uselessness, anger and self-pity associated with perceived put-downs, or when things don't go our way, will begin to disappear. Our continual urge to **prove** ourselves will begin to be replaced by an inner desire to **improve** ourselves. We will begin to criticize ourselves more and others less. And when we make a mistake we will automatically accept responsibility, and then work to responsibly correct it instead of attempting to hide from it.

In time we will lose interest in all the selfish, irresponsible things that ruled our lives before. And, we will gain more of an interest in helping others and providing some meaning and purpose to our lives. We will begin to feel a strong sense of self-disgust when we think of our past criminal way of life or see others who are involved in criminal behavior, sorrow for the many victims of these crimes, and shame and pity for the active criminal. And, we will begin to understand the concepts behind a responsible way of life. Concepts such as:

- consistency
- purpose
- honesty
- interdependence
- trust
- continual growth
- integrity
- personal direction

If we are sincere in our desire to change, we will consistently take stock of ourselves and maintain a view of ourselves as criminals. We will live with a fear of returning to our past way of life and continually review our life's purpose in order to help us sustain our desire to live responsibly. We will budget, save money, responsibly delay gratification, and plan for the future. We will always make the effort to be productive, allowing little free time in our responsible routine, and give an honest day's work for an honest day's pay. We will actively practice having empathy for others, sincerely look to see things from others' points of view, and implement a responsible decision-making process that helps us cause the consequences we want in life. We will keep a daily journal, fulfill all of our obligations, follow a responsible routine, and always follow the rules, regardless of what excuses we may come up with. We will hold ourselves totally responsible for the problems in our lives and quit blaming others.

If we truly desire to be successful, we will consistently live with integrity. We will always be honest, open, and truthful in all our dealings with others. Irresponsible and criminal thoughts and ideas will quickly be eliminated if they ever enter our thinking, because they are contrary to who we are inside and what we want out of life. We will be more aware of ourselves and continuously struggle to control our emotions instead of allowing them to control us. We will take minor obstacles, mistakes and inconveniences in stride, and not allow ourselves to return to our past pattern of going to extremes in thought, feeling or behavior. We will abdicate control, eliminate our quest for power in words and action, and allow others to have the power and control every once in a while. We will consistently use our moral abilities, maintain a clear conscience, and allow this conscience to help us responsibly guide our lives. We will sincerely struggle to correct all of our errors in thought and perception. And, we will make the sacrifice and effort necessary to consistently implement all of the components of a responsible way of life.

As a final warning, there will be times during our lives when things start running smoothly and we will be tempted to relax. However, we must not ever allow ourselves to become complacent. Complacency can lead to failure. Thus, we must continually struggle to improve and use every opportunity life may afford us to responsibly grow and fulfill our purpose.

For those of us in prison, we must also be aware that once we are released, we will be exposed to a greater variety of choices. Thus, more criminal thinking errors are likely to surface. As the authors of *The Criminal Personality* write, "We have found that when external restraints are reduced, every criminal, no matter how much he seems to be progressing, undergoes an increase in criminal thinking and is more likely to violate."[7] So, when our restraints are lifted and we regain our freedom, we must not allow ourselves to celebrate and throw caution to the wind. Instead, we must struggle even harder and become even more vigilant. With increased freedom comes increased responsibility. Realistically, our struggle to change and live responsibly doesn't end when we are released - it just begins.

Over the years, I have gained a better understanding of the concept of continual growth towards personal perfection. The more I change, the more I recognize that I need to change. And the more I grow, the more I realize I need to grow. As I move forward in life, I continue to learn more and more about the fundamental truths and realities of responsible living as these principles build upon themselves.

I don't profess to know all the answers, and I am by no means perfect myself. As I have responsibly progressed in life it has become easier for me to live responsibly, but it hasn't become easy. I still have problems with some of the things I talked about in this book and continue to struggle to implement all the principles and components of a responsible way of life. However, I have discovered that it is this struggle itself that brings much of the inner sense of peace, happiness and satisfaction that is the result of living responsibly, not to mention that it is being successful in this struggle that helps me to gain confidence in myself and develop a healthy self-esteem. I have learned to love the struggle.

Living a responsible way of life isn't easy, but it is possible. To be successful, you must simply believe in yourself and recognize that if you truly want to be happy, then you have no other choice than to work hard and cause the consequences you want in your life. As far as I am concerned, failure is not an option. I love my family, my freedom, and myself too much. I have too many things that I want to do with my life, and sitting in a prison cell isn't one

7   Yochelson, Samuel, and Samenow, Stanton E., "THE CRIMINAL PERSONALITY - VOLUME TWO: THE CHANGE PROCESS" (New Jersey, Jason Aronson Inc., 1977) pp.383

of them. The choice is yours – peace, joy, success and self-respect … or continuing to live a life of lies. Each moment we are faced with a choice. We can choose to continue doing what is wrong, or we can *Choose to do Right.*

Appendix

Suggested Reading for Further Growth

THE CRIMINAL PERSONALITY - VOLS. I, II & III, by Samuel Yochelson and Stanton E. Samenow (New Jersey: Jason Aronson Inc., 1976)

INSIDE THE CRIMINAL MIND, by Stanton E. Samenow, Ph.D. (New York: Times Books, 1984)

PEOPLE OF THE LIE: the hope for healing human evil, by M. Scott Peck M.D. (New York: Simon & Schuster, 1983)

MANS SEARCH FOR MEANING - AN INTRODUCTION TO LOGOTHERAPY, by Viktor E. Frankl (New York: Simon & Schuster, 1984)

THE SIX PILLARS OF SELF-ESTEEM, by Nathaniel Branden (New York: Bantam Books, 1994)

EMOTIONAL INTELLIGENCE, by Daniel Golkman (New York: Bantam Books, 1995)

TAKING RESPONSIBILITY, by Nathaniel Branden, Ph.D. (New York: Simon & Schuster, 1996)

A.A. BLUE BOOK THIRD EDITION, by Alcoholics Anonymous (New York: A.A. World Services Inc., 1976)

THINKING CRITICALLY: 4TH EDITION, by John Chafee (Boston: Houghton Mifflin Company, 1994)

HIDDEN POWER: HOW TO UNLEASH THE POWER OF YOUR SUBCONSCIOUS MIND, by James K. Vanfleet (New York: Parker Publishing, 1987)

THE SEVEN HABITS OF HIGHLY EFFECTIVE PEOPLE - POWERFUL LESSONS IN PERSONAL CHANGE, by Stephen R. Covey (New York: Simon & Schuster, 1989)

PHILOTHEA, OR AN INTRODUCTION TO THE DEVOUT LIFE, by St. Francis De Sales (Rockford: Tan Books and Publishers, 1994)

THE MIRACLE OF FORGIVENESS, by Spencer W. Kimball (Salt Lake City: Bookcraft Inc., 1969)

THE HOLY BIBLE

THE BOOK OF MORMON, Translated by Joseph Smith, Jun. (The Church of Jesus Christ of Latter-day Saints, Salt Lake City, Utah.)

THE MORAL COMPASS, edited by William Bennett (New York: Simon & Schuster, 1995)

THE VANISHING CONSCIENCE - DRAWING THE LINE IN A NO FAULT, GUILT FREE WORLD, by John F. MacArthur Jr. (Dallas World Publishing, 1995)

DON'T SWEAT THE SMALL STUFF....AND IT'S ALL SMALL STUFF, by Richard Carlson, Ph.D. (New York: Hyperion, 1997)

THE VOICE OF THE SAINTS, selected and arranged by Francis W. Johnston (Rockford: Tan Books and Publishers, 1986)

ADDICTIVE THINKING: UNDERSTANDING SELF DECEPTION, by Abraham Twerski M.D. (New York: Harper Collins Publishers)

THE ADDICTIVE PERSONALITY: ROOTS, RITUALS AND RECOVERY, by Craig Nakken (St. Paul: Hazelden Foundation)

CHOICES & CONSEQUENCES, by Dick Schaefer (Minneaplis: Johnson Institute)

LaVergne, TN USA
26 October 2009
161957LV00001B/1/P